Taste of Home
30-Minute Cookbook

Editors: Julie Schnittka, Julie Landry
Food Editor: Coleen Martin
Associate Food Editor: Sue A. Jurack
Art Director: Ellen Lloyd
Assistant Editor: Kristine Krueger
Test Kitchen Assistant: Suzi Hampton
Production: Claudia Wardius
Food Photography Artist: Stephanie Marchese
Photography: Scott Anderson, Glenn Thiesenhusen, Mike Huibregste, Judy Anderson
Photo Studio Coordinator: Anne Schimmel

PICTURED ABOVE: Italian Vegetable Soup (recipe on p. 111)
PICTURED ON THE COVER: Clockwise from upper right:
Favorite Fruit Salad (p. 60), Cheese Biscuits (p. 89), Zesty Buttered Peas (p. 169),
Salisbury Steak (p. 140) and Hazelnut Chocolate Chip Cookies (p. 190).

Here's All You'll Need to Beat the Kitchen Clock…

IF TIME is money, this *30-Minute Cookbook*—from the editors of *Taste of Home*, the leading food magazine in the country—should quickly become the most valuable you own. *Every one* of the *527 recipes* on the following pages can be prepared—not just cooked, *fully prepared*—in only half an hour or less!

You'll be amazed at how quickly you can whip up delicious main dishes like zesty Chicken Tamale Pie (page 128), mouth-watering Salisbury Steak (page 140) or savory Pork Tenderloin Diane (page 150). Or choose a hearty main-dish salad like Pork and Spinach Salad (page 45) or Creamy Chicken Crunch (page 50) for a tasty, time-saving change of pace.

Chapters on Vegetables & Side Dishes, Side Salads & Dressings and Muffins & Breads will help you round out a satisfying meal for your hungry family—while still getting you out of the kitchen in a hurry.

Be sure your gang saves room for dessert. There are plenty of scrumptious treats to choose from that also can be ready in a jiffy. Surprise them with elegant Raspberry Trifle (page 191) or luscious meringue-topped Raisin Custard Pie (page 194).

Again, each of these flavorful recipes can be fully prepared in a half hour or under!

The *30-Minute Cookbook* even has chapters on eye-opening breakfast dishes, tantalizing appetizers, hearty soups, finger-licking sandwiches and more…all equally fast to fix.

For those on restricted diets, look for the 45 recipes marked with this ✓. It quickly alerts you that those dishes are prepared with less salt, sugar and fat, and that the recipes include Diabetic Exchanges.

Finally, since the recipes in this book rely on ingredients you likely already have right on hand (no goat cheese or sun-dried tomatoes!), you can instantly add several of them to today's menu. And when your family tells you those dishes taste like you spent all day preparing them? Well, no one says a cook can't have a *few* secrets!

Taste of Home

30-Minute Cookbook

Breakfast & Brunch

PANCAKES FOR TWO

Annemarie Pietila, Farmington Hills, Michigan

(PICTURED AT RIGHT)

This recipe is perfect when you want to enjoy pancakes without having a bowlful of leftover batter.

1-1/4 cups all-purpose flour
1 tablespoon sugar
1 teaspoon baking powder
1/2 teaspoon baking soda
1/2 teaspoon salt
1-1/4 cups buttermilk
2 tablespoons vegetable oil
1 egg
1 cup fresh *or* frozen blueberries, optional

In a bowl, combine flour, sugar, baking powder, baking soda and salt. Combine buttermilk, oil and egg; stir into dry ingredients and mix well. Fold in blueberries if desired. Pour batter by 1/3 cupfuls onto a hot lightly greased griddle; turn when bubbles form on top of pancakes. Cook until second side is golden brown. **Yield:** 8 pancakes.

DELUXE HAM OMELET

Iola Egle, McCook, Nebraska

(PICTURED AT RIGHT)

This omelet is my family's favorite. Ham, vegetables and seasonings make it a hearty meal.

3 eggs
2 tablespoons half-and-half cream
2 tablespoons minced chives
1/2 teaspoon garlic salt
1/4 teaspoon pepper
1 tablespoon olive *or* vegetable oil
1/2 cup chopped fully cooked ham
2 tablespoons chopped green pepper
2 tablespoons chopped tomato
2 fresh mushrooms, sliced
2 tablespoons shredded cheddar cheese
2 tablespoons shredded mozzarella cheese

In a small bowl, beat the eggs, cream, chives, garlic salt and pepper. In a large skillet over medium heat, heat oil; pour egg mixture into skillet. As the eggs set, lift edges, letting uncooked portion flow underneath. Sprinkle with ham, green pepper, tomato and mushrooms. When eggs are completely set, remove from the heat and fold omelet in half. Sprinkle with cheeses; cover for 1-2 minutes or until melted. **Yield:** 1-2 servings.

CINNAMON-HONEY GRAPEFRUIT

Mrs. Carson Sadler, Souris, Manitoba

(PICTURED AT RIGHT)

Naturally delicious grapefruit gains even more terrific flavor in this recipe.

1 grapefruit, halved
2 teaspoons honey
Dash ground cinnamon

Place grapefruit halves, cut side up, in an ovenproof pan. Loosen grapefruit sections. Drizzle each half with 1 teaspoon honey; sprinkle with cinnamon. Broil 4 in. from the heat for 2-3 minutes or until bubbly. Garnish with maraschino cherries if desired. Serve warm. **Yield:** 2 servings.

FRIED SHREDDED WHEAT

Barbara Van Slyke, Verona, New York

My mother-in-law came up with this unique dish. Its great flavor has survived the generations.

4 large shredded wheat biscuits
3/4 cup milk
Maple syrup

Soak cereal in milk for 5 minutes on each side. Remove with a slotted spoon; drain slightly. Fry and flatten in a greased skillet until brown on both sides. Serve with syrup. **Yield:** 4 servings.

> **RISE AND SHINE!** *Pictured at right, top to bottom: Pancakes for Two, Deluxe Ham Omelet and Cinnamon-Honey Grapefruit (all recipes on this page).*

BIG DUTCH PANCAKE WITH LITTLE BERRIES

Debbie Johanesen, Missoula, Montana

This is a really fun recipe to prepare because the pancake puffs up into unique shapes. The custard-like texture and buttery flavor make it fun to eat, too!

> **1 cup halved strawberries**
> **1 cup fresh *or* frozen raspberries**
> **1 cup fresh *or* frozen blackberries *or* boysenberries**
> **1/4 cup butter *or* margarine, cubed**
> **1 cup milk**
> **4 eggs**
> **1/2 teaspoon vanilla extract**
> **1 cup all-purpose flour**
> **2 tablespoons sugar**
> **Confectioners' sugar**

In a bowl, combine berries; set aside. Place butter in an 8-in. square baking pan; place pan in a 425° oven for 2 minutes or until butter melts and pan is very hot. Combine milk, eggs and vanilla in a bowl. Stir in flour and sugar; beat until smooth. Pour into hot pan. Bake for 18-20 minutes or until puffed and brown on top. Spoon berries over top and dust with confectioners' sugar. **Yield:** 6 servings.

FRENCH TOAST SUPREME

Janis Hoople, Stanton, Michigan

(PICTURED BELOW)

As teachers, my husband and I rarely have time for breakfast during the week. So we look forward to relaxing breakfasts with our daughters on weekends. The cinnamon bread is a nice touch.

> **3 eggs**
> **1/4 cup milk**
> **1 tablespoon sugar**

1 teaspoon vanilla extract
4 ounces cream cheese, softened
12 slices cinnamon bread
Kiwifruit and starfruit, optional

In a shallow bowl, beat eggs, milk, sugar and vanilla. Spread 1 tablespoon cream cheese on six slices of bread; top with remaining slices to make six sandwiches. Dip sandwiches in egg mixture. Cook in a lightly greased skillet until golden brown on both sides. Garnish with kiwi and starfruit if desired. **Yield:** 4-6 servings.

BREAKFAST CUSTARD

Arlene Bender, Martin, North Dakota

My family delights in waking up to this custard. It tastes great with sausage or bacon.

4 eggs
1 cup milk
2 tablespoons butter *or* **margarine, melted**
1 teaspoon cornstarch
1/8 teaspoon baking powder
1/4 teaspoon salt
Dash pepper
1/2 cup shredded cheddar cheese

In a bowl, beat eggs. Add the next six ingredients. Stir in cheese. Pour into four buttered 4-oz. custard cups. Place cups in a baking pan. Fill pan with boiling water to a depth of 1 in. Bake, uncovered, at 425° for 15-20 minutes or until a knife inserted near the center comes out clean. **Yield:** 4 servings.

MUSHROOM OMELET

Christine Walker, Oklawaha, Florida

This tasty variation of a basic omelet reminds me of my childhood, when I'd help my father search for mushrooms in the forest near our home.

4 medium fresh mushrooms, sliced
1/8 teaspoon caraway seeds
1/8 teaspoon lemon-pepper seasoning
1 tablespoon butter *or* **margarine**
3 eggs
2 tablespoons milk
1/8 teaspoon salt
Dash pepper

In an 8-in. skillet, saute mushrooms, caraway and lemon pepper in butter for 3-5 minutes. In a small bowl, beat eggs, milk, salt and pepper. Pour over mushroom mixture. Cook over medium heat. As eggs set, lift edges, letting the uncooked

portion flow underneath. When eggs are completely set, fold omelet in half. **Yield:** 1-2 servings.

WAKE-UP SANDWICHES

Kayla Thielen, Carroll, Iowa

Like most people, we always have leftover hard-cooked eggs after Easter. But my family doesn't mind because they know I'll be making these breakfast sandwiches.

4 ounces cream cheese, softened
2 tablespoons milk
1 package (2-1/2 ounces) sliced corned beef, chopped
1/2 cup shredded Swiss cheese
2 hard-cooked eggs, chopped
3 English muffins, split and toasted
Sliced hard-cooked egg, optional
Minced fresh parsley, optional

In a bowl, combine cream cheese and milk until smooth. Fold in the corned beef, cheese and chopped eggs. Spread 1/3 cup mixture on each muffin half. Place on a baking sheet. Bake, uncovered, at 450° for 10-12 minutes or until heated through. If desired, garnish each sandwich with an egg slice and parsley. **Yield:** 2-3 servings.

HAM AND CHEESE WAFFLES

Doris Wright, Graham, Washington

My children love pizza...given the chance, they'd probably eat it for every meal! So their eyes lit up when I first served these waffles with pizza-like ingredients for breakfast.

3 eggs
2 cups milk
1/3 cup vegetable oil
2-1/2 cups all-purpose flour
2 teaspoons baking powder
1/2 teaspoon salt
1-1/2 cups (6 ounces) shredded mozzarella cheese
1/2 to 3/4 cup cubed fully cooked ham *or* **Canadian bacon**
Fried eggs, optional

In a bowl, beat eggs; add milk and oil. Combine flour, baking powder and salt; add to egg mixture and beat until smooth. Fold in cheese and ham or bacon. Bake in a preheated waffle iron according to manufacturer's directions until golden brown. Top each waffle with a fried egg if desired. **Yield:** 8-10 waffles (6-1/2 inches).

SHEEPHERDER'S POTATOES

Deborah Hill, Coffeyville, Kansas

Thyme adds a nice flavor surprise to this hearty casserole. Serve it as the main course at breakfast or brunch—or as a side dish at dinner.

    5 to 6 medium potatoes (about 2 pounds),
       cooked, peeled and sliced
   12 bacon strips, cooked and crumbled
    1 large onion, chopped
    6 eggs
 1/4 cup milk
    2 tablespoons dried parsley flakes
    1 teaspoon salt
 1/2 teaspoon pepper
 1/2 teaspoon dried thyme
 1/2 cup shredded cheddar cheese

In a greased 13-in. x 9-in. x 2-in. baking dish, layer potatoes, bacon and onion. In a bowl, beat eggs; add milk, parsley, salt, pepper and thyme. Pour over potato mixture. Bake, uncovered, at 350° for 15 minutes or until eggs are almost set. Sprinkle with cheese; bake 5 minutes longer or until cheese melts and eggs are completely set. **Yield:** 6-8 servings.

SPICED PEARS

Sue Fisher, Northfield Falls, Vermont

(PICTURED BELOW)

I try to serve a fruit dish with every breakfast to get some extra vitamins in our diet. Not only are these pears quick and easy to prepare, they're delicious.

    1 can (16 ounces) pear halves
 1/3 cup packed brown sugar
 3/4 teaspoon ground nutmeg
 3/4 teaspoon ground cinnamon

Drain pears, reserving syrup; set the pears aside. Place syrup, brown sugar, nutmeg and cinnamon in a saucepan; bring to a boil. Reduce heat and simmer, uncovered, for 5 minutes, stirring frequently. Add pears and simmer 5 minutes longer or until heated through. **Yield:** 4 servings.

PUMPKIN PANCAKES

Nancy Horsburgh, Everett, Ontario

For Halloween, my kindergarten class prepares these pancakes. They think they taste wonderful!

    1 cup all-purpose flour
    1 cup quick-cooking oats
    2 tablespoons wheat germ
    2 teaspoons sugar
    2 teaspoons baking powder
 1/2 teaspoon salt
Pinch ground cinnamon
    1 cup milk
 3/4 cup canned *or* cooked pumpkin
    1 egg
    2 tablespoons vegetable oil
Chocolate chips *or* raisins, optional

In a bowl, combine the flour, oats, wheat germ, sugar, baking powder, salt and cinnamon. Combine milk, pumpkin, egg and oil; stir into dry ingredients just until moistened. Pour batter by 1/4 cupfuls onto a hot greased griddle; turn when bubbles

form on top of pancakes. Cook until second side is golden brown. Decorate with chocolate chips or raisins if desired. **Yield:** 10-12 pancakes.

MUSHROOM BRUNCH TOAST

Ann Nace, Perkasie, Pennsylvania

(PICTURED AT RIGHT)

There are a lot of mushrooms grown in Pennsylvania, so this is a good recipe to represent our area. Guests enjoy this dish with hot ham slices.

>   **8 ounces fresh mushrooms, sliced**
>   **1/4 cup butter or margarine**
>   **2 garlic cloves, minced**
>   **1/4 cup whipping cream**
>   **1 teaspoon lemon juice**
>   **1/2 teaspoon salt**
> **Dash** *each* **pepper and ground nutmeg**
> **Toast points**
> **Chopped fresh parsley**

In skillet, saute mushrooms in butter until lightly browned. Add garlic, cream, lemon juice, salt, pepper and nutmeg. Cook and stir until thickened. Spoon over toast; sprinkle with parsley. **Yield:** 4 servings.

HONEY-APPLE TOPPING

Kathi Jessee, Woodland, California

I look forward to spending time with family and preparing a special breakfast of homemade pancakes or waffles served with this tasty topping.

>   **1/3 cup apple juice *or* cider**
>   **2 medium tart apples, peeled and chopped**
>   **2 tablespoons honey**
>   **1/8 teaspoon ground cinnamon**
> **Waffles *or* pancakes**

Combine all ingredients in a blender; cover and process until smooth. Serve over waffles or pancakes. **Yield:** 1-1/2 cups.

TOAD IN THE HOLE

Ruth Lechleiter, Breckenridge, Minnesota

This is one of the first recipes I had my children prepare when they were learning to cook. My "little ones" are now grown, but this continues to be a traditional standby in my home and theirs.

>   **1 slice of bread**
>   **1 teaspoon butter *or* margarine**

>   **1 egg**
> **Salt and pepper to taste**

Cut a 3-in. hole in the center of the bread and discard. In a small skillet, melt the butter; place the bread in the skillet. Break egg into the hole. Cook for about 2 minutes over medium heat until the bread is lightly browned. Turn and cook the other side until egg is completely set. Season with salt and pepper. **Yield:** 1 serving.

FAST AND FLAVORFUL EGGS

Michele Christman, Sidney, Illinois

With a small ingredient list and short cooking time, this delicious recipe is one of my favorites. And with two toddlers vying for my attention, I need all the free time I can get!

>   **1/4 cup chopped green pepper**
>   **1 tablespoon butter *or* margarine**
>   **6 eggs**
>   **1 can (10-3/4 ounces) condensed cream of chicken soup, undiluted, *divided***
>   **3/4 teaspoon salt**
>   **1/2 teaspoon pepper**
>   **6 bacon strips, cooked and crumbled**
>   **1/2 cup milk**

In a skillet, saute green pepper in butter until tender. Combine eggs, 1/2 cup soup, salt and pepper. Add to skillet; cook and stir gently until the eggs are completely set. Stir in bacon. Heat milk and remaining soup; stir until smooth. Serve over eggs. **Yield:** 3-4 servings.

CURRIED SCRAMBLED EGG

Lorraine Wiech, San Luis Obispo, California

The chives and curry powder in this recipe pack the right amount of punch and add even more flavor to eggs than salt ever could.

    1 egg
    1 teaspoon water
    1 teaspoon minced chives
    1/8 to 1/4 teaspoon curry powder
    1 teaspoon olive *or* vegetable oil

In a small bowl, beat the egg, water, chives and curry powder. In a small skillet, heat oil over medium heat; add egg mixture. Cook and stir gently until the egg is completely set. **Yield:** 1 serving.

KATE SMITH COFFEE CAKE

Ruth Nast, Waterford, Connecticut

(PICTURED BELOW)

I had been making this coffee cake for years before I realized that it came from Kate Smith's very own cookbook. I was delighted to know I had been using one of her favorite recipes!

    1/3 cup milk
      1 egg
    1/4 cup butter *or* margarine, melted

      1 cup all-purpose flour
    1/4 cup sugar
      2 teaspoons baking powder
    1/4 teaspoon salt
      1 cup bran flakes, crushed
TOPPING:
      2 teaspoons butter *or* margarine, softened
      2 tablespoons brown sugar
    1/3 cup bran flakes, crushed

In a mixing bowl, combine milk, egg and butter. Combine flour, sugar, baking powder and salt; stir into milk mixture. Add bran flakes. Spread into a greased 8-in. round baking pan. Combine topping ingredients; sprinkle over batter. Bake at 375° for 18-22 minutes or until cake tests done. Serve warm. **Yield:** 6 servings.

GOLDEN FRUIT COCKTAIL

Jenny Hughson, Mitchell, Nebraska

My family and friends enjoy the combination of the many fruits and fruit juices in this sweet hot fruit cocktail.

    3/4 cup packed brown sugar
    1/3 cup orange juice
    1/4 cup butter *or* margarine
      2 tablespoons lemon juice
      1 tablespoon cornstarch
      2 teaspoons grated orange peel
      1 cup sliced canned peaches
      1 cup sliced canned pears
      1 cup canned pineapple chunks
      1 cup canned mandarin orange segments
     12 maraschino cherries

In a large saucepan, combine brown sugar, orange juice, butter, lemon juice, cornstarch and orange peel. Bring to a boil over medium heat; cook and stir 2 minutes longer. Add fruit; heat through. **Yield:** 6-8 servings.

SLICED APPLE FRITTERS

Dolores Tolson, Oklahoma City, Oklahoma

Apple lovers will love these fast, flavorful fritters! They're good for breakfast or any meal.

      1 cup (8 ounces) sour cream
    1/2 cup milk
      1 egg
      2 teaspoons sugar
      1 teaspoon ground cinnamon
      1 cup self-rising flour*

1/4 cup cooking oil
3 medium tart apples, peeled and sliced
1/8 inch thick
Confectioners' sugar

In a bowl, combine the first six ingredients. In a large skillet, heat oil over medium-high. Dip apple slices into batter and fry until golden brown, 3-4 minutes on each side. Drain on paper towels. Dust with confectioners' sugar. Serve hot. **Yield:** 4-6 servings. ***Editor's Note:** As a substitute for self-rising flour, place 1-1/2 teaspoons baking powder and 1/2 teaspoon salt in a measuring cup. Add all-purpose flour to equal 1 cup.

BISCUIT EGG SCRAMBLE

Jacqueline Boyden, Sparks, Nevada

I like the convenience of baking biscuits along with the egg dish. It's a hearty meal anytime of day.

2 tablespoons butter *or* margarine
8 eggs, beaten
1 can (5 ounces) evaporated milk
1/2 pound process American cheese, cubed
1 tablespoon prepared mustard
1 cup cubed fully cooked ham
1 tube (10 ounces) refrigerator biscuits

In a 10-in. skillet over medium heat, melt butter. Add eggs; cook and stir until set. Set aside. In a medium saucepan, combine milk, cheese and mustard; cook over medium-low heat until cheese is melted. Remove from the heat; fold in ham and eggs. Pour into a greased 8-in. square baking dish.

Separate biscuits and arrange on top. Bake, uncovered, at 375° for 15-20 minutes or until the biscuits are golden brown. **Yield:** 4-6 servings.

CREAMED HAM AND ASPARAGUS

Linda Hartline, Marietta, Ohio

(PICTURED ABOVE)

To be truthful, asparagus is my least favorite vegetable. But I make an exception with this recipe my mom and I came up with together. The ham and cheese really lend a tasty difference.

1 pound fresh *or* frozen asparagus, cut into 1-inch pieces
2 tablespoons butter *or* margarine
1 tablespoon cornstarch
1 teaspoon salt
1/2 teaspoon pepper
1-1/2 cups milk
1-1/2 pounds fully cooked ham, cubed
2 cups (8 ounces) shredded cheddar cheese
3 hard-cooked eggs, chopped
1/2 teaspoon dried parsley flakes
Toast points *or* biscuits

In a saucepan, cook asparagus in a small amount of water until crisp-tender, about 3-4 minutes; drain and set aside. In a medium saucepan, melt butter; stir in cornstarch, salt and pepper. Gradually add milk; bring to a boil over medium heat, stirring constantly. Reduce heat; add ham, cheese, eggs, parsley and asparagus; cook and stir until ham is warmed and cheese is melted. Serve over toast points or biscuits. **Yield:** 4-6 servings.

VEGETABLE SCRAMBLED EGG

Marilyn Ipson, Rogers, Arkansas

(PICTURED ABOVE)

I like to have friends and family over for a special Sunday brunch, especially when there's a "big game" on television. These colorful eggs go perfectly with sausage, English muffins and fruit.

    4 eggs
    1/4 cup milk
    1/2 cup chopped green pepper
    1/4 cup sliced green onions
    1/2 teaspoon salt
    1/8 teaspoon pepper
    1 tablespoon butter *or* margarine
    1 small tomato, chopped and seeded

In a small bowl, beat eggs and milk. Add green pepper, onions, salt and pepper. In a small skillet, melt butter; add egg mixture. Cook and stir over medium heat until eggs are nearly set. Add the tomato; cook and stir until heated through and eggs are completely set. **Yield:** 2 servings.

SPICED DATE OATMEAL

Patricia Kaliska, Phillips, Wisconsin

You can prepare this hearty oatmeal in a hurry. And if you don't have dates available, try substituting raisins. Everyone will love this filling dish.

    2 cups apple juice
    1 cup quick-cooking oats
    1/2 cup chopped dates

    1/4 teaspoon ground cinnamon
Dash ground nutmeg
Milk
Coconut, optional

In a saucepan, bring apple juice to a boil. Stir in oats; cook for 1 minute. Remove from the heat; stir in dates, cinnamon and nutmeg. Cover and let stand for 5 minutes. Serve with milk; sprinkle with coconut if desired. **Yield:** 2 servings.

POTATAS FORRADAS

Mary Jo Amos, Noel, Missouri

Served with eggs, salsa and refried beans, these bacon-wrapped potatoes are part of a traditional Mexican breakfast. But they're just as good with toast and fresh fruit.

    3 tablespoons butter *or* margarine, melted
Garlic salt to taste
    4 medium potatoes, cooked and peeled
    1/2 teaspoon dried parsley flakes *or* cilantro
Salt to taste
    4 bacon strips
    1 green onion, thinly sliced

In a small bowl, combine butter and garlic salt. Brush over potatoes. Sprinkle with parsley and salt. Wrap a bacon slice around each potato; secure with a toothpick. Place in an ungreased baking dish. Bake, uncovered, at 375° for 25-30 minutes or until bacon is crisp. Sprinkle with onion. Remove toothpick before serving. **Yield:** 4 servings.

German Apple Pancake

Judi Van Beek, Lynden, Washington

If you're looking for a pretty dish to make when having guests for brunch, try this. Everyone I've served it to has enjoyed it.

PANCAKE:
- 3 eggs
- 1 cup milk
- 3/4 cup all-purpose flour
- 1/2 teaspoon salt
- 1/8 teaspoon ground nutmeg
- 3 tablespoons butter *or* margarine

TOPPING:
- 2 tart apples, peeled and sliced
- 3 to 4 tablespoons butter *or* margarine
- 2 tablespoons sugar

Confectioners' sugar
Lemon wedges

Preheat oven and 10-in. cast-iron skillet to 425°. In a blender, combine eggs, milk, flour, salt and nutmeg; cover and process until smooth. Add butter to skillet; return to oven until butter bubbles. Pour batter into skillet. Bake, uncovered, for 20 minutes or until pancake puffs and edges are crisp and browned. Meanwhile, place apples, butter and sugar in a saucepan; cook and stir over medium heat until apples are tender. Spoon into baked pancake. Dust with confectioners' sugar. Cut and serve with lemon wedges. **Yield:** 6-8 servings.

Strawberry-Stuffed French Toast

Julie Vogl, Cumberland, Iowa

This simple stuffed French toast is great to serve the family for weekend breakfasts. The creamy filling is sure to satisfy anyone's sweet tooth.

- 1 package (3 ounces) cream cheese, softened
- 1/2 cup strawberry yogurt
- 1-1/2 teaspoons vanilla extract, *divided*
- 8 slices bread
- 4 eggs
- 1/4 cup milk
- 1 tablespoon butter *or* margarine
- 1 cup sliced fresh strawberries

In a small mixing bowl, mix cream cheese, yogurt and 1/2 teaspoon of vanilla until smooth. Spread 2 tablespoons on four slices of bread; top with remaining bread to make four sandwiches. In a shallow bowl, beat eggs, milk and remaining vanilla; dip sandwiches in egg mixture. In a skillet over medium heat, melt butter. Cook sandwiches until golden brown on both sides. To serve, top each sandwich with 1 tablespoon of cream cheese mixture and 1/4 cup strawberries. **Yield:** 4 servings.

Breakfast Pizza

Marsha Benda, Round Rock, Texas

This unique stovetop "pizza" features a hearty hash brown crust and an egg, ham and cheese topping.

- 1/4 cup butter *or* margarine
- 3 cups frozen shredded hash browns
- 1/8 teaspoon salt

Dash pepper
- 4 eggs, beaten
- 1/2 pound fully cooked ham, julienned
- 1/2 cup shredded cheddar cheese

In a medium skillet over low heat, melt butter. Add hash browns, salt and pepper; cover and cook for 15 minutes, stirring occasionally. Pour eggs over the hash browns; sprinkle with ham. Cover and cook for 10-12 minutes or until the eggs are completely set. Sprinkle with cheese; cover and let stand until melted. Cut into wedges. **Yield:** 6 servings.

Southwestern Omelet

Patricia Collins, Imbler, Oregon

Hearty home-style food is popular in our small farming and timber community. Flavors of another region add spark to these eggs.

- 1/2 cup chopped onion
- 1 jalapeno pepper, seeded and minced
- 1 tablespoon cooking oil
- 6 eggs, beaten
- 6 bacon strips, cooked and crumbled
- 1 small tomato, chopped
- 1 ripe avocado, cut into 1-inch slices
- 1 cup (4 ounces) shredded Monterey Jack cheese, *divided*

Salt and pepper to taste
Salsa, optional

In a skillet, saute onion and jalapeno in oil until tender; remove with a slotted spoon and set aside. Pour eggs into the same skillet; cover and cook over low heat for 3-4 minutes. Sprinkle with onion mixture, bacon, tomato, avocado and 1/2 cup cheese. Season with salt and pepper. Fold omelet in half. Cover and cook for 3-4 minutes or until eggs are completely set. Sprinkle with remaining cheese. Serve with salsa if desired. **Yield:** 4 servings.

PORKY-PINE WAFFLES

Ferne Lanou Moe, Northbrook, Illinois

(PICTURED BELOW)

This recipe originated with a cousin of mine. For a change of taste, I sometimes substitute apple-sauce and sauteed apple chunks for pineapple.

1/2 pound fresh pork sausage links
1 can (8 ounces) pineapple tidbits
1 cup maple syrup
2 cups mashed potatoes
1/2 cup shredded cheddar cheese
3 eggs
1/2 cup milk
2 tablespoons butter *or* margarine, melted
1 cup all-purpose flour
2 teaspoons baking powder

Brown sausages; drain and cut into bite-size pieces. Drain pineapple, reserving juice. In a saucepan, combine sausages, pineapple and maple syrup; heat through. Combine the potatoes and cheese in a mixing bowl. Beat eggs with milk, butter and reserved pineapple juice; stir into potato mixture and mix well. Combine flour and baking powder; stir into potato mixture and mix well. Bake in a preheated waffle iron according to manufacturer's directions until golden brown. Top waffles with sausage mixture. **Yield:** 6-8 servings.

OLD-FASHIONED APPLESAUCE

Doris Natvig, Jesup, Iowa

We had all kinds of apple trees in the yard when I was growing up, so I don't know for sure which ones Mother liked best for applesauce. No matter what kind you use, this applesauce turns out terrific every time.

4 pounds tart apples
1 cup water
1 cinnamon stick *or* 1/2 teaspoon ground cinnamon
1/2 to 1 cup sugar

Peel, core and quarter the apples. In a Dutch oven over medium heat, bring apples, water and cinnamon to a boil. Reduce heat; cover and simmer for 10-15 minutes or until the apples are tender. Remove from the heat. Add sugar to taste and stir until dissolved. If cinnamon stick was used, remove and discard. Mash apples until desired texture is reached. Serve warm or chilled. **Yield:** 6 cups.

MEXICAN CORN SCRAMBLE

Brenda Spann, Granger, Indiana

Once my family tasted this zesty down-home dish, they never requested ordinary scrambled eggs again.

1 small onion, chopped
3 tablespoons butter *or* margarine
1 can (11 ounces) whole kernel corn with peppers, drained
1 can (2-1/4 ounces) sliced ripe olives, drained
8 eggs, beaten
1 cup cubed fully cooked sausage *or* ham
3/4 cup shredded cheddar cheese
Tortilla chips and picante sauce

In a large skillet, saute onion in butter until tender. Stir in corn and olives. Add eggs; cook and stir over medium heat until eggs just begin to set. Add sausage and cheese. Cook until eggs are completely set and cheese is melted. Serve with tortilla chips and picante sauce. **Yield:** 6 servings.

FRESH CORN CAKES

Gaynelle Fritsch, Welches, Oregon

(PICTURED AT RIGHT)

Corn's always been the basis of many of my recipes—in fact, these corn cakes were one of the first things I made for my husband.

- 1 cup all-purpose flour
- 1/2 cup yellow *or* blue cornmeal
- 1 tablespoon sugar
- 1 tablespoon baking powder
- 1/2 teaspoon salt
- 2 eggs, *separated*
- 1 cup milk
- 1/4 cup butter *or* margarine, melted
- 1 cup fresh corn, cooked
- 4 green onions, thinly sliced
- 1/2 medium sweet red pepper, finely chopped
- 1 can (4 ounces) chopped green chilies

Maple syrup, optional

In a medium bowl, combine flour, cornmeal, sugar, baking powder and salt. In a small bowl, beat egg yolks; blend in milk and butter. Add to dry ingredients; stir just until moistened (batter may be slightly lumpy). Stir in the corn, onions, red pepper and chilies; set aside. In a small bowl, beat egg whites until stiff peaks form. Gently fold into batter. For each pancake, pour about 1/4 cup batter onto a hot lightly greased griddle; turn when bubbles form on tops of cakes. Cook until second side is golden brown. Serve with syrup if desired. **Yield:** 20 pancakes.

WAKE-UP BACON OMELET

Mary Rayunec, Homosassa, Florida

The hot pepper sauce adds the right amount of zip to this delicious omelet. And because it's so easy to prepare, it's perfect for both hurried weekday breakfasts and leisurely weekend brunches.

- 2 eggs
- 2 tablespoons water
- 2 teaspoons minced chives
- 3 to 5 drops hot pepper sauce

Salt and pepper to taste
- 2 bacon strips, cooked and crumbled
- 1 tablespoon butter *or* margarine

In a small bowl, beat eggs, water, chives, hot pepper sauce, salt and pepper. Add bacon. In an 8-in. skillet over medium heat, melt butter. Add egg mixture. As the eggs set, lift edges, letting uncooked portion flow underneath. When eggs are completely set, fold the omelet in half. **Yield:** 1 serving.

SALMON SCRAMBLE

Janine Baker, Kansas City, Missouri

One morning, my husband and I whipped up this dish as a way to use leftover smoked salmon...it caught on! Now we always make extra portions of this tasty fish at dinner so we can have our family favorite in the morning.

- 8 eggs
- 3/4 cup milk
- 1/2 teaspoon salt
- 1/8 teaspoon pepper
- 1 cup smoked salmon *or* 1 can (7-1/2 ounces) pink salmon, drained, bones and skin removed
- 1/2 cup shredded Monterey Jack cheese
- 1/4 cup minced fresh parsley
- 2 tablespoons butter *or* margarine

In a bowl, beat eggs, milk, salt and pepper. Stir in salmon, cheese and parsley. In a large skillet over medium heat, melt butter; add egg mixture. Cook and stir gently until eggs are completely set, about 3-5 minutes. **Yield:** 4-6 servings.

Breakfast Burritos

Donna Poppe, Colfax, Illinois

This recipe is a nice change of pace from traditional breakfast food. Your family will love the zippy flavor.

     1 pound bulk pork sausage
    12 eggs, beaten
    10 flour tortillas (7 inches), warmed
     2 cups (16 ounces) sour cream
     1 jar (16 ounces) picante sauce
     1 can (2-1/4 ounces) sliced ripe olives,
       optional

In a large skillet over medium heat, cook sausage until no longer pink; drain. Add eggs and cook for 5-7 minutes or until completely set. Spoon about 1/4 cup egg mixture down the center of each tortilla. Top each with sour cream, picante sauce and olives if desired. Fold in sides and ends of tortilla. **Yield:** 6-8 servings.

Stewed Rhubarb

Caroline Simpson, Fredericton, New Brunswick

This is my husband's favorite way to enjoy rhubarb. He has it for breakfast over his cereal.

    5 to 6 cups chopped fresh *or* frozen
       rhubarb
     1 cup water
     2 cups sugar
    1/2 teaspoon ground cinnamon

In a saucepan, bring rhubarb and water to a boil. Add sugar and cinnamon; return to a boil. Reduce heat and simmer, uncovered, for 10-15 minutes or until sauce reaches desired consistency. Cool. **Yield:** 5 cups.

Kiwifruit Danish

Debbie Shick, McFarland, California

Kiwi's brilliant color and fresh flavor make this Danish extra special. It's an easy, pretty treat.

     1 tube (8 ounces) refrigerated crescent rolls
     1 package (3 ounces) cream cheese,
       softened
     1 egg yolk
     2 tablespoons sugar
    1/2 teaspoon almond extract
    2 to 3 kiwifruit, peeled and sliced
    1/2 cup apricot jam, warmed

Unroll crescent roll dough and shape into eight tri-angles with equal sides. Combine cream cheese, egg yolk, sugar and extract; blend well. Place 1 tablespoon cream cheese mixture in center of each triangle; top with a kiwi slice. Pull points of triangle to center and pinch to seal. Place on a greased baking sheet. Bake at 375° for 12-15 minutes or until golden brown. Cool on a wire rack. Top each with another kiwi slice; brush with jam. **Yield:** 8 servings.

Open-Faced Chicken Benedict

Cathy Tyrrell, Colorado Springs, Colorado

My husband enjoyed this recipe as a child, so my mother-in-law passed it on to me.

     6 boneless skinless chicken breast halves
    1/2 cup all-purpose flour
     1 teaspoon paprika
    1/2 teaspoon salt
    1/4 teaspoon pepper
     2 tablespoons cooking oil
     6 slices Canadian bacon
    SAUCE:
    1/2 cup sour cream
    1/2 cup mayonnaise
     1 tablespoon lemon juice
     1 teaspoon prepared mustard
    1/8 teaspoon pepper
     3 English muffins, split and toasted

Flatten chicken to 1/4-in. thickness. In a large resealable plastic bag, combine flour, paprika, salt and pepper. Add chicken, one piece at a time, and shake to coat. In a large skillet over medium heat, cook chicken in oil until browned and juices run clear. Transfer to a platter and keep warm. Brown Canadian bacon in the same skillet; remove and keep warm. For sauce, combine sour cream, mayonnaise, lemon juice, mustard and pepper in a small saucepan. Cook, stirring constantly, over low heat until heated through (do not boil). Place English muffin halves on a baking sheet. Top each with a slice of bacon, one chicken breast half and 2 tablespoons sauce. Broil until bubbly. **Yield:** 6 servings. **Editor's Note:** One envelope of Hollandaise sauce mix prepared according to package directions may be substituted for the homemade sauce.

> **KIWIFRUIT FACTS.** Ripen kiwi at room temperature until slightly soft. Then store in the refrigerator for up to 1 week.

BANANA-STUFFED FRENCH TOAST

Susan Seymour, Valatie, New York

My family liked this French toast so much when they first tried it on vacation that I came up with my own version at home.

> **4 slices sourdough *or* Italian bread (1 inch thick)**
> **2 large ripe bananas**
> **2 eggs**
> **1/2 cup milk**
> **1 teaspoon vanilla extract**
> **Maple syrup, optional**

Cut a 3-in. pocket in the crust of each slice of bread. Slice the bananas in half lengthwise and then into 3-in. pieces. Place two pieces of banana in each pocket. In a shallow bowl, beat eggs, milk and vanilla; soak bread for 2 minutes on each side. Cook on a greased griddle over medium heat until golden brown on both sides. Serve with syrup if desired. **Yield:** 2-4 servings.

ZUCCHINI FRITTATA

Carol Blumenberg, Lehigh Acres, Florida

(PICTURED BELOW)

When we plan a trip by car, I make this frittata the night before, stuff it into pita bread in the morning and microwave each one for a minute or two. Then I wrap them in a towel, and down the road, we enjoy a still-warm breakfast!

> **1 cup shredded zucchini**
> **1/2 cup chopped onion**
> **1 teaspoon cooking oil**
> **3 eggs, beaten**
> **1/4 teaspoon salt**
> **1 cup (4 ounces) shredded Swiss cheese**

In an 8-in. ovenproof skillet over medium heat, saute zucchini and onion in oil for 2-3 minutes or until tender. Pour eggs over top; sprinkle with salt. Cook until almost set, 6-7 minutes. Sprinkle with cheese. Bake, uncovered, at 350° for 4-5 minutes or until the cheese melts. **Yield:** 2 servings.

CHEESE DANISH

Mary Margaret Merritt, Washington Court House, Ohio

(PICTURED ABOVE)

This Danish has become standard fare at our house. Family and friends love this sweet treat, and so do I—it's delicious, and preparation time is minimal.

  1 tube (4 ounces) refrigerated crescent rolls
  1 package (3 ounces) cream cheese, softened
  1/4 cup sugar
  1/4 teaspoon vanilla extract
  1 teaspoon butter *or* margarine, melted
Cinnamon-sugar, optional

Unroll crescent roll dough and separate into two rectangles; place on an ungreased baking sheet and press the perforations together. In a small mixing bowl, beat cream cheese, sugar and vanilla until smooth. Spread over half of each rectangle; fold over opposite half of rectangle and pinch to seal. Brush with butter; sprinkle with cinnamon-sugar if desired. Bake at 350° for 15-20 minutes or until golden brown. **Yield:** 2 servings.

SCRAMBLED FRENCH TOAST

Torrey Stuart, Eugene, Oregon

I make a point of saving my leftover bread just so I can make this much-requested recipe. Everyone enjoys eating this sticky "scrambled" version of French toast.

  4 eggs
  2 cups milk
  2 teaspoons vanilla extract
  1 teaspoon ground cinnamon
  1/2 teaspoon ground nutmeg
  12 cups cubed day-old bread (1/2-inch cubes)
  3 tablespoons butter *or* margarine
  1/2 to 2/3 cup sugar

In a large bowl, beat the eggs. Add milk, vanilla, cinnamon and nutmeg. Add bread cubes and toss; let stand for 5 minutes. Melt butter in a large skillet. Add bread mixture; cook and stir until browned. Gradually add sugar; stir to coat evenly. Cook until all sugar is dissolved, about 5 minutes. **Yield:** 6-8 servings.

HOT CINNAMON WHEAT CEREAL

Michelle Bently, Niceville, Florida

Here's a quick warm breakfast for mornings when there's a chill in the air. For variety, we often top it with a spoonful of our favorite fruit preserves.

  1 large shredded wheat biscuit
  1 cup hot milk
Cinnamon-sugar to taste
  1 tablespoon butter *or* margarine

Place biscuit in a serving bowl; add milk. Sprinkle with cinnamon-sugar. Dot with butter. Serve immediately. **Yield:** 1 serving.

STRAWBERRY RHUBARB COMPOTE

Faye Bellgardt, Montrose, Colorado

This extra-speedy compote deliciously tops off waffles, pancakes and French toast. You can serve it warm or cold.

 1/2 cup water
   5 cups chopped fresh *or* frozen rhubarb
   2 to 4 tablespoons sugar
   2 cups fresh strawberries, halved
 1/8 teaspoon ground ginger

In a medium saucepan, bring water to a boil. Add rhubarb and sugar. Reduce heat and cook, uncovered, 5-10 minutes or until rhubarb is tender, stirring occasionally. Remove from heat; stir in strawberries and ginger. **Yield:** 6 servings.

MULTIGRAIN PANCAKES

Ann Harris, Lancaster, California

I developed this recipe to appeal to our kids' love of sweet toppings while giving them a taste of whole-grain cooking. They can't get enough of these pancakes.

✓ This tasty dish uses less sugar, salt and fat. Recipe includes *Diabetic Exchanges*.

 1/2 cup all-purpose flour
 1/4 cup whole wheat flour
 1/4 cup cornmeal
   2 tablespoons sugar
 1/2 teaspoon baking soda
 1/2 teaspoon salt
   1 egg
   1 cup buttermilk
   2 tablespoons butter *or* margarine, melted
Maple syrup

In a large bowl, combine dry ingredients. In a small bowl, beat egg; add buttermilk and butter. Stir into dry ingredients just until moistened. Pour batter by 1/4 cupfuls onto a hot lightly greased griddle; turn when bubbles form on top of pancakes. Cook until second side is golden brown. Serve with syrup. **Yield:** 4 servings. **Diabetic Exchanges:** Two pancakes (prepared with margarine and served with 2 tablespoons sugar-free maple-flavored syrup) equals 2-1/2 starch, 1-1/2 fat; also, 250 calories, 621 mg sodium, 55 mg cholesterol, 38 gm carbohydrate, 7 gm protein, 8 gm fat.

GRANDPA'S AUTUMN WAFFLES

June Formanek, Belle Plaine, Iowa

(PICTURED BELOW)

This is my father's original recipe. I've now handed it down to my children.

   7 tablespoons butter, melted, *divided*
 1/4 cup packed brown sugar
   2 medium tart apples, sliced
 1/4 cup raisins
 1/4 cup chopped pecans
   3 eggs
 3/4 cup milk
 3/4 cup half-and-half cream
   2 cups all-purpose flour
   2 teaspoons sugar
   2 teaspoons baking powder
 1/4 teaspoon salt
Maple syrup

In skillet, combine 2 tablespoons butter and brown sugar. Add the apples, raisins and pecans. Cook over medium heat until apples are tender, about 3-4 minutes; keep warm. In a bowl, beat eggs; add milk, cream and remaining butter. Combine flour, sugar, baking powder and salt; stir into egg mixture just until moistened. Bake in a preheated waffle iron according to manufacturer's directions until golden brown. Serve with apple topping and maple syrup. **Yield:** 5 waffles (7-1/2 inches).

SKIER'S SKILLET

Lynn Cronk, Indianapolis, Indiana

(PICTURED ABOVE)

With its great combination of flavors and ease of preparation. I often rely on this dish when we have overnight guests.

> 1 package (12 ounces) fresh pork sausage links
> 5 medium tart apples, peeled and quartered
> 3 tablespoons brown sugar
> 1 tablespoon lemon juice
> 1/8 teaspoon salt

In a 10-in. skillet over medium-high heat, cook sausages for 10 minutes or until no longer pink, turning occasionally; drain. Add apples. Sprinkle with brown sugar, lemon juice and salt. Cover and cook over medium heat for 10-15 minutes or until sausages are fully cooked and apples are tender. **Yield:** 6 servings.

QUICK CHERRY TURNOVERS

Elleen Oberrueter, Danbury, Iowa

These fruity pastries are my family's favorite at breakfast. You can substitute other fillings for cherry.

> 1 tube (8 ounces) refrigerated crescent rolls
> 1 cup cherry pie filling
> 1/2 cup confectioners' sugar
> 1 to 2 tablespoons milk

Unroll dough and separate into eight triangles; make four squares by pressing the seams of two triangles together and rolling into shape. Place on an ungreased baking sheet. Spoon 1/4 cup pie filling near one corner of each square. Fold to make triangles; pinch to seal. Bake at 375° for 10-12 minutes or until golden. Combine confectioners' sugar and milk; drizzle over turnovers. Serve warm. **Yield:** 4 servings.

BUTTERSCOTCH OATMEAL

Janet Nielsen, New Brighton, Minnesota

This sweet version of oatmeal is so good we could eat it almost every day!

> 1-3/4 cups milk
> 1/2 cup packed brown sugar
> 1 egg
> 1 cup quick-cooking oats
> 1 tablespoon butter *or* margarine

In a saucepan over medium heat, combine milk, brown sugar and egg. Cook, stirring constantly, for 5-7 minutes or until mixture boils. Add oats;

cook and stir for 1 minute. Remove from the heat. Add butter; cover and let stand for 3-5 minutes. **Yield:** 3-4 servings.

Hot Jam Breakfast Sandwiches

Gloria Jarrett, Loveland, Ohio

This recipe gives a whole new meaning to grilled sandwiches. The combination of flavors appeals to everyone.

   1/4 cup butter *or* margarine, softened
   1/4 cup flaked coconut
   1/2 cup apricot jam
   1/2 teaspoon ground cinnamon
   12 slices raisin bread

In a bowl, mix butter and coconut; stir in jam and cinnamon. Spread between slices of bread. Cook on a hot greased griddle until golden brown on both sides. **Yield:** 6 servings.

Yogurt Parfait

Dottye Wolf, Rolla, Missouri

This is a delicious breakfast or luncheon treat. It's also easy to adjust the amounts to serve any number of people.

   1 carton (6 ounces) yogurt flavor of your
      choice
   1/4 cup granola
   1/2 cup sliced fresh fruit (apple,
      strawberries, banana, etc.)

In a parfait glass or large glass mug, layer a third of the yogurt, half of the granola and half of the fruit. Repeat layers. Top with the remaining yogurt. **Yield:** 1 serving.

Country Crunch Pancakes

Anita Harmala, Howell, Michigan

(PICTURED AT RIGHT)

I adapted this from a regular pancake recipe. My kids think they're simply delicious!

   2 cups all-purpose flour
   1/3 cup whole wheat flour
   1/3 cup quick-cooking oats
   2 tablespoons sugar
   2 teaspoons baking powder
   1 teaspoon baking soda
   1 teaspoon salt

   1 teaspoon ground cinnamon
   2-1/4 cups buttermilk
   2 eggs
   2 tablespoons vegetable oil
   1 cup fresh *or* frozen blueberries, optional
CRUNCHY TOPPING:
   1/2 cup quick-cooking oats
   1/4 cup chopped slivered almonds
   1/4 cup packed brown sugar
   1 teaspoon ground cinnamon

In a mixing bowl, combine flours, oats, sugar, baking powder, baking soda, salt and cinnamon. Combine buttermilk, eggs and oil; stir into dry ingredients just until blended. Fold in blueberries if desired. Combine topping ingredients; sprinkle about 1 teaspoon for each pancake onto a hot lightly greased griddle; pour 1/4 cup of batter over topping. Immediately sprinkle with another teaspoonful of topping; turn when bubbles form on top of pancake. Cook until second side is golden brown. **Yield:** 14-16 pancakes.

Appetizers & Beverages

ANGEL FROST

Susan O'Brien, Scottsbluff, Nebraska

(PICTURED AT RIGHT)

I've served this refreshing beverage for holiday breakfasts and brunches for 20 years.

- **1 can (6 ounces) frozen pink lemonade concentrate, thawed**
- **1 cup milk**
- **1 package (10 ounces) frozen strawberries in syrup, partially thawed**
- **1 pint vanilla ice cream**

Fresh strawberries, optional

In a blender, place first four ingredients in the order given; cover and blend until smooth. Pour into glasses. Garnish with fresh strawberries if desired. **Yield:** 4-6 servings.

PRONTO MINI PIZZAS

Debbi Smith, Crossett, Arkansas

(PICTURED AT RIGHT)

These quick savory pizzas on pita bread are an excellent snack anytime.

- **1 pound ground beef *or* turkey**
- **1 cup sliced fresh mushrooms**
- **1/2 cup chopped green pepper**
- **1/2 cup chopped onion**
- **2 garlic cloves, minced**
- **1 can (8 ounces) tomato sauce**
- **1 teaspoon fennel seed**
- **1/2 teaspoon salt**
- **1/2 teaspoon dried oregano**
- **4 pita breads (6 inches)**
- **1 cup (4 ounces) shredded mozzarella cheese**

In a skillet, cook the meat, mushrooms, green pepper, onion and garlic until the meat is browned and the vegetables are tender; drain. Stir in tomato sauce, fennel, salt and oregano. Simmer for 1-2 minutes. Meanwhile, warm pitas in the microwave. Top each with a fourth of the meat mixture; sprinkle with a fourth of the cheese. Microwave or broil until cheese is melted. Cut into quarters. **Yield:** 16 wedges.

LINDA'S BLT DIP

Linda Nilsen, Anoka, Minnesota

(PICTURED AT RIGHT)

This spread is a different way to enjoy the winning combination of bacon, lettuce and tomato.

- **1/2 cup sour cream**
- **1/2 cup mayonnaise *or* salad dressing**
- **1/2 pound bacon, cooked and crumbled**
- **1 small tomato, diced**

Fresh vegetables

In a bowl, combine sour cream, mayonnaise and bacon; mix well. Stir in tomato. Use as a dip for vegetables. **Yield:** 1-1/2 cups. **Editor's Note:** This dip may also be served on crackers or on bread with lettuce.

FRUITY BREAKFAST BEVERAGE

Debbie Rohler, Indianapolis, Indiana

This drink is a real winner. I especially like to serve it to guests because it's so pretty and tasty.

- **2 cups orange juice**
- **1 peeled quartered banana, frozen**
- **1/2 cup unsweetened frozen strawberries**
- **1/2 cup unsweetened frozen raspberries**
- **1 teaspoon honey**

In a blender, combine all ingredients; cover and blend until smooth. Pour into glasses. **Yield:** 3-4 servings.

SIMPLE SNACKS. *Pictured at right, clockwise from top left: Angel Frost, Linda's BLT Dip and Pronto Mini Pizzas (all recipes on this page).*

POTATO NACHOS

Deb Helmer, Winfield, Kansas

(PICTURED BELOW)

These extra-prompt potato snacks are one of my family's favorites. They're heartier than most appetizers and so good, too.

    1 large baking potato
1/8 teaspoon salt
    1 jar (8 ounces) taco sauce
1/2 cup sliced green onions
1/2 cup chopped green chilies
1/2 cup shredded cheddar *or* Monterey
        Jack cheese
1/2 cup sliced ripe olives

Scrub the potato and cut it into 1/4-in. slices. Arrange the slices in a single layer on a greased broiler pan; sprinkle with salt. Broil 4 in. from the heat until golden brown. Turn; broil until brown and tender. Drizzle with taco sauce; garnish with onions, chilies, cheese and olives. Broil until the cheese melts. **Yield:** 2 servings. **Microwave Directions:** Arrange potato slices in a single layer on a microwave-safe pie plate or baking dish; sprinkle with salt. Drizzle with half of the taco sauce. Cover with plastic wrap; cook on high for 4-5 minutes or until tender, rotating dish once. Drizzle with remaining taco sauce; garnish with onions, chilies, cheese and olives. Cover and microwave 30-60 seconds longer or until cheese melts. **Editor's Note:** This recipe was tested in a 700-watt microwave.

VEGETABLE APPETIZER PIZZA

Marcia Tiernan, Madrid, New York

My sister brought this recipe with her when she was visiting from California. We served it at a family get-together and everyone just loved it.

    3 tubes (8 ounces *each*) refrigerated
        crescent rolls
    2 packages (8 ounces *each*) cream cheese,
        softened
2/3 cup mayonnaise
    1 tablespoon dill weed
    4 tomatoes, seeded and chopped
    2 cups chopped fresh broccoli
    2 cups sliced fresh mushrooms
1/2 medium green pepper, chopped
1/2 medium sweet red pepper, chopped
    3 green onions, thinly sliced
    1 can (2-1/4 ounces) sliced ripe olives,
        drained
    2 cups (8 ounces) shredded cheddar cheese

Unroll crescent roll dough and place on two greased 15-in. x 10-in. x 1-in. baking pans. Flatten dough, sealing seams and perforations. Bake at 400° for 10 minutes or until light golden brown. Cool. In a small bowl, blend the cream cheese, mayonnaise and dill. Spread over crusts. Top with vegetables, olives and cheese. Cut into bite-size squares. Refrigerate until ready to serve. **Yield:** about 8 dozen.

CURRIED CHICKEN CHEESE BALL

Pauline Rhine, Bunker Hill, Indiana

I cater for parties and weddings, so I'm always searching for new menu ideas. I found a similar cheese ball recipe in a magazine, then adjusted the ingredients to suit my tastes.

✓ This tasty dish uses less sugar, salt and fat. Recipe includes *Diabetic Exchanges*.

    1 package (8 ounces) cream cheese,
        softened
    2 tablespoons orange marmalade

1-1/2 teaspoons curry powder
  1/2 teaspoon salt, optional
  1/4 teaspoon white pepper
    2 cups finely chopped cooked chicken
    2 tablespoons minced green onions
    2 tablespoons minced celery
  3/4 cup chopped toasted almonds *or*
       chopped fresh parsley
Crackers

In a mixing bowl, beat the cream cheese, marmalade, curry powder, salt if desired and pepper until smooth. Stir in chicken, onions and celery. Shape into a large ball. Roll in almonds or parsley. Cover and chill. Serve with crackers. **Yield:** 2 cups. **Diabetic Exchanges:** One 3-tablespoon serving (prepared with light cream cheese and parsley and without salt) equals 1/2 meat, 1/2 fat, 1/2 fruit; also, 89 calories, 135 mg sodium, 30 mg cholesterol, 5 gm carbohydrate, 7 gm protein, 5 gm fat.

PINTO BEAN DIP

Gladys DeBoer, Castleford, Idaho

(PICTURED BELOW)

Whether you're hosting a party or just treating yourself, this creamy dip is great to snack on with raw vegetables or tortilla chips.

✓ This tasty dish uses less sugar, salt and fat. Recipe includes *Diabetic Exchanges.*

    1 can (15 ounces) pinto beans, rinsed and
       drained
    3 tablespoons lemon juice
    3 tablespoons chopped green onions
    2 tablespoons mayonnaise
1-1/2 teaspoons minced seeded jalapeno
       pepper
    1 teaspoon Worcestershire sauce

  1/2 to 3/4 teaspoon salt, optional
  1/4 teaspoon sugar
Fresh vegetables *or* tortilla chips

In a blender or food processor, combine all ingredients; cover and process until smooth. Serve with vegetables or chips. **Yield:** 1-3/4 cups. **Diabetic Exchanges:** One 2-tablespoon serving (prepared with fat-free mayonnaise and without salt) equals 1 vegetable; also, 28 calories, 149 mg sodium, 0 cholesterol, 5 gm carbohydrate, 2 gm protein, trace fat.

ORIENTAL TRIANGLES

Violet Heaton, Portland, Oregon

Crunchy vegetables, savory meat and a flaky crust—there's a lot to like in these little pockets!

  1/2 pound lean ground beef
    1 cup canned bean sprouts, drained
  1/2 cup sliced water chestnuts, finely chopped
    2 tablespoons chopped onion
    1 envelope beef and mushroom dry
       soup mix
    2 tubes (8 ounces *each*) refrigerated
       crescent rolls
Prepared sweet-and-sour sauce, optional
Prepared hot mustard sauce, optional

In a skillet, combine the first five ingredients. Cook over medium heat, stirring often, until beef is browned and onion is tender. Separate crescent dough into triangles; cut each one in half diagonally. Place 1 rounded teaspoon of beef mixture in center of each triangle; fold dough over mixture and pinch corners together to seal edges. Place on an ungreased baking sheet. Bake, uncovered, at 375° for 15 minutes or until golden. Serve with sweet-and-sour sauce and hot mustard sauce if desired. **Yield:** about 3 dozen.

BUTTERMILK SHAKE

Gloria Jarrett, Loveland, Ohio

(PICTURED ABOVE)

This rich shake tastes like liquid cheesecake! It makes a nice addition to a brunch.

- 1 pint vanilla ice cream
- 1 cup buttermilk
- 1 teaspoon grated lemon peel
- 1/2 teaspoon vanilla extract
- 1 drop lemon extract

In a blender, combine all ingredients; cover and blend until smooth. Serve immediately **Yield:** 4 servings.

CHILAQUILAS

Joy Frost, Wood River, Illinois

I learned how to make this recipe when I was attending high school in California. It's been a family favorite for years.

- 1 pound ground beef
- 1 can (16 ounces) diced tomatoes, undrained
- 1 can (16 ounces) chili beans, undrained
- 1 can (6 ounces) sliced ripe olives, drained
- 6 green onions with tops, sliced
- 1 to 2 tablespoons chili powder
Salt and pepper to taste

- 1 package (20 ounces) tortilla *or* corn chips
- 1 to 2 cups (4 to 8 ounces) shredded cheddar cheese

In a skillet over medium heat, brown meat; drain. Add tomatoes, beans, olives, onions, chili powder, salt and pepper. Simmer until thickened, about 20 minutes. Arrange chips on a platter; top with meat mixture and sprinkle with cheese. **Yield:** 8-10 servings.

TASTY TEXAS TENDERS

Joan Dinger, Fulshear, Texas

When time gets away from you and your clan is hungry, prepare this fun fast finger food. The chicken is crispy outside and tender inside.

- 1 pound chicken tenders *or* boneless skinless chicken breasts
- 3 cups crisp rice cereal, crushed
- 1 teaspoon garlic salt
- 1 teaspoon dill weed
- 1/4 cup vegetable oil
Sour cream, optional

If using chicken breasts, cut into 4-in. strips; set aside. Combine cereal, garlic salt and dill. Dip chicken tenders or strips in oil, then roll in cereal mixture. Place on a foil-lined baking sheet. Bake, uncovered, at 375° for 25 minutes or until juices run clear. Serve with sour cream for dipping if desired. **Yield:** 6-8 servings.

RASPBERRY CIDER

Pat McIlrath, Grinnell, Iowa

Here's a refreshing cooler for a late-summer afternoon. The cider is so pretty served in a clear sparkling glass!

1 pint (2 cups) fresh *or* frozen raspberries
4 cups apple cider
Mint sprigs, optional

In a bowl, crush berries. Add cider and mix well. Strain through a fine sieve or cheesecloth. Chill. Garnish with mint sprigs if desired. **Yield:** about 5 cups.

CHEESEBURGER BITES

Holly Camozzi, Petaluma, California

This is a recipe from my mother. I like to make up a batch or two and store them in the freezer till I'm ready to cook them.

1/2 pound lean ground beef
2 tablespoons grated onion
1 egg yolk
1/2 teaspoon salt
Dash pepper
6 slices bread
24 cubes cheddar cheese (1/2-inch cubes)

In a bowl, combine beef, onion, egg yolk, salt and pepper. Shape into 3/4-in. balls. Remove crusts from bread; roll flat and cut into 1-1/2-in. rounds. Place meatballs on bread rounds, making sure bread is covered with meat mixture. Make an indentation in each meatball; place a cheese cube in the center. Place on baking sheet. Broil about 6 in. from the heat for 3-5 minutes or until no longer pink. Garnish with ketchup, mustard, sliced green onions or sliced dill pickles if desired. **Yield:** 2 dozen.

SESAME CHICKEN WITH HONEY SAUCE

Donna Shull, Pipersville, Pennsylvania

(PICTURED AT RIGHT)

Between working and raising three children, we don't have much time on our hands. These crunchy chicken bites can be prepared in a hurry for a super snack or light dinner.

1/2 cup dry bread crumbs
1/4 cup sesame seeds
1/2 cup mayonnaise
1 teaspoon ground mustard
1 teaspoon dried minced onion
4 cups cubed cooked chicken
SAUCE:
1/2 cup mayonnaise
1/4 cup honey

In a resealable plastic bag, mix bread crumbs and sesame seeds; set aside. In a small bowl, combine mayonnaise, mustard and onion. Coat chicken pieces with mayonnaise mixture; toss in crumb mixture. Place on a greased baking sheet. Bake, uncovered, at 425° for 10-12 minutes or until lightly browned. Combine sauce ingredients; serve with the hot chicken. **Yield:** 4-6 servings.

BAKED ASPARAGUS DIP

Sandra Baratka, Phillips, Wisconsin

Since I'm from Wisconsin, I thought it was only logical to put together a vegetable and a cheese... two of the things this state produces in abundance.

> **1 pound fresh asparagus, diced, cooked and drained**
> **1 cup grated Parmesan cheese**
> **1 cup mayonnaise**
> **Snack rye bread**

Combine asparagus, cheese and mayonnaise. Place in an ungreased 2-cup ovenproof bowl. Bake, uncovered, at 375° for 20 minutes. Serve with bread. **Yield:** 6-8 servings.

MAPLE HOT CHOCOLATE

Darlene Miller, Linn, Missouri

(PICTURED BELOW)

When I first developed this version of hot chocolate, my husband was quite skeptical. But after one taste, his doubts were erased.

> **1/4 cup sugar**
> **1 tablespoon baking cocoa**
> **1/8 teaspoon salt**

> **1/4 cup hot water**
> **1 tablespoon butter *or* margarine**
> **4 cups milk**
> **1 teaspoon maple flavoring**
> **1 teaspoon vanilla extract**
> **12 large marshmallows**

In a large saucepan, combine sugar, cocoa and salt. Stir in hot water and butter; bring to a boil. Add the milk, flavorings and 8 marshmallows. Heat through, stirring occasionally, until marshmallows are melted. Pour into mugs and top each with a marshmallow. **Yield:** 4 servings.

QUICK GUACAMOLE

Linda Fox, Soldotna, Alaska

This delicious dip always hits the spot when we have a craving for something to munch on. For a quick recipe, it really has authentic guacamole taste.

> **1 medium ripe avocado**
> **1/2 cup small-curd cottage cheese**
> **1/3 cup picante sauce *or* salsa**
> **1/2 teaspoon minced seeded jalapeno pepper, optional**
> **Tortilla chips *or* fresh vegetables**

In a bowl, mash the avocado. Stir in cottage cheese and picante sauce. Add jalapeno if desired. Serve with chips or vegetables. **Yield:** about 1-1/2 cups.

APPLE PIE A LA MODE SHAKE

Tina Wilson, Panama City, Florida

I'm always looking for good-tasting yet nutritious treats for our toddler. This shake complements any breakfast and also makes a great snack.

> **1 cup (8 ounces) plain yogurt**
> **1/2 cup applesauce, frozen**
> **2 tablespoons brown sugar**
> **1/2 teaspoon ground cinnamon**
> **1/2 teaspoon vanilla extract**

In a blender, combine all ingredients; cover and blend until smooth. Serve immediately. **Yield:** 1-2 servings.

CHEESE CRISPS

Janelle Lee, Sulphur, Louisiana

The surprising crunch of these fun snacks makes them great for parties or anytime.

> **1 cup butter *or* margarine, softened**
> **2 cups all-purpose flour**

1/2 teaspoon salt
1/4 teaspoon cayenne pepper
3 cups crisp rice cereal
2 cups (8 ounces) shredded sharp cheddar
cheese

In a mixing bowl, cream the butter. Slowly mix in flour, salt and cayenne pepper. Stir in cereal and cheese. Shape into 1-1/2-in. balls; place on ungreased baking sheets. Bake at 350° for 15-17 minutes or until lightly browned. Serve warm or cold. **Yield:** 3 dozen.

COUNTRY CHEESE SNACKS

Sandy Thorn, Sonora, California

(PICTURED AT RIGHT)

This is one of my favorite appetizers. They take just minutes to prepare.

1 cup mayonnaise
1 cup grated Parmesan cheese
1 package (8 ounces) cream cheese,
softened
2 green onions, minced
18 slices snack rye bread
Parsley sprigs
Sliced stuffed olives

In a small bowl, combine the first four ingredients. Spread on bread; place on a baking sheet. Broil 4 in. from the heat for 1-2 minutes or until golden and bubbly. Garnish with parsley and olives. Serve immediately. **Yield:** 1-1/2 dozen.

TACO TARTLETS

Mary Little, Richardson, Texas

The bright colors in these zippy little tarts make any gathering a festive one. They freeze well, too.

FILLING:
1 cup (8 ounces) sour cream
3 tablespoons chopped ripe olives
2 tablespoons taco sauce
1 cup coarsely crushed tortilla chips
MEAT SHELLS:
1 pound ground beef
2 tablespoons taco seasoning
2 tablespoons water
1 cup (4 ounces) shredded cheddar
cheese

In a mixing bowl, combine filling ingredients; set aside. In another bowl, combine beef, taco seasoning and water; mix well. Press onto the bottom and sides of mini-muffin cups. Place a teaspoonful of filling into each meat shell; sprinkle with cheese. Bake at 425° for 7-8 minutes or until meat is no longer pink and filling is bubbly. Remove immediately from pan. Serve warm. **Yield:** about 2 dozen.

FRUIT PUNCH

Ruth Tacoma, Falmouth, Michigan

This punch really fills the bill for those on special diets. You'd never know it's good for you!

✓ This tasty dish uses less sugar, salt and fat. Recipe includes *Diabetic Exchanges*.

1 package (5 ounces) sweetened tropical
punch flavored soft drink mix
4-3/4 cups water
1 can (12 ounces) frozen orange juice
concentrate, thawed
4 quarts white soda

In a large pitcher, combine soft drink mix and water; mix well. Add orange juice concentrate; mix well. Just before serving, pour into punch bowl and add the white soda. **Yield:** 20 servings (5 quarts). **Diabetic Exchanges:** One 1-cup serving (prepared with sugar-free punch mix, unsweetened orange juice concentrate and diet soda) equals 1/2 fruit; also 38 calories, 3 mg sodium, 0 cholesterol, 9 gm carbohydrate, trace protein, trace fat.

CALIFORNIA FRESH FRUIT DIP

Nancy Cutright, San Jose, California

(PICTURED ABOVE)

I tried this dip at a potluck lunch and loved it. I think it represents California because of the abundance of fresh fruit grown here.

✓ This tasty dish uses less sugar, salt and fat. Recipe includes *Diabetic Exchanges*.

- 1 cup plain yogurt
- 2 tablespoons honey
- 2 tablespoons lime juice
- 1 teaspoon grated lime peel
- 1/4 teaspoon ground ginger

Fresh fruit

In a small bowl, combine the first five ingredients. Chill until serving. Serve with fruit. **Yield:** about 1 cup. **Diabetic Exchanges:** One 2-tablespoon serving (prepared with low-fat yogurt) equals 1/4 fruit, 1/4 skim milk; also, 33 calories, 22 mg sodium, 1 mg cholesterol, 7 gm carbohydrate, 2 gm protein, trace fat.

BEST DEVILED EGGS

Anne Foust, Bluefield, West Virginia

Herbs lend a nice zest to these pick-up-and-eat accompaniments. Everyone enjoys them.

- 12 hard-cooked eggs
- 1/2 cup mayonnaise

- 2 tablespoons milk
- 1 teaspoon dried parsley flakes
- 1/2 teaspoon dried chives
- 1/2 teaspoon ground mustard
- 1/2 teaspoon dill weed
- 1/4 teaspoon salt
- 1/4 teaspoon paprika
- 1/8 teaspoon pepper
- 1/8 teaspoon garlic powder

Fresh parsley and additional paprika

Slice eggs in half lengthwise; remove yolks and set whites aside. In a small bowl, mash yolks. Add the next 10 ingredients; mix well. Evenly fill the whites. Garnish with parsley and paprika. Refrigerate until ready to serve. Refrigerate leftovers. **Yield:** 2 dozen.

WHITE CHOCOLATE PARTY MIX

Norene Wright, Manilla, Indiana

You won't be able to stop eating this irresistible mix. The lightly sweet coating is great over cereal, peanuts, pretzels and M&M's.

- 5 cups Cheerios
- 5 cups Corn Chex
- 2 cups salted peanuts
- 1 pound M&M's
- 1 package (10 ounces) miniature pretzels
- 2 packages (12 ounces *each*) vanilla baking chips
- 3 tablespoons vegetable oil

In a large bowl, combine the first five ingredients; set aside. In a microwave-safe bowl, heat vanilla chips and oil on medium-high for 2 minutes, stirring once. Microwave on high for 10 seconds; stir until smooth. Pour over cereal mixture and mix well. Spread onto three waxed paper-lined baking sheets. Cool; break apart. Store in an airtight container. **Yield:** 5 quarts. **Editor's Note:** This recipe was tested in a 700-watt microwave.

STRAWBERRY YOGURT DIP

Nancy Johnson, Laverne, Oklahoma

When I was hostess for our monthly ladies' meeting years ago, I served this light, fluffy dip with a variety of fruit.

- 1-1/2 cups frozen whole strawberries, thawed
- 1 carton (8 ounces) strawberry yogurt
- 1 cup whipped topping

Fresh fruit *or* angel food cake

In a bowl, mash berries. Add yogurt and mix well. Fold in whipped topping. Serve with fruit or cake. **Yield:** 2-3/4 cups.

HOMEMADE ORANGE REFRESHER

Iola Egle, McCook, Nebraska

Family and friends will thank you for serving this cool, tangy orange drink on warm evenings.

   3/4 cup cold water
   1 can (6 ounces) frozen orange juice
      concentrate, thawed
   1/3 cup sugar
   1/3 cup instant nonfat dry milk powder
   2 teaspoons vanilla extract
   10 to 12 ice cubes
Orange slices and mint, optional

In a blender, combine the first five ingredients; cover and blend on high. Add ice cubes, a few at a time, blending until slushy. Garnish with orange slices and mint if desired. Serve immediately. **Yield:** 4 servings.

FAST PUNCH. Don't throw away that juice from canned fruit. Pour leftover juice into a container—combining different flavors if you like—and freeze. Thaw later for an easy-to-make punch.

FIESTA APPETIZERS

Sharon Skildum, Maple Grove, Minnesota

The fact that these appetizers go from freezer to oven means less last-minute kitchen fuss...and more time to spend with guests.

   1 pound ground beef
   1 pound bulk pork sausage
   1 medium onion, chopped
   1 pound Mexican-style process
      American cheese, cubed
   1 tablespoon Worcestershire sauce
   1 teaspoon dried oregano
Salt and pepper to taste
   1 loaf (1 pound) sliced snack rye bread

In a skillet over medium heat, cook beef, sausage and onion until meat is browned and onion is tender; drain well. Stir in the cheese, Worcestershire sauce and seasonings. Spread 1 heaping tablespoon of mixture onto each slice of bread. Broil 4 in. from the heat for 3 minutes or until hot and bubbly. **Yield:** about 4 dozen. **Editor's Note:** These may be frozen and broiled without defrosting.

HONEY-GLAZED SNACK MIX

Jan Olson, New Hope, Minnesota

(PICTURED BELOW)

This recipe earned me a blue ribbon at a local fair. I hope you enjoy its slightly sweet flavor.

   8 cups Crispix cereal
   3 cups miniature pretzels
   2 cups pecan halves
   2/3 cup butter *or* margarine
   1/2 cup honey

In a large bowl, combine the cereal, pretzels and pecans; set aside. In a small saucepan, melt butter; stir in honey until well blended. Pour over cereal mixture and stir to coat. Spread into two greased 15-in. x 10-in. x 1-in. baking pans. Bake at 350° for 12-15 minutes or until mixture is lightly glazed, stirring occasionally. Cool in pan for 3 minutes; remove from pan and spread on waxed paper to cool completely. Store in an airtight container. **Yield:** about 12 cups.

HAMBURGER-BROCCOLI DIP

Marvel Maki, Ponca City, Oklahoma

Here's an appetizer that's guaranteed to keep hunger pangs at bay until dinner's ready!

- 1/2 pound ground beef
- 1/2 teaspoon salt
- 1 pound process American cheese, cubed
- 1 can (10 ounces) diced tomatoes with green chilies, undrained
- 1 package (10 ounces) frozen chopped broccoli, cooked and drained

Corn chips

In a skillet over medium heat, brown beef and salt; drain. Add cheese; cook and stir until melted. Add tomatoes and broccoli; mix well. Serve with chips. **Yield:** 8-10 servings.

ASPARAGUS APPETIZER ROLL-UPS

Mrs. Howard Lansinger, Pineola, North Carolina

(PICTURED BELOW)

This is a wonderful warm appetizer for spring-time entertaining. It's perfect for showers and also makes a tasty first course for Easter dinner.

- 12 slices white bread, crusts removed
- 1 carton (8 ounces) soft cream cheese
- 8 bacon strips, cooked and crumbled
- 2 tablespoons chopped green onions
- 24 fresh asparagus spears
- 1/4 cup butter *or* margarine, melted
- 3 tablespoons grated Parmesan cheese

Flatten bread with a rolling pin. In a small bowl, combine the cream cheese, bacon and onions. Spread mixture over bread. Cut asparagus to fit bread; place two spears on each slice. Roll up and place, seam side down, on a greased baking sheet. Brush with butter; sprinkle with Parmesan cheese. Bake, uncovered, at 400° for 10-12 minutes or until lightly browned. Serve immediately. **Yield:** 1 dozen.

HOT CHEESE DIP

Ardyce Piehl, Wisconsin Dells, Wisconsin

I'm a teacher, and when a colleague brought this dip to our regular staff potluck, I immediately gave it an A+.

- 2 cups (8 ounces) shredded mozzarella cheese
- 2 cups (8 ounces) shredded sharp cheddar cheese
- 2 cups mayonnaise
- 1 medium onion, diced
- 1 can (4 ounces) chopped green chilies, drained

1-1/2 ounces sliced pepperoni
1/2 cup sliced ripe olives
Rye chips, crackers *or* fresh vegetables

In an ungreased shallow baking dish or pie plate, combine the first five ingredients. Top with pepperoni and olives. Bake, uncovered, at 325° for 25 minutes or until bubbly. Serve with rye chips, crackers or vegetables. **Yield:** 36 servings.

CAPPUCCINO SHAKE

Paula Pelis, Rocky Point, New York

I created this quick and easy shake as a special treat for my mom. She was tickled pink!

✓ This tasty dish uses less sugar, salt and fat. Recipe includes *Diabetic Exchanges*.

1 cup milk
1-1/2 teaspoons instant coffee crystals
4 teaspoons sugar *or* sugar substitute equivalent
2 drops vanilla *or* rum extract
Dash ground cinnamon

In a blender, combine milk, coffee crystals, sugar and vanilla. Cover and blend until coffee is dissolved. Serve immediately. Garnish with a dash of cinnamon. For a hot drink, pour into a mug and heat in a microwave. **Yield:** 1 serving.
Diabetic Exchanges: One serving (prepared with skim milk and sugar substitute) equals 1 skim milk; also, 100 calories, 128 mg sodium, 4 mg cholesterol, 15 gm carbohydrate, 9 gm protein, trace fat.

THREE-HERB POPCORN

Flo Burtnett, Gage, Oklahoma

This snack rates as the No. 1 nighttime treat in my family. The herbs and nuts put a different twist on plain popcorn.

6 quarts (24 cups) popped popcorn
Salt to taste
1/2 cup butter *or* margarine
1 teaspoon dried basil
1 teaspoon dried chervil *or* oregano
1/2 teaspoon dried thyme
1 can (12 ounces) mixed nuts, optional

Place popcorn in a large container or roasting pan. Salt to taste and set aside. Melt butter; stir in basil, chervil and thyme. Drizzle over popcorn and toss lightly to coat evenly. Stir in nuts if desired. **Yield:** about 20 cups.

SPICY CRANBERRY WARMER

Marlene Cartwright, Sierra City, California

(PICTURED ABOVE)

I like serving this drink to winter guests at our bed-and-breakfast as they warm up in front of our stone fireplace—it's a favorite with everyone for its heavenly scent!

4 cups apple cider
3 whole cloves
2 cinnamon sticks (3 inches)
2 whole allspice
1/3 cup packed brown sugar
4 cups cranberry juice
Additional cinnamon sticks, optional

Pour cider into a large saucepan. Tie cloves, cinnamon and allspice in a small cheesecloth bag; add to saucepan. (Or place loose spices in saucepan and strain before serving.) Cover and simmer for 5 minutes. Stir in sugar and simmer 5 minutes longer. Add cranberry juice and heat through. Remove spice bag. Serve hot in mugs. Garnish with cinnamon sticks if desired. **Yield:** 8-10 servings (2 quarts).

2 packages (8 ounces *each*) cream cheese,
   softened
1 cup (4 ounces) shredded cheddar cheese
1 to 2 tablespoons chopped onion
1 to 2 tablespoons chopped fresh parsley
1 to 2 teaspoons lemon juice
1 to 2 teaspoons Worcestershire sauce
1-1/2 to 2 cups ground walnuts
Crackers

In a small bowl, combine the first six ingredients;
mix well. Shape into 1-1/2-in. balls. Roll in nuts.
Chill. Serve with crackers. **Yield:** 20 servings.

BLACK BEAN SALSA

Susan Cochran, Anaheim, California

*Why serve store-bought salsa when you can
make this fast-to-fix homemade version? It's filling and flavorful.*

1 can (15 ounces) black beans, *divided*
2 tablespoons lime juice
3 plum tomatoes, seeded and chopped
1 medium onion, chopped
2 to 4 tablespoons chopped fresh parsley
   or cilantro
1 garlic clove, minced
Salt to taste
Tortilla chips

Drain beans, reserving 1 tablespoon liquid. In a
bowl, combine liquid, half the beans and lime
juice; mash until smooth. Stir in the tomatoes,
onion, parsley, garlic, salt and remaining beans.
Serve with chips. **Yield:** 4-6 servings.

CROWD-PLEASING PUNCH

Ruby Andersen, Walnut, Iowa

*I first made this punch to serve at each of our
children's wedding receptions. Since then, I've
taken it to many get-togethers.*

3 quarts water
2 cans (46 ounces *each*) pineapple juice
2 cans (46 ounces *each*) apricot nectar
3 cans (12 ounces *each*) frozen orange
   juice concentrate, thawed
3 cans (12 ounces *each*) frozen lemonade
   concentrate, thawed
3 cups sugar
4 packages (.15 ounce *each*) orange-
   flavored soft drink mix
3 bottles (28 ounces *each*) ginger ale,
   chilled

HOLIDAY NOG

Nancy Schickling, Bedford, Virginia

(PICTURED ABOVE)

*I developed this delicious recipe for my diabetic
mother. This festive drink has real taste appeal.*

✓ This tasty dish uses less sugar, salt and fat. Recipe includes *Diabetic Exchanges*.

1 package (3.4 ounces) instant vanilla
   pudding mix
7 cups cold milk, *divided*
1 to 2 teaspoons vanilla *or* rum extract
2 tablespoons sugar *or* sugar substitute
   equivalent
1 cup evaporated milk

Combine pudding mix, 2 cups of milk, vanilla and
sugar in a bowl; mix according to package directions. Pour into a half-gallon container with a tight-
fitting lid. Add 3 cups milk; cover and shake well.
Add evaporated milk and shake. Add remaining
milk; shake well. Chill. **Yield:** 8 servings. **Diabetic
Exchanges:** One serving (prepared with sugar-free
pudding mix, skim milk, sugar substitute and evaporated skim milk) equals 1 skim milk, 1/4 starch; also, 107 calories, 187 mg sodium, 1 mg cholesterol,
15 gm carbohydrate, 10 gm protein, 1 gm fat.

INDIVIDUAL CHEESE BALLS

Mildred Sherrer, Bay City, Texas

*With their creamy, nutty flavor, these small
cheese balls work great in a bag lunch.*

In a 6-gal. container, combine the first seven ingredients; mix well. Just before serving, pour one-third of punch mixture into a punch bowl; add 1 bottle of ginger ale. Repeat with remaining punch mixture and ginger ale as needed. **Yield:** 100 servings (about 3-1/2 gallons).

Italian Stuffed Mushrooms

Virginia Slater, West Sunbury, Pennsylvania

(PICTURED BELOW)

These appealing appetizers get hearty flavor from the ham, bacon and cheese. They look lovely and really curb hunger.

    4 **bacon strips, diced**
  24 **to 30 large fresh mushrooms**
1/4 **pound ground fully cooked ham**
    1 **cup onion and garlic salad croutons, crushed**
    1 **cup (4 ounces) shredded mozzarella cheese**
1/4 **cup grated Parmesan cheese**
    1 **medium tomato, finely chopped**
    2 **tablespoons minced fresh parsley**
1-1/2 **teaspoons minced fresh oregano *or* 1/2 teaspoon dried oregano**

In a skillet, cook the bacon until crisp. Meanwhile, remove mushroom stems from caps; set caps aside. Mince half the stems and discard the rest; add minced stems to bacon and drippings. Saute for 2-3 minutes. Remove from the heat and stir in remaining ingredients. Firmly stuff mushroom caps. Place in a greased 15-in. x 10-in. x 1-in. baking pan. Bake at 425° for 12-15 minutes or until tender. **Yield:** 2-1/2 to 3 dozen.

Mexican Deviled Eggs

Susan Klemm, Rhinelander, Wisconsin

We live on a beautiful lake and host lots of summer picnics and cookouts. Folks who are expecting the same old deviled eggs are surprised when they try this delightful tangy variation.

    8 **hard-cooked eggs**
1/2 **cup shredded cheddar cheese**
1/4 **cup mayonnaise**
1/4 **cup salsa**
    2 **tablespoons sliced green onions**
    1 **tablespoon sour cream**
Salt to taste

Slice the eggs in half lengthwise; remove yolks and set whites aside. In a small bowl, mash yolks. Add the next six ingredients. Evenly fill the whites. Refrigerate until ready to serve. **Yield:** 16 servings.

East Coast Crab Appetizers

Mrs. William Hitchens, Georgetown, Delaware

(PICTURED ABOVE)

These appetizers are simple to make and absolutely delicious. We love seafood here on the East Coast, so I make these often.

- 1/2 pound process American cheese
- 3/4 cup butter *or* margarine
- 1 pound cooked crabmeat *or* 3 cans (6 ounces *each*) crabmeat, drained
- 1 can (4 ounces) mushrooms, chopped
- 12 English muffins, split, toasted and quartered

In a saucepan over low heat, melt cheese and butter. Add crab and mushrooms. Spoon onto muffins; place on baking sheet. Broil 4 in. from the heat until lightly browned. **Yield:** 8 dozen.

Shrimp and Cheddar Snacks

Margery Bryan, Royal City, Washington

If time is short, prepare the spread ahead. When guests arrive, quickly assemble and bake.

- 2 cups (8 ounces) shredded cheddar cheese
- 1 cup mayonnaise
- 1 can (6 ounces) broken shrimp, rinsed and drained
- 1 small onion, finely chopped
- 1/4 teaspoon garlic powder
- 42 slices snack rye bread, toasted

In a bowl, combine cheese, mayonnaise, shrimp, onion and garlic powder; mix well. Spread 1 tablespoon over each slice of bread; place on ungreased baking sheets. Bake at 350° for 7-9 minutes or until bubbly. Serve hot. **Yield:** 3-1/2 dozen.

Tuna Dill Spread

Geraldine Grisdale, Mt. Pleasant, Michigan

Although I most frequently serve this as a snack, it also makes a wonderful sandwich spread.

- 1 can (6-1/8 ounces) tuna, drained and flaked
- 1 package (3 ounces) cream cheese, softened
- 1/3 cup finely chopped seeded cucumber
- 2 tablespoons lemon juice
- 1 to 2 tablespoons minced fresh dill
- 1/2 teaspoon salt
- 1/4 teaspoon pepper

Crackers *or* snack rye bread

In a bowl, combine the first seven ingredients; mix well. Serve with crackers or bread. **Yield:** 1-1/4 cups.

White Bean Dip

Linn Landry, Honeydew, California

My family and I enjoy eating this with tortilla chips, crackers and just about anything else we can find to dip into it—including our fingers!

✓ This tasty dish uses less sugar, salt and fat. Recipe includes *Diabetic Exchanges.*

- 1 can (15-1/2 ounces) great northern beans, rinsed and drained
- 2 tablespoons plain yogurt
- 2 tablespoons chopped fresh parsley
- 1 tablespoon lemon juice
- 1/2 teaspoon pepper
- 1/4 teaspoon hot pepper sauce
- 2 to 3 garlic cloves

Salt to taste, optional

Pita bread, corn chips *or* fresh vegetables

In a blender or food processor, combine the first eight ingredients; cover and process until smooth.

Chill. Serve with toasted pita bread triangles, corn chips or vegetables. **Yield:** 1-1/4 cups. **Diabetic Exchanges:** One 1-tablespooon serving (prepared with nonfat yogurt and without salt) equals 1/2 starch; also, 29 calories, 78 mg sodium, trace cholesterol, 6 gm carbohydrate, 2 gm protein, trace fat.

PEACHY YOGURT SHAKE

Charity Lovelace, Anchorage, Alaska

Here's a unique way to eat fruit for breakfast. My two preschoolers think they're really getting away with something when I serve these "milk shakes".

3/4 cup milk
2 cups sliced peeled peaches
1 cup peach yogurt
1 cup cracked ice
2 tablespoons sugar
2 drops almond extract

In a blender, place all ingredients in the order given; cover and blend until smooth. Serve immediately. **Yield:** 3-4 servings.

MOZZARELLA PUFFS

Joan Mousley Dziuba, Waupaca, Wisconsin

These savory cheese biscuits go over great at my house. Since they're so quick to make, I can whip up a batch anytime my family asks for them.

1 tube (7-1/2 ounces) refrigerated buttermilk biscuits
1 teaspoon dried oregano
1 block (2 to 3 ounces) mozzarella cheese
2 tablespoons pizza sauce

Make an indentation in the center of each biscuit; sprinkle with oregano. Cut the mozzarella into 10 cubes, 3/4 in. each; place a cube in the center of each biscuit. Pinch dough tightly around cheese to seal. Place, seam side down, on an ungreased baking sheet. Spread pizza sauce over tops. Bake at 375° for 10-12 minutes or until golden brown. **Yield:** 10 servings.

ORANGE TEA

Sally Mueller, Loveland, Colorado

(PICTURED AT RIGHT)

My children always appreciated a hot cup of this beverage after walking home from school. The tea is refreshing and tasty, and it warms you up.

7 cups water
1 can (12 ounces) frozen orange juice concentrate
1/2 cup sugar
2 tablespoons lemon juice
5 teaspoons instant tea
1 teaspoon whole cloves

In a large saucepan, combine water, orange juice concentrate, sugar, lemon juice and tea. Tie the cloves in a small cheesecloth bag; add to saucepan. (Or place the cloves in saucepan and strain before serving.) Simmer, uncovered, for 15-20 minutes. Remove spice bag. Serve hot. Store leftovers in a glass container in the refrigerator. **Yield:** 8 servings (2 quarts).

MEXICAN HOT CHOCOLATE

Kathy Young, Weatherford, Texas

(PICTURED BELOW)

This delicious, not-too-sweet hot chocolate is richly flavored with cocoa and delicately seasoned with spices. The blend of cinnamon and chocolate flavors is wonderful!

  1/4 cup baking cocoa
   2 tablespoons brown sugar
   1 cup boiling water
   3 cups milk
  1/4 teaspoon ground cinnamon
Dash ground cloves *or* nutmeg
   1 teaspoon vanilla extract
Whipped cream
Cinnamon sticks, optional

In a large saucepan, combine cocoa and sugar; stir in water. Bring to boil; reduce heat and cook for 2 minutes, stirring constantly. Add milk, cinnamon and cloves. Simmer for 5 minutes (do not boil). Whisk in vanilla. Pour into mugs and top with whipped cream. Garnish with cinnamon sticks if desired. **Yield:** 4 servings.

CHICKEN NUGGETS

Annette Ellyson, Carolina, West Virginia

I like to make these golden chicken nuggets because they're so quick and easy and the whole family loves them.

   1 cup all-purpose flour
   4 teaspoons seasoned salt
   1 teaspoon paprika
   1 teaspoon poultry seasoning
   1 teaspoon ground mustard
  1/2 teaspoon pepper
   8 boneless skinless chicken breast halves
  1/4 cup olive *or* vegetable oil

In a large resealable plastic bag, combine the first six ingredients. Flatten chicken to 1/2-in. thickness and cut into 1-1/2-in. pieces. Place chicken pieces, a few at a time, into bag and shake to coat. Heat oil in a skillet; cook chicken, turning frequently, for 6-8 minutes or until browned and juices run clear. **Yield:** 8-10 servings.

FRUIT ON A STICK

Faye Hintz, Springfield, Missouri

In the summer, my family loves this fun finger food with its smooth, creamy dip.

   1 package (8 ounces) cream cheese, softened
   1 jar (7 ounces) marshmallow creme
   3 to 4 tablespoons milk
Whole strawberries
Melon and kiwifruit, cut into bite-size pieces

Mix cream cheese, marshmallow creme and milk until smooth. Thread fruit on skewers; serve with dip. **Yield:** 1-1/2 cups dip.

RHUBARB PUNCH

Patty Hamm, Kuna, Idaho

This is a lively new twist on lemonade and a fun way to use up some of your extra rhubarb.

   1 pound fresh *or* frozen rhubarb, chopped
   1 cup water
  1/2 cup sugar
   1 can (6 ounces) frozen pink lemonade concentrate, thawed
   1 bottle (1 liter) lemon-lime soda

In a large saucepan, combine rhubarb, water and sugar. Bring to a boil; reduce heat and simmer 5-10 minutes or until rhubarb is tender. Cool slightly. Place half the mixture at a time in a blender; cover and process until smooth. Pour into a large container; add lemonade concentrate, soda and enough water to make 1 gal. Serve on ice. **Yield:** 16 servings (1 gallon).

TRAIL MIX

Sandra Thorn, Sonora, California

This is a super snack. In small gingham bags, it made wonderful party favors for the cowboy-theme wedding shower I hosted.

- **2 pounds dry roasted peanuts**
- **2 pounds cashews**
- **1 pound raisins**
- **1 pound M&M's**
- **8 ounces flaked coconut**

Combine all ingredients in a large bowl. Store in an airtight container. **Yield:** 6 quarts.

SWEET MINGLERS

Mary Obeilin, Selinsgrove, Pennsylvania

This snack mix is perfect for a late-night treat or a pick-me-up anytime of the day. It's a slightly different cereal snack because of the chocolate and peanut butter.

- **1 cup (6 ounces) semisweet chocolate chips**
- **1/4 cup creamy peanut butter**

6 cups Corn *or* Rice Chex cereal
1 cup confectioners' sugar

In a large microwave-safe bowl, melt chocolate chips on high for 1 minute. Stir; microwave 30 seconds longer or until the chips are melted. Stir in peanut butter. Gently stir in cereal until well coated; set aside. Place confectioners' sugar in a 2-gal. resealable plastic bag. Add cereal mixture and shake until well coated. Store in an airtight container in the refrigerator. **Yield:** about 6 cups. **Editor's Note:** This recipe was tested in a 700-watt microwave.

VEGGIE CHRISTMAS TREE

Leola Seltmann, Wichita, Kansas

(PICTURED ABOVE)

I have served this festive dish for years. Everyone comments on how pretty it is.

✓ This tasty dish uses less sugar, salt and fat. Recipe includes *Diabetic Exchanges*.

- **1 bottle (8 ounces) ranch salad dressing**
- **4 cups broccoli florets**
- **1 broccoli stem**
- **3 to 4 cups cauliflowerets**
- **4 to 5 cherry tomatoes, quartered**
- **1 medium carrot, sliced**

Cover the bottom of a 13-in. x 9-in. x 2-in. glass dish with dressing. Arrange broccoli in a tree shape, using the stem as the trunk. Place cauliflower around tree. Add tomatoes and carrot slices as ornaments. **Yield:** 20 servings. **Diabetic Exchanges:** One serving (prepared with low-fat dressing) equals 1 vegetable; also, 37 calories, 102 mg sodium, 0 cholesterol, 4 gm carbohydrate, 2 gm protein, 2 gm fat.

Hearty Main Salads

STRAWBERRY-ORANGE CHICKEN SALAD

Jerry Minerich, Westminster, Colorado

(PICTURED AT RIGHT)

This salad is light and tasty and good enough for special guests. Folks are surprised to hear syrup is an ingredient.

2 cups torn spinach
2 cups torn leaf lettuce
3/4 cup cubed cooked chicken
2/3 cup sliced fresh strawberries
1 orange, peeled and sectioned
1/4 cup strawberry-flavored pancake syrup
2 tablespoons cider *or* red wine vinegar
1/4 cup cashews *or* pecans, optional

Arrange spinach and lettuce on two salad plates. Top with chicken, strawberries and orange sections. Combine syrup and vinegar; drizzle over salads. Top with nuts if desired. **Yield:** 2 servings.

BEEF AND PASTA MEDLEY

Jo Ann Satsky, Bandera, Texas

(PICTURED AT RIGHT)

My husband and I like zesty pasta salads and have tried many different types. This delightful dish can be eaten warm or cold, so it's a perfect meal anytime of year.

3 cups spiral pasta, cooked and drained
1 medium green pepper, julienned
1 cup halved cherry tomatoes
1/2 cup sliced ripe olives
1 pound boneless top sirloin, cut into strips
2 tablespoons cooking oil
1 bottle (8 ounces) Italian salad dressing
1-1/2 cups (6 ounces) shredded provolone *or* mozzarella cheese
Breadsticks, optional

In a large bowl, combine pasta, green pepper, tomatoes and olives. In a skillet over medium-high heat, stir-fry beef in oil until cooked as desired; drain. Spoon meat over pasta. Add dressing to skillet and bring to a boil. Pour over pasta mixture; toss to coat. Add cheese. Serve with breadsticks if desired. **Yield:** 4-6 servings.

SALMON PASTA SALAD

Mary Dennis, Bryan, Ohio

I've used this recipe for years. In fact, I've had it so long that I don't even remember where it came from originally. This salad is a nice light meal for a hot summer day, and it lets the salmon flavor come through.

1 package (8 ounces) spiral pasta, cooked and drained
2 cups fully cooked salmon chunks *or* 1 can (14-3/4 ounces) pink salmon, drained, bones and skin removed
1-1/2 cups quartered cherry tomatoes
1 medium cucumber, quartered and sliced
1 small red onion, sliced
1/2 cup vegetable oil
1/3 cup lemon *or* lime juice
1-1/2 teaspoons dill weed
1 garlic clove, minced
3/4 teaspoon salt
1/4 teaspoon pepper
1 head iceberg lettuce, torn

In a large bowl, toss the pasta, salmon, tomatoes, cucumber and onion. For dressing, combine oil, lemon juice, dill, garlic, salt and pepper; mix well. Pour over pasta mixture and toss to coat. Serve over lettuce. **Yield:** 6-8 servings.

> **LIVELY LUNCHES.** *Pictured at right, top to bottom: Strawberry-Orange Chicken Salad and Beef and Pasta Medley (both recipes on this page).*

HAM SALAD

Patricia Reed, Pine Bluff, Arkansas

I first made this for a shower and everyone raved about it. Now when I go to a potluck, I take this salad...and copies of the recipe.

3/4 cup mayonnaise
1/2 cup finely chopped celery
1/4 cup thinly sliced green onions
2 tablespoons minced chives
1 tablespoon honey
2 teaspoons spicy brown mustard
1/2 teaspoon Worcestershire sauce
1/2 teaspoon seasoned salt
5 cups diced fully cooked ham *or* turkey
1/3 cup chopped pecans *and/or* almonds, toasted
Cantaloupe wedges, optional

In a large bowl, combine the first eight ingredients; mix well. Fold in ham. Add nuts and toss. Serve on cantaloupe wedges if desired. **Yield:** 4-6 servings.

STIR-FRY SPINACH SALAD

Victoria Schreur, Lowell, Michigan

I'm sure you and your family will like the slightly sweet-and-sour sauce in this unique salad.

✓ This tasty dish uses less sugar, salt and fat. Recipe includes *Diabetic Exchanges*.

1 can (8 ounces) pineapple chunks
1 pound boneless skinless chicken breasts, julienned
2 tablespoons cooking oil
1 medium green pepper, julienned
3 tablespoons brown sugar
1 tablespoon cornstarch
1/4 cup ketchup
3 tablespoons vinegar
2 tablespoons soy sauce
6 cups torn fresh spinach
1 cup cherry tomato halves

Drain pineapple, reserving 3 tablespoons juice; set pineapple aside. (Discard remaining juice or save for another use.) In a skillet or wok, stir-fry chicken in oil for 5 minutes or until juices run clear. Add green pepper; stir-fry for 2-4 minutes or until crisp-tender. Meanwhile, add brown sugar and cornstarch to reserved pineapple juice; mix well. Stir in ketchup, vinegar and soy sauce until smooth; add to skillet. Cook and stir over medium heat for 2 minutes. Arrange spinach, pineapple and tomatoes on a large serving platter. Top with chicken mixture. **Yield:** 6 servings. **Diabetic Exchanges:** One serving (prepared with unsweetened pineapple and light soy sauce) equals 2 lean meat, 2 vegetable, 1 fruit; also, 230 calories, 480 mg sodium, 53 mg cholesterol, 22 gm carbohydrate, 21 gm protein, 8 gm fat.

BLACK-EYED PEA SALAD

Reesa Byrd, Enterprise, Alabama

Once my family knows I'm making their most-requested dish, it disappears quickly! If there are any leftovers, they taste great the next day.

2 cups cubed cooked chicken
2 teaspoons seasoned salt
1 can (15-1/2 ounces) black-eyed peas, rinsed and drained
1 can (15 ounces) white *or* yellow corn, drained
1 can (8 ounces) sliced water chestnuts, drained
1 cup mayonnaise
1 cup sliced celery
1 cup cooked wild rice
3/4 cup chopped cucumber
1/2 cup fresh broccoli florets
1/2 cup chopped green pepper
1/4 teaspoon pepper

Place the chicken in a large bowl; sprinkle with seasoned salt. Add remaining ingredients and mix well. Cover and refrigerate until ready to serve. **Yield:** 6-8 servings.

SPICY BARBECUE CHICKEN SALAD

Michele Armentrout, New Hope, Virginia

I came up with this one-of-a-kind salad as a way to use leftover barbecued chicken. People who try it can't figure out what makes it so delicious!

3 cups cubed cooked *or* barbecued chicken
1/2 cup chopped celery
1/4 cup finely chopped onion
1/2 cup mayonnaise
3 tablespoons barbecue sauce
1 tablespoon sweet pickle relish
1/4 teaspoon ground mustard
1/4 teaspoon hot pepper sauce
Lettuce leaves, optional

In a large bowl, toss chicken, celery and onion. Combine mayonnaise, barbecue sauce, relish, mustard and hot pepper sauce until well mixed. Stir into chicken mixture. Serve on lettuce if desired. **Yield:** 4-6 servings.

PORK AND SPINACH SALAD

Marian Platt, Sequim, Washington

(PICTURED ABOVE)

You just can't beat this salad. It tastes great and is good for you, too.

✓ This tasty dish uses less sugar, salt and fat. Recipe includes *Diabetic Exchanges*.

    1 package (10 ounces) fresh spinach, torn
    1 can (15-1/2 ounces) black-eyed peas,
      rinsed and drained
  1/2 cup sliced fresh mushrooms
  1/3 cup Italian salad dressing
  1/4 cup sliced green onions
  1/4 cup sliced celery
    1 jar (2 ounces) sliced pimientos, drained
    2 tablespoons sliced ripe olives
    2 garlic cloves, minced
    1 tablespoon olive *or* vegetable oil
  1/2 pound pork tenderloin, cut into thin
      strips

Line four plates with spinach; set aside. In a bowl, combine the peas, mushrooms, dressing, onions, celery, pimientos and olives; set aside. In a medium skillet, saute garlic in oil for 30 seconds. Add pork and stir-fry for 2-3 minutes or until no longer pink. Remove from the heat; add vegetable mixture and mix well. Divide among spinach-lined plates. **Yield:** 4 servings. **Diabetic Exchanges:** One serving (prepared with fat-free Italian dressing) equals 2 oz. meat, 3 vegetable, 1 starch, 1 fat; also, 317 calories, 758 mg sodium, 56 mg cholesterol, 24 gm carbohydrate, 27 gm protein, 13 gm fat.

RANCH-STYLE SALAD

Carol Jacobson, Covina, California

This filling, flavorful salad features potatoes. It makes a hearty meal.

    1 pound bulk Italian sausage
    1 large sweet red pepper, chopped
    1 small onion, chopped
    8 medium potatoes, cooked, peeled and
      cubed
    6 hard-cooked eggs, chopped
    2 cups ranch salad dressing
    3 tablespoons minced watercress, optional

In a skillet, cook and crumble sausage until no longer pink; drain. Add red pepper and onion; saute until tender. Add potatoes and eggs; heat through. Add dressing and watercress if desired. Toss to coat. **Yield:** 6-8 servings.

TURKEY PASTA SALAD

Karen Harris, Lewisville, Indiana

(PICTURED BELOW)

I almost always make this salad when I have left-over turkey. It's inexpensive, delicious and easy to prepare. Plus, my family loves it!

2 cups spiral pasta
1 cup chopped cooked turkey
1 cup chopped celery
1 medium red onion, chopped
1 medium green pepper, chopped
1 cup (8 ounces) sour cream
1 cup mayonnaise *or* salad dressing
1 envelope ranch dressing mix
1 teaspoon garlic salt
1/2 cup slivered almonds
1 teaspoon paprika
Green pepper rings and tomato wedges, optional

Cook the pasta according to package directions; rinse in cold water and drain. In a large bowl, toss pasta, turkey, celery, onion and green pepper. Combine sour cream, mayonnaise, dressing mix and garlic salt. Add to pasta mixture and mix well. Sprinkle with almonds and paprika. Garnish with pepper rings and tomatoes if desired. **Yield:** 6-8 servings.

CHICKEN CAESAR SALAD

Anne Frederick, New Hartford, New York

You'll find this salad makes a nice addition to any brunch buffet. The robust Caesar dressing adds some "zest" to the mild flavors of chicken and vegetables.

1/2 cup mayonnaise
2 anchovy fillets, finely chopped, optional
1 tablespoon grated Parmesan cheese
1 tablespoon cider *or* red wine vinegar
1 teaspoon Worcestershire sauce
1 teaspoon Dijon mustard
1 garlic clove, minced
2 cups cooked chicken strips
1/2 large bunch romaine, torn
1 small red onion, sliced into rings
1 carrot, julienned

In a large bowl, combine the first seven ingredients. Add chicken, romaine, onion and carrot; toss to coat. **Yield:** 4 servings.

TEXICAN RICE SALAD

Rebecca Mininger, El Campo, Texas

This dish is a favorite of my husband's and makes use of the plentiful rice grown in our area.

> 1 pound ground beef
> 1/2 cup chopped onion
> 1/2 cup chili sauce
> 2 garlic cloves, minced
> 1/2 teaspoon salt
> 1 teaspoon chili powder
> 3 cups cooked rice
> 1 can (15 ounces) garbanzo beans, drained
> 1 can (4 ounces) chopped green chilies
> 1 to 2 medium tomatoes, seeded and chopped

Shredded lettuce
Shredded cheddar cheese

In a skillet, brown beef and onion until beef is no longer pink and onion is tender; drain. In a small bowl, combine chili sauce, garlic, salt and chili powder; add to meat mixture. Add rice, beans and chilies; mix well. Cover and cook over medium until heated through. Add tomato; cook 5 minutes more. For each serving, spoon 1 cup meat mixture over lettuce and sprinkle with cheese. **Yield:** 8-10 servings.

CHEF'S SALAD

Eleanore Hill, Fresno, California

(PICTURED ABOVE)

This traditional salad appeared on the menu of the restaurant we owned years ago. The homemade Thousand Island dressing was a hit.

> 1/2 head iceberg lettuce, torn
> 1 can (15 ounces) garbanzo beans, drained, optional
> 1 small cucumber, chopped
> 1 small red onion, chopped
> 1/2 cup sliced radishes
> 1 small tomato, chopped
> 1 cup julienned fully cooked ham
> 1 cup julienned Swiss *or* cheddar cheese

THOUSAND ISLAND DRESSING:

> 1 cup mayonnaise *or* salad dressing
> 1/2 cup *each* ketchup, sweet pickle relish and chopped onion

Dash garlic salt

In a large salad bowl, combine lettuce, beans if desired, cucumber, onion, radishes and tomato. Arrange ham and cheese on top. In a small bowl, combine all dressing ingredients; stir until well blended. Serve with the salad. **Yield:** 6 servings.

SUMMERTIME SALAD WITH HONEY DRESSING

Tami Harrington, Scottsdale, Arizona

My family is delighted whenever I serve this re-freshing salad.

> 4 cups cubed cooked chicken
> 1-1/2 cups fresh peach chunks (about 2 peaches)
> 1-1/2 cups fresh pineapple chunks
> 1 cup sliced fresh strawberries
> 1 cup chopped celery
> 3/4 cup slivered almonds
> 1/2 cup chopped red onion

HONEY DRESSING:

> 1 cup mayonnaise
> 3/4 cup peach preserves *or* orange marmalade
> 1 tablespoon honey
> 2 teaspoons Dijon mustard
> 1/2 teaspoon salt

In a large bowl, combine chicken, fruit, celery, almonds and onion. Mix dressing ingredients in a small bowl. Pour over chicken mixture; toss to coat. **Yield:** 6-8 servings.

SEAFOOD MACARONI SALAD

Frances Harris, Coeur d'Alene, Idaho

(PICTURED BELOW)

My mother said this recipe just "evolved", because she kept adding ingredients until it tasted right. It really does have great flavor!

- 3 cups uncooked elbow macaroni (about 10 ounces)
- 6 ounces cooked salad shrimp
- 1 can (6 ounces) crabmeat, drained and cartilage removed
- 2 cups sliced celery
- 1/2 small onion, finely chopped
- 3 to 4 hard-cooked eggs, coarsely chopped
- 1 cup mayonnaise
- 3 tablespoons sweet pickle relish *or* finely chopped sweet pickles
- 1 tablespoon prepared mustard
- 1 tablespoon vinegar
- 1 teaspoon paprika

Salt and pepper to taste

Cook macaroni according to package directions; rinse in cold water and drain. In a large bowl, toss macaroni, shrimp, crab, celery, onion and eggs; set aside. In a small bowl, mix the mayonnaise, pickle relish, mustard, vinegar and paprika. Add to macaroni mixture; toss to coat. Season with salt and pepper. **Yield:** 8 servings.

PERFECT CHICKEN SALAD

Lora Schnurr, Fort Wayne, Indiana

My godchild doesn't care for vegetables, but he loves this salad...even the peas and carrots!

- 2 cups cubed cooked chicken
- 1/2 cup frozen peas, thawed
- 1/4 cup chopped ripe olives
- 2 tablespoons shredded carrot
- 2 tablespoons finely chopped onion

DRESSING:
- 1/2 cup mayonnaise
- 1 tablespoon yellow *or* spicy brown mustard
- 1/4 teaspoon Worcestershire sauce
- 1/4 teaspoon seasoned salt
- 1/8 teaspoon pepper

In a medium bowl, combine the chicken, peas, olives, carrot and onion. Mix dressing ingredients in a small bowl; pour over salad and toss to coat. **Yield:** 2-3 servings.

REFRESHING TURKEY SALAD

Carolyn Lough, Medley, Alberta

When the heat of summer hits, I want to spend time with my family, not with my oven! So I'll often cook a turkey, then dice and freeze leftovers for fast hearty dishes like this.

✓ This tasty dish uses less sugar, salt and fat. Recipe includes *Diabetic Exchanges*.

- 3 cups cooked wild rice
- 2 cups cubed cooked turkey
- 2 cups thinly sliced celery
- 1/2 cup seedless green grapes, halved
- 1/2 cup seedless red grapes, halved
- 1/4 cup chopped green pepper
- 1/4 cup chopped sweet red pepper
- 1 jar (2 ounces) sliced pimientos, drained
- 1/2 cup mayonnaise
- 1/2 cup sour cream
- 1 tablespoon honey
- 1 teaspoon Dijon mustard
- 1 teaspoon celery seed
- 1/2 teaspoon poppy seeds
- 1/2 teaspoon salt, optional
- 1/4 teaspoon pepper
- 1 tablespoon slivered almonds, toasted, optional

In a large bowl, combine rice, turkey, celery, grapes, peppers and pimientos; set aside. In a small bowl, combine mayonnaise, sour cream, honey, mustard, celery seed, poppy seeds, salt if

desired and pepper; mix well. Pour over rice mixture; toss to coat. Garnish with almonds if desired. **Yield:** 8 servings. **Diabetic Exchanges:** One 1-cup serving (prepared with turkey breast, unsweetened pineapple and fat-free mayonnaise and sour cream, and without salt and almonds) equals 1 starch, 1 very lean meat, 1 vegetable, 1/2 fruit; also, 160 calories, 340 mg sodium, 13 mg cholesterol, 27 gm carbohydrate, 9 gm protein, 1 gm fat.

SPICY GRILLED CHICKEN SALAD

Brenda Eichelberger, Williamsport, Maryland

(PICTURED ABOVE)

I look forward to this filling salad after working in the garden all day.

✓ This tasty dish uses less sugar, salt and fat. Recipe includes *Diabetic Exchanges*.

    1 can (8 ounces) sliced pineapple
    3 tablespoons vegetable oil
    2 tablespoons soy sauce
    1 tablespoon vinegar
    1 tablespoon honey
  1/4 teaspoon ground ginger
  1/4 teaspoon cayenne pepper
    4 boneless skinless chicken breast halves
      (1 pound)
  1/2 to 1 teaspoon seasoned *or* black pepper
    5 cups torn lettuce
    1 small green pepper, julienned
    1 small sweet red pepper, julienned
    1 cup sliced fresh mushrooms
    1 small onion, sliced into rings

Drain pineapple, reserving 2 tablespoons juice; set pineapple aside. In a jar with a tight-fitting lid, combine pineapple juice, oil, soy sauce, vinegar, honey, ginger and cayenne; shake well. Brush some over pineapple slices; set aside. Sprinkle both sides of chicken with pepper; grill or broil for 4-5 minutes on each side or until juices run clear. Cut into strips. Grill or broil pineapple slices on both sides for 2-3 minutes or until heated through. To serve, toss lettuce, peppers, mushrooms and onion in a large bowl and top with chicken and pineapple; or arrange on four plates. Drizzle with remaining dressing. **Yield:** 4 servings. **Diabetic Exchanges:** One serving with 2 tablespoons dressing (prepared with unsweetened pineapple and light soy sauce) equals 3 lean meat, 2 vegetable, 1 fat, 1 fruit; also, 323 calories, 659 mg sodium, 73 mg cholesterol, 21 gm carbohydrate, 29 gm protein, 14 gm fat.

BUSY DAY SALAD

Bettie Walker, Lancaster, California

With our children gone from home, I'm able to make simple, satisfying foods like this for just my husband and me.

    4 cups torn lettuce
  1/4 cup julienned fully cooked ham
  1/4 cup julienned salami
    2 hard-cooked eggs, sliced
DRESSING:
  1/4 cup mayonnaise *or* salad dressing
    4 teaspoons ketchup
    2 teaspoons sweet pickle relish
    2 teaspoons chopped green onion
  1/2 teaspoon lemon juice
  1/4 teaspoon salt

On a serving plate or two individual plates, arrange lettuce, ham, salami and eggs. In a jar with a tight-fitting lid, combine dressing ingredients; shake well. Serve with salad. **Yield:** 2 servings.

CREAMY CHICKEN CRUNCH

Denise Goedeken, Platte Center, Nebraska

(PICTURED ABOVE)

Whenever I take this salad to church functions and family picnics, I always come home with an empty bowl. As any cook knows, that's a sure sign of success!

- 1-1/2 cups cubed cooked chicken
- 1 cup frozen peas, thawed
- 1/2 cup sliced celery
- 1/2 cup chopped green pepper
- 1/2 cup fresh pea pods, halved
- 1/4 cup sliced green onions
- 1 cup mayonnaise
- 2 tablespoons lemon juice
- 1 teaspoon soy sauce
- 1/4 teaspoon ground ginger
- 1 can (3 ounces) chow mein noodles (1-1/2 cups)
- 1/4 cup salted peanuts

In a large bowl, combine the first six ingredients. Stir together mayonnaise, lemon juice, soy sauce and ginger; pour over chicken mixture and toss to coat. Fold in chow mein noodles and peanuts. **Yield:** 4-6 servings.

TURKEY-BLUE CHEESE PASTA SALAD

Angela Leinenbach, Newport News, Virginia

Blue cheese dressing makes this salad unique. I've served it many times, and family and friends never tire of it.

✓ This tasty dish uses less sugar, salt and fat. Recipe includes *Diabetic Exchanges*.

- 1 package (16 ounces) pasta shells, cooked and drained
- 3 cups cubed cooked turkey *or* chicken
- 1 cup diced green pepper
- 1/4 cup chopped onion
- 1 cup blue cheese salad dressing
- 1/4 cup sour cream
- 2 teaspoons celery seed
- 1/2 teaspoon salt, optional
- 1/4 teaspoon pepper

Combine pasta, turkey, green pepper and onion in a large bowl. In a small bowl, combine dressing, sour cream, celery seed, salt if desired and pepper; pour over salad and toss. **Yield:** 12 servings. **Diabetic Exchanges:** One 1-cup serving (prepared with turkey breast and fat-free salad dressing and sour cream and without salt) equals 2 starch, 1 very lean meat, 1 vegetable; also, 213 calories, 240 mg sodium, 22 mg cholesterol, 38 gm carbohydrate, 11 gm protein, 2 gm fat.

TURKEY CASHEW SALAD

Phyllis Barkey, Warren, Michigan

This salad has appeared at many bridal and baby showers I've attended, and I finally received the recipe. The salty crunchy cashews work nicely with the sweet tangy dressing.

> 1 cup small ring pasta
> 4 cups cubed cooked turkey *or* chicken
> 1 cup thinly sliced celery
> 1 cup halved green grapes
> 1 cup mayonnaise
> 2 tablespoons orange juice
> 2 tablespoons vinegar
> 1 tablespoon olive *or* vegetable oil
> 1-1/2 teaspoons grated orange peel
> 3/4 teaspoon salt
> 1/4 teaspoon ground ginger
> 3/4 cup salted cashews

Cook pasta according to package directions; rinse in cold water and drain. Place in a large bowl. Add the turkey, celery and grapes. In a small bowl, combine mayonnaise, orange juice, vinegar, oil, orange peel, salt and ginger. Pour over salad; toss to coat. Stir in cashews just before serving. **Yield:** 8 servings.

CHICKEN SALAD MEXICANA

Kay Goldman, Punta Gorda, Florida

This salad was served at a local spring festival and was enjoyed by all. The slightly spicy seasonings add just the right amount of festive flair.

> 4 cups chopped cooked chicken
> 2 cups (8 ounces) shredded cheddar cheese
> 1 can (16 ounces) kidney beans, rinsed and drained
> 1 medium onion, chopped
> 1 can (4 ounces) chopped green chilies
> 1/2 cup sliced ripe olives
> 1/2 cup sour cream
> 1/2 cup mayonnaise
> 1 envelope taco seasoning mix
> 2 tablespoons chopped sweet red pepper
> 2 tablespoons chopped green pepper
> 5 to 6 cups shredded lettuce
> 2 medium tomatoes, chopped
> 4 cups corn chips

In a large bowl, combine the first 11 ingredients; mix well. Serve on a bed of lettuce; top with tomatoes and corn chips. **Yield:** 8 servings.

SESAME BEEF AND ASPARAGUS SALAD

Tamara Steeb, Issaquah, Washington

(PICTURED BELOW)

When I prepare this dish for guests, I'll also serve rice and bread—it's quick and easy, but it always wins me many compliments!

✓ This tasty dish uses less sugar, salt and fat. Recipe includes *Diabetic Exchanges*.

> 1 pound top round steak
> 4 cups sliced fresh asparagus (2-inch pieces)
> 3 tablespoons soy sauce
> 2 tablespoons sesame oil
> 1 tablespoon cider *or* red wine vinegar
> 1/2 teaspoon grated fresh gingerroot *or*
> 1/8 teaspoon ground ginger

Sesame seeds

Broil steak to desired doneness. Cool and cut into thin diagonal strips. Cook asparagus in a small amount of water for 30-60 seconds. Drain and cool. Combine beef and asparagus. Blend soy sauce, oil, vinegar and ginger; pour over beef and asparagus. Sprinkle with sesame seeds and toss. **Yield:** 6 servings. **Diabetic Exchanges:** One serving equals 2 lean meat, 1-1/2 vegetable, 1/2 fat; also, 179 calories, 696 mg sodium, 48 mg cholesterol, 6 gm carbohydrate, 21 gm protein, 8 gm fat.

ASPARAGUS SHRIMP SALAD

Roberta Hulsizer, Yakima, Washington

(PICTURED BELOW)

Southeast Washington is a prime growing area for asparagus, and this recipe is one of the best I've tried using this delicious vegetable.

- 1 package (8 ounces) spiral pasta
- 1 garlic clove, crushed
- 1 slice (1/4 inch) fresh gingerroot, minced, optional
- 1 tablespoon cooking oil
- 1 pound fresh asparagus, cut into 1-1/2-inch pieces
- 1/2 pound uncooked shrimp, peeled and deveined
- 2 tablespoons water
- 1 can (8 ounces) sliced water chestnuts, drained *or* 1 cup sliced celery
- 1/4 pound fully cooked ham, julienned *or* cubed
- 1/3 cup sliced ripe olives

DRESSING:
- 6 tablespoons vegetable oil
- 2 tablespoons cider *or* white wine vinegar
- 1 tablespoon soy sauce
- 1/4 teaspoon salt
- 1/8 teaspoon pepper
- 1/8 teaspoon ground mustard

Cook the pasta according to package directions. Meanwhile, in a large skillet, saute garlic and gingerroot if desired in oil over medium-high heat for 1-2 minutes. Add asparagus, shrimp and water; cook until asparagus is crisp-tender and shrimp are pink, about 8 minutes. Stir in water chestnuts, ham and olives. Remove from the heat. Rinse and drain pasta. Place in a large salad bowl; add asparagus mixture and keep warm. Combine all dressing ingredients; pour over salad and toss. **Yield:** 4-6 servings.

GREEK RICE SALAD

Barbara Nowakowski, North Tonawanda, New York

I love cooking. My husband even had to build another room especially for the cookbooks I collected! No matter how many salad recipes I try, this one is still at the top of my list.

✓ This tasty dish uses less sugar, salt and fat. Recipe includes *Diabetic Exchanges*.

- 4 cups cooked brown rice
- 2 cups julienned cooked turkey breast
- 2 cups halved cherry tomatoes

1 cup halved ripe olives
3/4 cup plain yogurt
3 to 4 tablespoons minced fresh mint
2 tablespoons cider *or* red wine vinegar
1/2 teaspoon lemon-pepper seasoning
1/2 cup crumbled feta cheese, optional

Combine rice, turkey, tomatoes and olives. In a small bowl, combine yogurt, mint, vinegar and lemon pepper; mix well. Pour over rice mixture; toss to coat. Sprinkle with feta cheese if desired. **Yield:** 8 servings. **Diabetic Exchanges:** One 1-cup serving (prepared with nonfat yogurt and without feta cheese) equals 1-1/2 starch, 1 meat; also, 174 calories, 258 mg sodium, 15 mg cholesterol, 25 gm carbohydrate; 11 gm protein, 3 gm fat.

HOT TURKEY PECAN SALAD

Ethel Brown, Decatur, Illinois

As a way to use leftovers from the holidays, I substituted turkey for chicken in this traditional hot salad. My family always says this country-style dish reminds them of home.

2 cups cubed cooked turkey *or* chicken
2 cups thinly sliced celery
1/2 cup sliced stuffed olives
1/2 cup chopped pecans
1 tablespoon finely chopped onion
1 cup mayonnaise
2 tablespoons lemon juice
1/2 teaspoon salt
3/4 to 1 cup crushed potato chips
1/2 cup shredded cheddar cheese

In a large bowl, combine turkey, celery, olives, pecans and onion. Combine mayonnaise, lemon juice and salt; pour over turkey mixture and toss. Pour into a greased 8-in. square baking dish. Sprinkle with potato chips and cheese. Bake, uncovered, at 375° for 20-25 minutes or until bubbly. **Yield:** 4 servings.

SOUTHWEST SALAD

Jeannie Daubar, Todd, North Carolina

(PICTURED ABOVE)

I invented this recipe several years ago. It's quick to make and uses ingredients I usually have on hand in my pantry and refrigerator.

1 pound ground beef
1/2 teaspoon salt
1/4 teaspoon pepper
1 can (16 ounces) hot chili beans with gravy
4 to 6 cups corn chips
1 cup (4 ounces) shredded cheddar cheese
2 cups shredded lettuce
1 large tomato, chopped
1 small green pepper, chopped
6 green onions with tops, chopped
1 small avocado, chopped, optional
1/2 cup sliced ripe olives, optional
1 cup (8 ounces) sour cream
Salsa

In a skillet, brown beef; drain. Sprinkle with salt and pepper; set aside. Heat beans in a saucepan or in the microwave. On six plates, layer corn chips, beef, cheese, beans and lettuce. Sprinkle with tomato, green pepper, onions, and avocado and olives if desired. Top with sour cream and salsa. **Yield:** 6 servings.

Smoked Turkey and Apple Salad

Carolyn Popwell, Lacey, Washington

(PICTURED ABOVE)

An eye-catching dish, this refreshing salad is a great main course. The dressing's Dijon flavor goes nicely with the turkey, and the apples add crunch.

✓ This tasty dish uses less sugar, salt and fat. Recipe includes *Diabetic Exchanges*.

DRESSING:
 5 tablespoons olive *or* vegetable oil
 2 tablespoons cider vinegar
 1 tablespoon Dijon mustard
 1 teaspoon lemon-pepper seasoning
 1/2 teaspoon salt, optional
SALAD:
 1 bunch watercress *or* romaine, torn into bite-size pieces
 1 carrot, julienned
 10 cherry tomatoes, halved
 8 ounces smoked turkey, julienned
 4 medium apples, sliced
 1/3 cup chopped walnuts, toasted

Whisk together dressing ingredients and set aside. Arrange greens on a platter or individual plates. Top with carrot, tomatoes, turkey and apples. Drizzle with dressing and sprinkle with walnuts. **Yield:** 8 servings. **Diabetic Exchanges:** One serving (prepared with romaine and without salt) equals 2 fat, 1-1/2 vegetable, 1 meat; also, 195 calories, 267 mg sodium, 8 mg cholesterol, 10 gm carbohydrate, 6 gm protein, 16 gm fat.

Tuna Salad for Two

Sharon Balzer, Phoenix, Arizona

We have long hot summers here in the desert Southwest, so I try to get creative with salads and come up with cool dinners for my husband and me. We think this one is simply scrumptious!

 2 cups torn lettuce
 1 package (5 ounces) spiral pasta, cooked and drained
 1 cup broccoli florets
 1 can (6 ounces) tuna, drained and flaked
 1 small cucumber, sliced
 1 medium tomato, cut into wedges
 1 celery rib, sliced
 1 carrot, peeled and sliced
 1/2 cup julienned provolone *or* mozzarella cheese
 1/4 cup julienned green pepper
DRESSING:
 1/4 cup olive *or* vegetable oil
 1 tablespoon lemon juice
 1 small garlic clove, minced
 1-1/2 teaspoons cider *or* white wine vinegar
 3/4 teaspoon Italian seasoning
 1/4 teaspoon salt
 1/8 teaspoon pepper

On two salad plates, arrange the first 10 ingredients in order listed. In a jar with a tight-fitting lid, combine dressing ingredients; shake well. Pour over salads. **Yield:** 2 servings.

CHOPPED SALAD WITH PARMESAN DRESSING

Marilyn Norrie, King City, Ontario

(PICTURED BELOW)

This attractive salad has been enjoyed wherever I've served it. It's an especially welcome dish at our family's annual Father's Day gathering.

- 1/2 **head iceberg lettuce, chopped into bite-size pieces**
- 1 **small bunch romaine, chopped into bite-size pieces**
- 1 **cup canned garbanzo beans, rinsed and drained**
- 1/4 **pound salami, finely diced**
- 1/4 **pound mozzarella cheese, finely chopped**

DRESSING:

- 5 **tablespoons vegetable oil**
- 2 **tablespoons cider *or* white wine vinegar**
- 1 **teaspoon ground mustard**
- 1 **teaspoon salt, optional**
- 1/2 **teaspoon black pepper**
- 1/2 **cup grated Parmesan cheese**

In a large bowl, toss salad ingredients. In a jar with a tight-fitting lid, combine dressing ingredients; shake well. Pour over salad; toss to coat. **Yield:** 6-8 servings.

EASY TACO SALAD

Faye Shaw, Medicine Hat, Alberta

This salad goes over well at any social function. (Teenagers just love it!) I usually double the recipe because it disappears so fast.

- 1 **pound ground beef**
- 1 **envelope taco seasoning mix**
- 1 **medium head iceberg lettuce, shredded**
- 2 **medium tomatoes, seeded and chopped**
- 1 **cup Catalina salad dressing**
- 4 to 5 **cups corn chips, crushed**
- 2 **cups (8 ounces) shredded cheddar cheese**

In a skillet, brown beef until no longer pink; drain. Stir in taco seasoning. Place in a large bowl; add lettuce, tomatoes, dressing, corn chips and cheese. Toss well. **Yield:** 6-8 servings.

CHICKEN 'N' FRUIT MEDLEY

Jodi Cigel, Stevens Point, Wisconsin

You'll especially appreciate this salad in winter, when fresh fruit isn't readily available. Serving a smaller crowd? No problem! The recipe can easily be cut in half.

- 8 **cups cubed cooked chicken**
- 3 **cups sliced celery**
- 1 **can (16 ounces) apricot halves, drained and chopped**
- 2 **cans (16 ounces *each*) chunky mixed fruit, drained**
- 3 **cups mayonnaise**
- 1/2 **cup French salad dressing**
- 3 **tablespoons cider *or* red wine vinegar**
- 2 **tablespoons honey**
- 1 **tablespoon curry powder**
- 1 **cup chopped pecans, toasted**

In a large bowl, combine chicken, celery and fruit. Combine mayonnaise, salad dressing, vinegar, honey and curry powder. Pour over chicken mixture and toss to coat. Sprinkle with pecans. **Yield:** 20 servings.

> **SAVORY SALAD.** Perk up your tuna salad by adding 1/8 teaspoon of garlic powder for a salad made with two cans of tuna.

Side Salads & Dressings

SNAPPY POTATO SALAD

Madeleine Haney, San Carlos, California

(PICTURED AT RIGHT)

Some potato salads require lots of ingredients and preparation time, but not this one. Plus, horseradish adds a little extra "zip".

   8 medium potatoes, peeled, cubed and cooked
   8 bacon strips, cooked and crumbled
   1 cup chopped onion
3/4 teaspoon salt
   2 cups mayonnaise
1/4 cup prepared mustard
1/4 cup prepared horseradish
   1 cup sliced celery
1/4 cup shredded carrots
Celery leaves, optional

In a large bowl, combine potatoes, bacon, onion and salt; set aside. In a small saucepan, combine mayonnaise, mustard and horseradish; cook until heated through, stirring constantly. Add celery and carrots; mix well. Pour over potato mixture and toss to coat. Serve warm. Garnish with celery leaves if desired. **Yield:** 8-10 servings.

FRESH FRUIT SALAD

Dianna Shimizu, Issaquah, Washington

(PICTURED AT RIGHT)

We enjoy picking our own raspberries for this scrumptious salad. Sometimes I'll add cold cubed chicken and serve it in cantaloupe shells. It's flavorful and filling!

   2 large cantaloupe, cubed
   1 cup green grapes
   1 cup fresh raspberries
   2 kiwifruit, peeled and sliced
DRESSING:
   1/2 cup honey
   1/3 cup lime juice

1/4 teaspoon ground coriander
1/4 teaspoon ground nutmeg

Toss fruit in a large bowl. In a small bowl, mix dressing ingredients; pour over fruit and toss to coat. **Yield:** 6-8 servings.

> **SALAD SECRET.** Wash and dry lettuce leaves thoroughly so they'll be crisp. To avoid a soggy salad, most greens should be served immediately after the dressing is added.

CAESAR SALAD

Schelby Thompson, Winter Haven, Florida

(PICTURED AT RIGHT)

This crunchy refreshing salad has a simple zesty dressing that provides a burst of flavor with each bite. It's a great salad to perk up any meal.

   1 large bunch romaine, torn
3/4 cup olive *or* vegetable oil
   3 tablespoons red wine vinegar
   1 teaspoon Worcestershire sauce
   1 garlic clove
1/2 teaspoon salt
1/4 teaspoon ground mustard
1/2 fresh lemon
Dash pepper
1/4 to 1/2 cup shredded Parmesan cheese
Caesar *or* garlic croutons

Place romaine in a large bowl. Place the next six ingredients in a blender; cover and process until smooth. Pour over romaine and toss. Squeeze lemon juice over salad. Sprinkle with pepper, Parmesan cheese and croutons. **Yield:** 6-8 servings.

> **GARDEN GOODNESS.** *Pictured at right, top to bottom: Snappy Potato Salad, Fresh Fruit Salad and Caesar Salad (all recipes on this page).*

APPLE-STRAWBERRY SPINACH SALAD

Carolyn Popwell, Lacey, Washington

(PICTURED ABOVE)

I created this salad myself and love to serve it in spring when strawberries are at their peak.

- 1 pound fresh spinach, torn
- 2 cups chopped unpeeled tart apples
- 3/4 cup fresh bean sprouts
- 1/2 cup sliced fresh strawberries
- 1/4 cup crumbled cooked bacon

DRESSING:
- 3/4 cup vegetable oil
- 1/2 cup sugar
- 1/3 cup cider *or* white wine vinegar
- 1 small onion, grated
- 2 teaspoons Worcestershire sauce
- 2 teaspoons salt

In a large salad bowl, combine the first five ingredients. In a small bowl, whisk together all dressing ingredients. Pour over salad and toss. **Yield:** 6-8 servings.

AMBROSIA WALDORF SALAD

Janet Smith, Smithton, Missouri

This recipe puts a different spin on traditional Waldorf salad. My family didn't think they liked cranberries until they tried this sweet crunchy salad.

- 2 cups fresh *or* frozen cranberry halves
- 1/2 cup sugar
- 3 cups miniature marshmallows
- 2 cups diced unpeeled apples
- 1 can (20 ounces) pineapple tidbits, drained
- 1 cup green grape halves
- 3/4 cup chopped pecans
- 1 cup whipping cream, whipped
- Shredded *or* flaked coconut

Combine cranberries and sugar. In a large bowl, combine the marshmallows, apples, pineapple, grapes and pecans. Add the cranberries and mix well. Fold in whipped cream and sprinkle with coconut. **Yield:** 12-14 servings.

ARTICHOKE POTATO SALAD

Lori Gleason, Minneapolis, Minnesota

Featuring a light vinaigrette dressing, this salad is a nice change of pace from traditional potato salads. It's one of my husband's favorite side dishes for barbecued chicken.

- 2 pounds red potatoes, cooked and cubed
- 1 can (8-1/2 ounces) quartered artichoke hearts (in water), drained
- 1 small red onion, chopped
- 1 cup cubed brick *or* Monterey Jack cheese
- 1/2 cup crumbled blue cheese
- 3/4 cup vegetable oil
- 1/4 cup cider *or* red wine vinegar
- 2 garlic cloves, minced
- 1 teaspoon dried rosemary, crushed
- 1 teaspoon dill weed
- 1/2 teaspoon salt
- 1/4 teaspoon pepper

In a large bowl, combine potatoes, artichokes, onion and cheeses. In a jar with tight-fitting lid, combine oil, vinegar, garlic, rosemary, dill, salt and pepper; shake well. Pour over potato mixture; toss to coat. **Yield:** 10-12 servings.

HARVEST LAYERED SALAD

Vera Ambroselli, Fort Myers, Florida

(PICTURED AT RIGHT)

Unlike most layered salads that have a mayonnaise topping, this version features a tasty vinegar-and-oil dressing. I often double it to serve for special occasions.

2-1/2 cups shredded carrots
2-1/2 cups sliced fresh mushrooms
2-1/2 cups shredded cabbage
2-1/2 cups sliced zucchini
    1 small red onion, thinly sliced
    1 cup (4 ounces) shredded Colby *or*
       cheddar cheese
DRESSING:
    1/4 cup vegetable oil
    2 tablespoons cider *or* red wine vinegar
    1/8 teaspoon ground mustard
    1/8 teaspoon sugar
    1/8 teaspoon garlic salt
    1/8 teaspoon pepper

In a 3-1/2-qt. bowl, layer the first six ingredients in order listed. Combine all dressing ingredients in a jar with tight-fitting lid; shake well. Pour over salad. Do not toss. **Yield:** 10-14 servings.

SIMPLE FRUIT SALAD

Debbie Zimmerman, East Alton, Illinois

This recipe is delicious with canned fruit, but fresh fruit can easily be substituted or added. It's also very versatile—you can use whatever fruit happens to be in season.

    1 can (29 ounces) sliced peaches, drained
    1 can (20 ounces) pineapple chunks,
       drained
    1 can (15 ounces) mandarin oranges,
       drained
    1 large firm banana, sliced, optional
1/4 cup maraschino cherries, halved
    1 cup sugar
    2 tablespoons cornstarch
1/8 to 1/4 teaspoon ground nutmeg
    1 cup water
    3 tablespoons peach *or* apricot gelatin

Toss fruit in a large bowl. In a saucepan, combine sugar, cornstarch and nutmeg; stir in water until smooth. Bring to a boil over medium heat; cook and stir for 2 minutes. Remove from the heat; stir in gelatin until dissolved. Pour over fruit and toss to coat. **Yield:** 8-10 servings. **Editor's Note:** Sauce will thicken upon standing.

DIJON VINAIGRETTE

Beth Philson, Lincoln, Nebraska

In this recipe, Dijon mustard adds a new twist to a traditional vinaigrette dressing. Olive oil gives it great flavor, but I have used vegetable oil in a pinch.

2/3 cup olive *or* vegetable oil
1/3 cup cider *or* red wine vinegar
    2 tablespoons Dijon mustard
1/2 teaspoon salt
1/4 teaspoon pepper
1/4 teaspoon sugar

Combine all ingredients in a jar with tight-fitting lid; shake until blended. **Yield:** about 1 cup.

GERMAN COLESLAW

Joyce Brown, Genesee, Idaho

This recipe has been handed down through generations of German families in northern Idaho. Everyone around here makes it. It's good served either warm or cold.

  1 medium head cabbage, finely shredded
  3 to 4 green onions, sliced
  3/4 cup sugar
  3/4 cup vinegar
  1-1/2 teaspoons celery seed
  1-1/2 teaspoons salt
  3/4 cup vegetable oil

In a large bowl, combine cabbage and onions. In a saucepan, mix sugar, vinegar, celery seed and salt; bring to a boil. Add oil; return to boiling and cook until sugar dissolves. Pour over cabbage; toss gently. **Yield:** 14-18 servings.

FESTIVE TOMATO WEDGES

Wilma Purcell, Alma, Illinois

(PICTURED BELOW)

Since I have a large vegetable and herb garden, many of the ingredients in this recipe are truly "homegrown". I found this simple recipe in a magazine years ago and it quickly became a favorite at family picnics.

  6 medium tomatoes, cored and cut into wedges
  2/3 cup vegetable oil
  1/4 cup cider *or* white wine vinegar
  1/4 cup snipped fresh parsley
  1/4 cup sliced green onions
  1 garlic clove, minced
  2 tablespoons mayonnaise
  1 teaspoon dill weed
  1 teaspoon dried basil
  1 teaspoon salt
  1/4 teaspoon pepper
  1/4 teaspoon dried oregano

Place tomato wedges in a large bowl. Place remaining ingredients in a blender or food processor; cover and process until blended. Pour over tomatoes and toss gently. **Yield:** 12 servings.

FAVORITE FRUIT SALAD

Doris Dion, Lake Ozark, Missouri

(PICTURED ON FRONT COVER)

I spend a lot of time in the kitchen, especially when our four children and nine grandchildren come to visit. This salad is always requested when they're here for dinner.

  1/4 cup *each* grapefruit, orange and pineapple juice
  2 teaspoons cornstarch
  8 cups torn iceberg lettuce

6 cups torn Bibb lettuce
3 cups orange sections
3 cups fresh pineapple chunks
3 cups sliced fresh strawberries
1/4 cup vinegar
2 tablespoons vegetable oil
1 garlic clove, minced
2 to 3 teaspoons sugar
1 teaspoon prepared mustard
1/2 teaspoon salt
1/2 teaspoon paprika
1/2 teaspoon ground nutmeg

In a saucepan, stir juices and cornstarch until smooth. Bring to a boil over medium heat; cook and stir for 2 minutes. Cool to room temperature. Meanwhile, in a salad bowl, toss lettuce and fruit. Stir vinegar, oil, garlic, sugar, mustard, salt, paprika and nutmeg into cooled juice mixture. Pour over salad and toss. **Yield:** 12-14 servings.

CRUNCHY PEA SALAD

Phyllis Barkey, Warren, Michigan

After I had this salad in two different restaurants—one here in Michigan and one in Florida —I finally decided to try my hand at duplicating the recipe. My family thinks I succeeded!

1/3 cup ranch salad dressing
1/3 cup mayonnaise
1 tablespoon lemon juice
1/4 teaspoon celery seed
1/4 teaspoon salt
1/8 teaspoon pepper
2 packages (10 ounces *each*) frozen peas, thawed
3 tablespoons finely chopped onion
3/4 cup salted peanuts

In a large bowl, combine salad dressing, mayonnaise, lemon juice, celery seed, salt and pepper. Add peas and onion; toss. Stir in peanuts. **Yield:** 6 servings.

SMALL-BATCH POTATO SALAD

June Schwanz, Saukville, Wisconsin

This recipe is handy when you have a taste for German-style potato salad but don't have a crowd to feed.

4 bacon strips
1/3 cup sugar
1 tablespoon cornstarch
1/2 cup water

1/4 cup vinegar
1/2 teaspoon salt
1/4 teaspoon pepper
1 can (15 ounces) sliced potatoes, drained
Minced fresh parsley

In a skillet, cook bacon until crisp. Drain, reserving 2 tablespoons of drippings. Crumble bacon and set aside. Combine sugar and cornstarch; stir into drippings until smooth. Add water, vinegar, salt and pepper; cook and stir over medium heat for 3-4 minutes or until thickened and bubbly. Stir in potatoes and bacon. Cook for 2-3 minutes or until heated through. Serve warm or at room temperature. Garnish with parsley. **Yield:** 2 servings.

HONEY FRUIT DRESSING

Dorothy Anderson, Ottawa, Kansas

(PICTURED ABOVE)

I love to use this dressing for a salad of colorful fresh fruits. Mix the dressing with a medley of watermelon, cantaloupe, peaches, grapes, strawberries or whatever you have on hand.

2/3 cup sugar
1 teaspoon ground mustard
1 teaspoon paprika
1 teaspoon celery seed
1/4 teaspoon salt
1/3 cup honey
1/3 cup vinegar
1 tablespoon lemon juice
1 teaspoon grated onion
1 cup vegetable oil

In a mixing bowl, combine sugar, mustard, paprika, celery seed and salt. Add honey, vinegar, lemon juice and onion. Gradually add oil, beating constantly. Serve with fresh fruit. Store in the refrigerator. **Yield:** 2 cups.

QUICK CORN SALAD

Priscilla Witthar, Marshall, Missouri

(PICTURED ABOVE)

This recipe was given to me by a friend and it's one the entire family likes. Whenever we have a family get-together, I'm asked to bring this salad.

✓ This tasty dish uses less sugar, salt and fat. Recipe includes *Diabetic Exchanges*.

- 1 can (16 ounces) whole kernel corn, drained
- 1 large tomato, seeded and chopped
- 1/2 cup chopped celery
- 1/2 cup chopped cucumber
- 1/3 cup finely chopped green pepper
- 1/4 cup finely chopped onion
- 1/4 cup sour cream
- 2 tablespoons mayonnaise
- 1 tablespoon cider vinegar
- 1/4 teaspoon salt, optional
- 1/4 teaspoon celery seed
- 1/8 teaspoon pepper

In a large salad bowl, combine the corn, tomato, celery, cucumber, green pepper and onion. In a small bowl, combine the remaining ingredients; gently blend into the salad. **Yield:** 8 servings. **Diabetic Exchanges:** One 1/2-cup serving (prepared with no-salt-added corn, light sour cream and fat-free mayonnaise and without added salt) equals 1 vegetable, 1/2 starch; also, 58 calories, 42 mg sodium, 3 mg cholesterol, 12 gm carbohydrate, 2 gm protein, 1 gm fat.

SPINACH SALAD WITH CREAMY PARMESAN DRESSING

Ruth Seitz, Conesville, Iowa

The savory from-scratch dressing is perfect over spinach or any of your favorite greens.

- 1/2 cup mayonnaise
- 1/2 cup grated Parmesan cheese
- 2 tablespoons evaporated milk
- 1-1/2 teaspoons dill weed
- 1-1/2 teaspoons dried minced onion
- 1-1/2 teaspoons lemon-pepper seasoning
- 4 cups torn fresh spinach

Combine the first six ingredients (thinning with additional milk if necessary). Toss with spinach or serve on the side. Refrigerate any leftover dressing. **Yield:** 6 servings.

THREE-PEPPER PASTA SALAD

Jan Malone, Arapaho, Oklahoma

I like to make this recipe during the summer when I can get the ingredients fresh from the garden. It not only tastes very good, it's a pretty addition to any meal.

- 1 package (12 ounces) tricolor spiral pasta
- 2/3 cup olive *or* vegetable oil
- 3 tablespoons cider *or* red wine vinegar
- 1/4 cup minced fresh basil *or* 1 tablespoon dried basil
- 2 tablespoons grated Parmesan cheese
- 1-1/4 teaspoons salt
- 1/4 teaspoon pepper
- 1 small sweet red pepper, julienned
- 1 small sweet yellow pepper, julienned
- 1 small green pepper, julienned
- 1 medium tomato, cut into thin wedges
- 1 can (2-1/4 ounces) sliced ripe olives, drained
- 2 tablespoons sliced green onions
- 8 ounces mozzarella cheese, cubed

Cook the pasta according to package directions. Meanwhile, in a blender or food processor, combine oil, vinegar, basil, Parmesan cheese, salt and pepper; cover and process until smooth. Rinse pasta in cold water; drain and place in a large bowl. Add peppers, tomato, olives and onions. Add dressing; toss to coat. Add mozzarella and toss. Serve at room temperature. **Yield:** 6-8 servings.

ITALIAN BROCCOLI SALAD

Patricia Free, Baton Rouge, Louisiana

I received this recipe from my cousin several years ago, and it remains a family favorite. It's also a real crowd-pleaser whenever I take it to a potluck.

2-1/2 pounds fresh broccoli
    1 pound sliced bacon, cooked and crumbled
    1 jar (5-1/4 ounces) stuffed olives, drained and sliced
    1 cup sliced green onions
    1 bottle (16 ounces) Italian salad dressing
    1 cup mayonnaise
    3/4 cup shredded Parmesan cheese

In a large saucepan, cook broccoli in a small amount of water until crisp-tender, about 5-8 minutes. Rinse in cold water; drain and cut into bite-size pieces. Place in a large bowl; add bacon, olives and onions. In a small bowl, combine salad dressing, mayonnaise and Parmesan cheese; mix well. Pour over vegetables and toss. **Yield:** 10-12 servings.

GUACAMOLE SALAD BOWL

Ann Eastman, Greenville, California

The bowl is usually "licked clean" when I make this hearty salad for our Grange group. I sometimes substitute tuna for the shrimp.

    5 cups torn leaf lettuce
    2 medium tomatoes, cut into wedges
    1 cup (4 ounces) shredded cheddar cheese
    1 cup cooked salad shrimp
    1 cup corn chips
1/2 cup sliced ripe olives
1/4 cup sliced green onions
AVOCADO DRESSING:
    1/2 cup mashed ripe avocado
      1 tablespoon lemon juice
    1/2 cup sour cream
    1/3 cup vegetable oil
      1 garlic clove, minced
    1/2 teaspoon sugar
    1/2 teaspoon chili powder

1/4 teaspoon salt
1/4 teaspoon hot pepper sauce

In a large salad bowl, combine the first seven ingredients. In a mixing bowl or blender, combine dressing ingredients; beat or process until smooth. Pour over salad and toss. **Yield:** 6-8 servings.

FRUIT 'N' NUT SALAD

Willie Mae Philen, Mexia, Alabama

(PICTURED BELOW)

My mother-in-law created this recipe using left-over fruit from holiday baking. It tasted so good that it became standard fare every time we had ham or turkey. It's a perfect side dish for those entrees.

    2 medium tart apples, chopped
    2 medium oranges, sectioned and cut into bite-size pieces
    1 cup raisins
    1 jar (10 ounces) maraschino cherries, drained and chopped
1-1/2 cups chopped pecans
    1 cup mayonnaise
  1/2 cup sugar
    1 tablespoon lemon juice
    2 medium firm bananas, sliced

In a large bowl, combine the apples, oranges, raisins, cherries and pecans. Combine mayonnaise, sugar and lemon juice; mix well. Add to fruit mixture and stir to coat. Stir in bananas. **Yield:** 12-16 servings.

BLUE CHEESE SALAD

Ann Berg, Chesapeake, Virginia

(PICTURED ABOVE)

A fresh salad is a wonderful way to round out any meal, but this colorful combination has eye appeal as well. I love the crispy crunch of croutons and tangy touch of dill in this recipe.

1/4 cup cider *or* white wine vinegar
1/4 cup olive *or* vegetable oil
1 garlic clove, minced
1/2 teaspoon dill weed
1/4 teaspoon pepper
1/4 teaspoon seasoned salt
1 small bunch romaine, torn
3 hard-cooked eggs, chopped
1 cup croutons
1/2 cup crumbled blue cheese

In a small bowl or jar with tight-fitting lid, combine the first six ingredients; mix or shake until well blended. Place romaine, eggs, croutons and blue cheese in a large salad bowl. Add dressing and toss. **Yield:** 4 servings.

HERBED TOMATO AND CHEESE SALAD

Sharon Miller, Olivenhain, California

A flavorful combination of ingredients and a tangy garlic-laced dressing make this salad a mouth-watering delight.

5 large tomatoes, cut into wedges
1 medium green pepper, chopped
1/2 small red onion, thinly sliced
1-1/2 cups (6 ounces) shredded Monterey Jack cheese
1/4 cup stuffed green olives, sliced
1/2 teaspoon dried basil
DRESSING:
6 tablespoons vegetable oil
2 tablespoons cider *or* red wine vinegar
2 tablespoons minced fresh parsley
1 tablespoon minced chives
1 garlic clove, minced
1/2 teaspoon salt
1/4 teaspoon pepper

Place tomato wedges in a shallow dish. Top with green pepper, onion, cheese and olives. Sprinkle with basil. In a small bowl, mix dressing ingredients. Spoon over salad. **Yield:** 6-8 servings.

LETTUCE WITH BUTTERMILK DRESSING

Jean Morgan, Roscoe, Illinois

I often serve my garden lettuce this way. The dressing lets the fresh flavor come through.

1/4 cup buttermilk
2 tablespoons mayonnaise *or* salad dressing
2 tablespoons sugar

1 tablespoon vinegar
6 cups torn leaf lettuce

In a small bowl, whisk the first four ingredients. Toss with lettuce or serve on the side. Refrigerate any leftover dressing. **Yield:** 4 servings.

DELUXE GERMAN POTATO SALAD

Betty Perkins, Hot Springs, Arkansas

I make this salad for all occasions—it goes well with any kind of meat. I often take it to potlucks, and there's never any left over. The celery, carrots and ground mustard are a special touch not usually found in traditional German potato salad.

　　1/2 pound sliced bacon
　　1 cup thinly sliced celery
　　1 cup chopped onion
　　1 cup sugar
　　2 tablespoons all-purpose flour
　　1 cup vinegar
　　1/2 cup water
　　1 teaspoon salt
　　3/4 teaspoon ground mustard
　　5 pounds red potatoes, cooked and sliced
　　2 medium carrots, shredded
　　2 tablespoons minced fresh parsley
Additional salt, optional

In a skillet, cook bacon until crisp. Drain, reserving 1/4 cup drippings. Crumble bacon and set aside. Saute the celery and onion in drippings until tender. Combine sugar and flour; add to skillet with vinegar, water, salt and mustard. Cook, stirring constantly, until mixture thickens and bubbles. In a large bowl, combine potatoes, carrots and parsley; pour the sauce over and stir gently to coat. Season with salt if desired. Garnish with crumbled bacon. Serve warm. **Yield:** 14-16 servings.

FLUFFY FRUIT DELIGHT

Margaret Naylor, Salt Lake City, Utah

I came up with this dish by combining several different recipes. It's light and refreshing...just perfect for picnics and potlucks on hot summer days.

　　1 carton (8 ounces) frozen whipped
　　　topping, thawed
　　3 tablespoons raspberry gelatin
　　1 can (20 ounces) pineapple tidbits,
　　　drained
　　1 can (16 ounces) fruit cocktail, drained

2 large apples, diced
2 large firm bananas, sliced

In a large bowl, combine whipped topping and gelatin. Stir in fruit. **Yield:** 12-16 servings.

FAVORITE FRENCH DRESSING

Linda Nilsen, Anoka, Minnesota

(PICTURED BELOW)

My mom and her cousin developed this tangy dressing many years ago. It really perks up salad greens and holds together well once mixed. Everyone wants the recipe once they try it.

　　1 cup vinegar
　　3/4 cup sugar
　　1/4 cup grated onion
　1-1/2 teaspoons salt
　1-1/2 teaspoons ground mustard
　1-1/2 teaspoons paprika
　　1 bottle (12 ounces) chili sauce
　　1 cup vegetable oil

In a bowl or jar with tight-fitting lid, mix vinegar, sugar and onion. Combine salt, mustard, paprika and 2 tablespoons chili sauce to form a paste. Add the remaining chili sauce and mix well. Pour into vinegar mixture; add oil and mix or shake well. Store in the refrigerator. **Yield:** 3-1/2 cups.

SUMMER SALAD WITH GOLDEN DRESSING

Belle Kemmerer, Stanfordville, New York

(PICTURED BELOW)

The golden dressing for this salad is also excellent served as a sauce for meat or used as a marinade for vegetables. The touch of curry gives any food a wonderfully tangy taste.

> 1 package (16 ounces) frozen French-style green beans, cooked and drained *or* 1 can (14-1/2 ounces) French-style green beans, drained
> 1/2 cup sliced celery
> 1/2 cup sliced cucumber
> 4 medium radishes, sliced
> 4 medium tomatoes, cut into wedges

Lettuce leaves
DRESSING:
> 1/2 cup vegetable oil
> 1/4 cup vinegar
> 1 tablespoon dried minced onion
> 1/2 teaspoon salt
> 1/8 teaspoon curry powder
> 1 hard-cooked egg, chopped

In a bowl, toss beans, celery, cucumber and radishes. Arrange tomatoes on a lettuce-lined platter. Fill center with bean mixture. Combine dressing ingredients; pour over salad. **Yield:** 8 servings.

MIXED GREENS WITH MUSHROOMS

Sue Walker, Greentown, Indiana

This is a great year-round salad because you can use whatever greens are in season. The tarragon in the dressing is subtle but really adds to the flavor.

✓ This tasty dish uses less sugar, salt and fat. Recipe includes *Diabetic Exchanges*.

> 6 cups mixed greens
> 1 cup halved cherry tomatoes
> 1/2 pound fresh mushrooms, sliced

DRESSING:
> 1 tablespoon cider *or* red wine vinegar
> 1 tablespoon lemon juice
> 1 tablespoon thinly sliced green onion
> 1 tablespoon Dijon mustard
> 1 tablespoon minced fresh parsley
> 1/4 teaspoon salt, optional
> 1/4 teaspoon sugar
> 1/8 teaspoon dried tarragon

Dash pepper

Toss greens, tomatoes and mushrooms in a large bowl. In a small bowl, whisk together dressing ingredients; pour over salad. **Yield:** 8 servings.
Diabetic Exchanges: One 1-cup serving (prepared without salt) equals 1 vegetable; also, 30 calories, 60 mg sodium, 0 cholesterol, 5 gm carbohydrate, 3 gm protein, trace fat.

FRUITED PEACH HALVES

Mrs. Damon Cross, Kenton, Tennessee

(PICTURED AT RIGHT)

This is my favorite recipe from an old cookbook. This time-tested recipe even won a contest sponsored by our local newspaper.

**1 can (29 ounces) peach halves
(6 to 7 halves)
1/3 cup finely chopped dried apricots
1/4 cup finely chopped dried figs
1/2 cup finely chopped pecans, *divided***
Lettuce leaves

Drain peaches, reserving 1 tablespoon juice. Set peaches aside. Combine peach juice, apricots, figs and 3 tablespoons pecans; mix well. Shape into 1-in. balls. Roll outside edges of peach halves in the remaining pecans. Place on a lettuce-lined plate; place a fruit ball on each. **Yield:** 6-7 servings.

SWEET POTATO SALAD

Mrs. Willard Wilson, Woodsfield, Ohio

My mother used to make this potato salad. We all liked it back then—and now my family likes it, too!

**3 pounds sweet potatoes, cooked, peeled
and cubed
1 cup chopped sweet red pepper
1/2 cup chopped onion
1-1/4 cups mayonnaise
1-1/2 teaspoons salt
1/2 teaspoon pepper
1/4 teaspoon hot pepper sauce**

In a large bowl, mix sweet potatoes, red pepper and onion. In a small bowl, blend remaining ingredients; add to potato mixture and toss to coat. **Yield:** 10-12 servings.

CRANBERRY CABBAGE SALAD

Connie Johnson, Litchfield, Minnesota

Fresh cranberries are abundant here during the holidays, so my family is always thrilled to see this colorful salad on the Christmas table.

**3/4 cup fresh *or* frozen cranberries, halved
1/4 cup sugar
6 cups shredded cabbage
1 cup green grapes, halved
1/2 cup thinly sliced celery
1/4 cup orange juice**
**3 tablespoons mayonnaise
1/2 teaspoon salt**

Toss cranberries with sugar and set aside. In a large bowl, combine the cabbage, grapes and celery. Add cranberries and toss. Combine orange juice, mayonnaise and salt; pour over salad and toss to coat. **Yield:** 6-8 servings.

TOMATO CUCUMBER SALAD

Margery Richmond, Lacombe, Alberta

My family expects to see this salad on the table several times a week in summer. They can't resist the refreshing flavor.

**3 medium tomatoes, sliced
1 small cucumber, thinly sliced
1 green onion, chopped
3 tablespoons Italian salad dressing
1 tablespoon vinegar
1 teaspoon chopped fresh basil *or* 1/4
teaspoon dried basil
1/4 teaspoon salt**
Pinch pepper
Pinch garlic salt

In a serving bowl, layer half the tomatoes, all of the cucumber, then remaining tomatoes. Sprinkle with onion. Combine remaining ingredients in a jar with a tight-fitting lid; shake well. Pour over salad. **Yield:** 4 servings.

PINEAPPLE COLESLAW

Betty Follas, Morgan Hill, California

(PICTURED ABOVE)

During the Depression, our good times were planned around simple foods and family activities. My fondest memories of those days are of family picnics featuring this tropical-tasting coleslaw.

    3/4 cup mayonnaise
    2 tablespoons vinegar
    2 tablespoons sugar
    1 to 2 tablespoons milk
    4 cups shredded cabbage
    1 can (8 ounces) pineapple tidbits, drained
Paprika, optional

In a mixing bowl, combine mayonnaise, vinegar, sugar and milk. Place cabbage and pineapple in a large salad bowl; add dressing and toss. Sprinkle with paprika if desired. **Yield:** 8 servings.

MARINATED ONION SALAD

Michelle Wrightsman, Linwood, Kansas

On days you find yourself rushing, reach for this recipe. Everyone cheers its fabulous old-fashioned taste.

    3 medium sweet onions, thinly sliced
    4 cups boiling water
    4 medium cucumbers, thinly sliced
    1 cup (8 ounces) plain yogurt
    1 teaspoon lemon juice
    1-1/2 teaspoons salt
    1/8 teaspoon pepper
Dash Worcestershire sauce
Dash vinegar
    1 teaspoon dill weed, optional
    2 tablespoons minced fresh parsley

Separate the onions into rings and place in a large bowl; pour water over onions. Let stand 1 minute; drain. Add cucumbers. In a small bowl, combine the yogurt, lemon juice, salt, pepper, Worcestershire sauce, vinegar and dill if desired; mix well. Pour over onion mixture and toss to coat. Sprinkle with parsley. Serve with a slotted spoon. **Yield:** 16-20 servings.

ROQUEFORT DRESSING

Evelyn Skaggs, Nixa, Missouri

I came up with this recipe after being disappointed by several store-bought varieties.

    1 cup (8 ounces) sour cream
    1/2 cup mayonnaise *or* salad dressing
    1 teaspoon tarragon vinegar
    1 teaspoon Worcestershire sauce
    1 teaspoon lemon juice
    1/2 teaspoon garlic salt
    1/2 teaspoon garlic powder
    1/2 teaspoon onion salt
Few drops hot pepper sauce

1 package (4 ounces) crumbled Roquefort cheese

In a small bowl, mix together all ingredients in the order listed. Store in the refrigerator. **Yield:** about 2 cups.

FESTIVE FRUIT SALAD

Gail Sellers, Savannah, Georgia

My bowl always comes home empty when I take this salad to a party or cookout. This recipe is a great way to take advantage of fresh fruit at its best.

- **1 medium fresh pineapple**
- **3 medium apples (1 red, 1 yellow and 1 green), cubed**
- **1 small cantaloupe, cubed**
- **4 cups seedless red and green grapes**
- **1 pint strawberries, halved**
- **1 pint blueberries**
- **3 kiwifruit, peeled and sliced**
- **1 large firm banana, sliced**

DRESSING:
- **1 package (3 ounces) cream cheese, softened**
- **1/2 cup confectioners' sugar**
- **2 teaspoons lemon juice**
- **1 carton (8 ounces) frozen whipped topping, thawed**

Additional berries for garnish, optional

Peel and core pineapple; cut into cubes. Place in a 3- or 4-qt. glass serving bowl. Add remaining fruit and stir to mix. In a mixing bowl, beat the cream cheese until smooth. Gradually add sugar and lemon juice; mix well. Fold in whipped topping. Spread over fruit. Garnish with additional berries if desired. Store leftovers in the refrigerator. **Yield:** 16-20 servings.

APPLE BEET SALAD

Shirley Glaab, Hattiesburg, Mississippi

Tart apples and pickled beets add zest to this colorful salad. It makes a satisfying side dish for casual picnics or fancy Sunday gatherings.

- **1/3 cup sweet pickle relish**
- **1/4 cup sliced green onions**
- **1/4 cup mayonnaise**
- **2 tablespoons cider vinegar**
- **1 tablespoon sugar**
- **1/4 teaspoon salt**
- **1/8 teaspoon pepper**
- **2 cups diced peeled tart apples**

- **2 cups diced pickled beets**
- **Lettuce leaves, optional**
- **1 hard-cooked egg, chopped, optional**

In a bowl, combine the first seven ingredients. Gently fold in apples and beets. If desired, serve on a lettuce-lined plate and top with chopped egg. **Yield:** 6-8 servings.

BLACK-AND-WHITE BEAN SALAD

Margaret Andersen, Greeley, Colorado

(PICTURED BELOW)

This zippy bean salad goes perfectly with a barbecued meal and is also great for a buffet or potluck. Best of all, it can be prepared in no time.

- **1 can (16 ounces) great northern beans, rinsed and drained**
- **1 can (15 ounces) black beans, rinsed and drained**
- **1-1/2 cups diced sweet red *or* yellow pepper**
- **1-1/4 cups chopped seeded tomato**
- **3/4 cup thinly sliced green onions**
- **1/2 cup salsa**
- **3 tablespoons cider *or* red wine vinegar**
- **2 tablespoons minced fresh parsley *or* cilantro**
- **1/4 teaspoon salt**
- **1/8 teaspoon pepper**

Combine the first five ingredients in a large bowl. In a small bowl, combine salsa, vinegar, parsley, salt and pepper. Pour over bean mixture; toss to coat. **Yield:** 6-8 servings.

GARDEN STATE SALAD

Mary Jane Ruther, Trenton, New Jersey

My state is known as the "Garden State" because it produces such a bounty of fine crops, and I like this recipe because it uses so many of them.

        1 small bunch romaine, torn
        2 medium potatoes, cooked and cubed
        2 large tomatoes, cut into wedges
        1 cup diced cucumber
    1/2 cup chopped celery
    1/2 medium green pepper, cut into strips
        1 small carrot, shredded
        3 hard-cooked eggs, chopped
    1/2 cup pitted whole ripe olives
        3 medium radishes, sliced
DRESSING:
    1-1/2 cups mayonnaise *or* salad dressing
        2 tablespoons Dijon mustard
        2 tablespoons cider *or* red wine vinegar
    1/2 teaspoon sugar
    1/4 teaspoon salt
    1/8 teaspoon pepper

In a large bowl, toss the first 10 ingredients. In a small bowl, combine dressing ingredients and stir well. Serve with the salad. **Yield:** 6-8 servings.

SOUR CREAM CUCUMBERS

Karen Holt, Redding, California

Not only is this the only way my kids will eat cucumbers, but they actually request it! The recipe is simple and delicious.

        2 large cucumbers, peeled and sliced
        1 large onion, sliced into rings
    3/4 cup sour cream

        3 tablespoons cider vinegar
        2 tablespoons sugar
Salt and pepper to taste

In a bowl, combine the cucumbers and onion. Combine remaining ingredients and pour over cucumbers. Mix well. **Yield:** 6-8 servings.

CALICO TOMATO SALAD

Donna Cline, Pensacola, Florida

(PICTURED BELOW)

This recipe has been in our family for years. We always appreciate this eye-catching salad because it's easy to prepare and delicious to eat.

✓ This tasty dish uses less sugar, salt and fat. Recipe includes *Diabetic Exchanges*.

        5 medium tomatoes
        1 small zucchini
        1 small sweet yellow pepper
    1/4 cup cider vinegar
        2 tablespoons olive *or* vegetable oil
        2 tablespoons minced fresh parsley
        2 teaspoons sugar
    1/2 teaspoon salt, optional
    1/2 teaspoon dried basil
    1/4 teaspoon dried marjoram
    1/8 teaspoon pepper

Cut tomatoes, zucchini and yellow pepper into 1/2-in. pieces; place in a large bowl. In a jar with a tight-fitting lid, combine remaining ingredients and shake well. Pour over vegetables and toss. **Yield:** about 8 servings. **Diabetic Exchanges:** One 3/4-cup serving (prepared without salt) equals 1 vegetable, 1/2 fat; also, 49 calories, 4 mg sodium, 0 cholesterol, 5 gm carbohydrate, 1 gm protein, 3 gm fat.

Festive Tossed Salad

Ruby Williams, Bogalusa, Louisiana

(PICTURED ABOVE)

This salad is always a hit—pretty to serve, adaptable to any number of servings and tasty, too.

>   2 tablespoons vegetable oil
>   1 tablespoon lemon juice
>   1 tablespoon honey
>   1/4 teaspoon sugar
>   1/4 teaspoon garlic powder
> Dash salt
>   2 to 3 cups torn lettuce
>   1 celery rib, sliced
>   1 medium carrot, shredded
>   2 green onions, sliced
>   1/2 cup mandarin oranges
>   1 tablespoon sliced almonds, toasted

In a jar with a tight-fitting lid, combine the first six ingredients; shake well. In a salad bowl, toss the lettuce, celery, carrot, onions and oranges. Add dressing and toss to coat; sprinkle with almonds. **Yield:** 2 servings.

Italian Salad

Regina Bianchi, Bessemer, Pennsylvania

This salad is super for summer with its light dressing and nice combination of fresh ingredients.

>   1/2 cup olive *or* vegetable oil
>   1/4 cup cider *or* red wine vinegar
>   2 garlic cloves, minced
>   1 teaspoon sugar
>   1/2 teaspoon dried oregano
>   1/2 teaspoon salt
>   1/4 teaspoon pepper
>   1 small head lettuce, torn

>   1/2 cup sliced green onions
>   1/2 cup chopped celery
>   1/2 cup shredded mozzarella cheese
>   1 can (2-1/4 ounces) sliced ripe olives, drained
>   1 medium tomato, cut into wedges
>   2 tablespoons shredded Parmesan cheese

In a jar with a tight-fitting lid, combine the first seven ingredients; shake well. In a large bowl, combine the lettuce, onions, celery, mozzarella cheese, olives and tomato. Add dressing and toss; sprinkle with Parmesan cheese. **Yield:** 6 servings.

Mexican Salad

Bernice Brown, Paradise, California

Much of my cooking—like this salad—is heavily influenced by the foods and flavors I tasted while growing up near the Mexican border.

>   8 cups torn mixed greens
>   2 medium tomatoes, cut into wedges
>   1 bunch green onions, sliced
>   1 can (2-1/4 ounces) sliced ripe olives, drained
>   1 to 2 cups corn chips
> AVOCADO DRESSING:
>   1 small ripe avocado, peeled
>   1/2 cup sour cream
>   1/4 cup vegetable oil
>   2 tablespoons lemon juice
>   1/2 teaspoon seasoned salt
>   1/2 teaspoon crushed red pepper flakes
>   1/2 teaspoon sugar

In a large bowl, toss the first five ingredients. In a small bowl, mash avocado with a fork. Add remaining dressing ingredients and mix well. Pour over salad and toss. **Yield:** 6-8 servings.

BUTTERMILK SALAD DRESSING

Mary Gehl, Victor, Montana

Your family will relish every bite of green salads when this is the zesty topping.

- **3/4 cup mayonnaise**
- **1/2 cup buttermilk**
- **1 garlic clove, minced**
- **1 teaspoon dried parsley flakes**
- **1/2 teaspoon dried minced onion**
- **1/4 to 1/2 teaspoon salt**
- **1/8 teaspoon pepper**

Combine all ingredients in a jar with a tight-fitting lid; shake until smooth. Chill for 25 minutes. Store in the refrigerator. **Yield:** 1-1/4 cups.

CRUNCHY SPINACH SALAD

Sharon Bickett, Chester, South Carolina

A fresh salad is the perfect complement to any meal. This salad, with its tangy dressing and crisp, crunchy ingredients, has become one of our very favorites.

- **2 quarts fresh torn spinach**
- **1 can (16 ounces) bean sprouts, drained** *or* **2 cups fresh bean sprouts**
- **1 can (8 ounces) sliced water chestnuts, drained**
- **4 hard-cooked eggs, chopped**
- **6 bacon strips, cooked and crumbled**
- **1 small onion, thinly sliced**

DRESSING:
- **1/2 cup packed brown sugar**
- **1/2 cup vegetable oil**
- **1/3 cup vinegar**
- **1/3 cup ketchup**
- **1 tablespoon Worcestershire sauce**

In a large bowl, combine spinach, bean sprouts, water chestnuts, eggs, bacon and onion. In a jar with a tight-fitting lid, combine all dressing ingredients; shake well. Pour over salad and toss. **Yield:** 8 servings.

ASPARAGUS MUSHROOM SALAD

Patsy Bell Hobson, Liberty, Missouri

(PICTURED ABOVE)

When I served this salad at a luncheon years ago, everyone asked for the recipe. Occasionally I'll garnish it with toasted walnut halves instead of tomatoes to give it some crunch.

- **1 pound fresh asparagus**
- **1 pound fresh mushrooms, sliced 1/4 inch thick**
- **4 tablespoons lemon juice,** *divided*
- **1 cup whipping cream**
- **1/2 teaspoon paprika**
- **1/2 teaspoon salt**
- **1/4 teaspoon pepper**
- **1 bunch romaine, torn**

Tomato wedges and additional paprika, optional

Cook asparagus spears in boiling water until crisp-tender, about 6-8 minutes; rinse in cold water and drain. In a bowl, toss mushrooms with 3 tablespoons lemon juice. Combine cream, paprika, salt, pepper and remaining lemon juice; whisk until smooth. Pour over mushrooms; toss to coat. Line a large serving platter with romaine. Arrange the asparagus in spoke fashion with stems toward center. Spoon mushrooms into center. If desired, garnish with tomato wedges and paprika. **Yield:** 8-10 servings.

ORANGE AND RED ONION SALAD

Nancy Schmidt, Gustine, California

It's true—orange and onion sounds like an unusual combination, but whenever I serve this salad, it quickly disappears.

    1 tablespoon butter *or* margarine
    1 cup sliced almonds
    2 tablespoons lemon juice
    1 teaspoon Dijon mustard
    1/2 teaspoon sugar
    1/2 teaspoon salt
    1/4 teaspoon white pepper
    1/2 cup vegetable oil
    1 bunch romaine, torn
    2 medium oranges, peeled and sectioned
    1 small red onion, thinly sliced

In a skillet, melt butter over medium heat. Saute the almonds until golden brown. Remove almonds to paper towels to drain. In a small bowl, combine lemon juice, mustard, sugar, salt and pepper; gradually beat in oil. In a large bowl, combine romaine, oranges, onion and almonds. Add dressing and toss. **Yield:** 6 servings.

> **AN A-PEEL-ING IDEA.** Hollowed-out orange halves make unique and pretty individual dishes for serving sherbet or ice cream.

TOMATO PARMESAN SALAD

Michelle Bently, Niceville, Florida

(PICTURED BELOW)

This salad makes regular appearances on our table. It's a great way to use garden tomatoes.

    2 bunches romaine, torn
    1 head iceberg lettuce, torn
    2 small red onions, thinly sliced
    2 large tomatoes, chopped
    1 jar (4 ounces) diced pimientos, drained
    2/3 cup shredded Parmesan cheese
1-1/3 cups vegetable *or* olive oil
    1 cup cider *or* red wine vinegar
    2 garlic cloves, minced
Salt and pepper to taste

In a large salad bowl, combine the first six ingredients. In a jar with a tight-fitting lid, combine oil, vinegar, garlic, salt and pepper; shake well. Pour over salad and toss. **Yield:** 14 servings.

BLUEBERRY SPINACH SALAD

Heidi Gilleland, Lees Summit, Missouri

(PICTURED ABOVE)

I received this recipe from a co-worker's wife and it's become one of my favorites. The blueberries give this salad a different twist.

  1/2 cup vegetable oil
  1/4 cup raspberry vinegar
    2 teaspoons Dijon mustard
    1 teaspoon sugar
  1/2 teaspoon salt
    1 package (10 ounces) fresh spinach, torn
    1 package (4 ounces) blue cheese, crumbled
    1 cup fresh blueberries
  1/2 cup chopped pecans, toasted

In a jar with a tight-fitting lid, combine the first five ingredients and shake well. In a large salad bowl, toss the spinach, blue cheese, blueberries and pecans. Add dressing and toss gently. **Yield:** 6-8 servings.

HERBED SALAD DRESSING

Marge Clark, West Lebanon, Indiana

I'm an avid gardener and have even published a cookbook featuring my favorite recipes using my favorite herb—thyme!

    1 to 1-1/3 cups tarragon vinegar
    1 cup vegetable oil

  2/3 cup olive oil
    4 teaspoons mayonnaise
    3 garlic cloves, minced
    1 tablespoon minced fresh thyme
    or 1 teaspoon dried thyme
    2 teaspoons Dijon mustard
1-1/2 teaspoons minced fresh tarragon
    or 1/2 teaspoon dried tarragon
    1 teaspoon brown sugar
    1 teaspoon salt

In a jar with a tight-fitting lid, combine all ingredients; shake well. **Yield:** 3 cups.

SWEET-AND-SOUR DRESSING

Marcia Orlando, Boyertown, Pennsylvania

When I was growing up, Dad made this so much it became our "house" dressing. This recipe makes a nice big batch that you can conveniently keep in your refrigerator.

1-1/2 cups sugar
    2 teaspoons dried minced onion
  1/2 teaspoon salt
  1/2 teaspoon chili powder
  1/2 teaspoon ground mustard
  1/4 teaspoon crushed red pepper flakes
    1 cup vinegar
    1 cup vegetable oil
  1/4 to 1/2 cup light corn syrup

In a bowl, combine sugar and seasonings. Add vinegar; stir until sugar is dissolved. Whisk in oil and corn syrup until well blended. **Yield:** 3 cups.

FESTIVE CORN BREAD SALAD

Dean Schrock, Jacksonville, Florida

(PICTURED BELOW)

This lightly sweet, fresh-tasting salad was devoured by the guests at a Southwestern theme party I hosted. The unusual combination of ingredients brought them back for seconds.

- **5 cups cubed corn bread *or* 6 corn bread muffins**
- **3 cups diced fresh tomatoes**
- **1 cup diced sweet onion**
- **1 cup diced green pepper**
- **1 pound sliced bacon, cooked and crumbled**
- **1/4 cup sweet pickle relish**
- **1 cup mayonnaise**
- **1/4 cup sweet pickle juice**
- **Shredded Parmesan cheese**

Place corn bread cubes in a large salad bowl (or crumble muffins into bowl). Combine tomatoes, onion, green pepper, bacon and relish; add to corn bread. Combine mayonnaise and pickle juice; mix well. Pour over corn bread mixture. Sprinkle with Parmesan cheese. **Yield:** 10-12 servings.

GERMAN POTATO SALAD

Sue Hartman, Parma, Idaho

I'd always loved my German grandmother's potato salad. So when I married a potato farmer—and had spuds in abundance—I played with several recipes that sounded similar and came up with this salad that reminds me of hers.

- **5 bacon strips**
- **3/4 cup chopped onion**
- **2 tablespoons all-purpose flour**
- **1-1/3 cups water**
- **2/3 cup cider vinegar**
- **1/4 cup sugar**
- **6 cups sliced cooked peeled potatoes**
- **1 teaspoon salt**
- **1/8 teaspoon pepper**

In a skillet, cook bacon until crisp; crumble and set aside. Drain, reserving 2 tablespoons of drippings; saute onion in drippings until tender. Stir in flour; blend well. Add water and vinegar; cook and stir until bubbly and slightly thick. Add sugar and stir until dissolved. Gently stir in bacon, potatoes, salt and pepper; heat through, stirring lightly to coat potatoes. Serve warm. **Yield:** 6-8 servings.

TOMATO-GARLIC DRESSING

Diane Hyatt, Renton, Washington

I've served this salad dressing many times when having company over for dinner, and everyone just loves it. I've had this recipe for so many years, I forgot where it came from!

2 cups mayonnaise
1 teaspoon lemon juice
1 teaspoon garlic powder
2 medium tomatoes, chopped

Combine all ingredients in a food processor or blender; cover and process until smooth. Store in the refrigerator. **Yield:** about 3 cups.

CARROT RAISIN SALAD

Denise Baumert, Jameson, Missouri

This colorful traditional salad is one of my mother-in-law's favorites. It's fun to eat because of its crunchy texture, and the raisins give it a slightly sweet flavor. Plus, it's easy to prepare.

✓ This tasty dish uses less sugar, salt and fat. Recipe includes *Diabetic Exchanges*.

4 cups shredded carrots (about 4 to 5 large)
1 cup raisins
1/4 cup mayonnaise *or* salad dressing
2 tablespoons sugar
2 to 3 tablespoons milk

Place carrots and raisins in a bowl. In another bowl, mix together mayonnaise, sugar and enough milk to reach a salad dressing consistency. Pour over carrot mixture and toss to coat. **Yield:** 8 servings. **Diabetic Exchanges:** One serving (prepared with salad dressing and skim milk) equals 1 fruit, 1 vegetable, 1/2 fat; also, 110 calories, 80 mg sodium, 2 mg cholesterol, 24 gm carbohydrate, 1 gm protein, 2 gm fat.

SPINACH SLAW

GaleLynn Peterson, Long Beach, California

(PICTURED BELOW)

This hearty slaw is a great side dish. Even people who don't like cabbage enjoy it prepared this way.

8 cups shredded iceberg lettuce
5 cups shredded spinach
4 cups shredded red cabbage
3 cups shredded green cabbage
1 cup mayonnaise *or* salad dressing
1/4 cup honey
3/4 to 1 teaspoon garlic powder
1/2 teaspoon salt
1/4 teaspoon pepper

In a large bowl, toss lettuce, spinach and cabbages. In a small bowl, combine remaining ingredients. Pour over salad and toss to coat. **Yield:** 12-16 servings.

WILTED LETTUCE

Rosemary Falls, Austin, Texas

(PICTURED ABOVE)

When I think of my favorite meals from childhood, this salad comes to mind. Nothing beats garden lettuce wilted with bacon drippings, and no other recipe better captures the taste of long ago.

    4 cups torn leaf lettuce
    1 small onion, sliced
    3 radishes, sliced
    6 bacon strips, diced
    2 tablespoons vinegar
    1 teaspoon brown sugar
    1/4 teaspoon ground mustard
    1/4 to 1/2 teaspoon salt
    1/8 teaspoon pepper

In a large salad bowl, toss the lettuce, onion and radishes; set aside. In a skillet, cook bacon until crisp; remove with a slotted spoon to drain on paper towel. To the drippings, add vinegar, brown sugar, mustard, salt and pepper; bring to a boil. Pour over lettuce and toss; sprinkle with bacon. **Yield:** 4-6 servings.

SUMMER APPLE SALAD

Kim Stoller, Smithville, Ohio

This apple salad really goes well with sandwiches and is especially nice for summer. It's a colorful combination of crunchy, fresh ingredients.

    3 medium tart red apples, diced
    1 can (8 ounces) pineapple tidbits,
        drained
1-1/2 cups sliced celery
    1 cup green grapes, halved

    1 medium carrot, shredded
1/2 cup coarsely chopped almonds
3/4 cup sour cream
    1 tablespoon sugar
1/2 teaspoon lemon juice

In a large salad bowl, combine apples, pineapple, celery, grapes, carrot and almonds. In a small bowl, combine sour cream, sugar and lemon juice; mix well. Add to apple mixture and toss to coat. **Yield:** 12 servings.

ASPARAGUS TOMATO SALAD

Anne Frederick, New Hartford, New York

This is a delicious way to start off any meal—and a nice change of pace from the usual tossed salad.

DRESSING:
    2 tablespoons lemon juice
    1 tablespoon olive *or* vegetable oil
    1 teaspoon cider *or* red wine vinegar
1/2 garlic clove, minced
1/2 teaspoon Dijon mustard
1/4 teaspoon dried basil
1/4 teaspoon salt
1/8 teaspoon pepper
SALAD:
    12 fresh asparagus spears, cut into
        1-1/2-inch pieces
    3 small tomatoes, seeded and diced
    1 small red onion, sliced

In a medium bowl, whisk together dressing ingredients; set aside. Cook asparagus in boiling water until crisp-tender, about 3-4 minutes. Rinse with cold water and drain. Place in a large bowl; add tomatoes and onion. Add dressing and toss to coat. **Yield:** 4 servings.

Muffins & Breads

Jellied Biscuits

Marsha Ransom, South Haven, Michigan

(PICTURED AT RIGHT)

These biscuits are a pleasure to serve breakfast guests because they look so lovely.

> 2 cups all-purpose flour
> 4 teaspoons baking powder
> 2 teaspoons sugar
> 1/2 teaspoon salt
> 1/2 teaspoon cream of tartar
> 1/2 cup shortening
> 3/4 cup milk
> 1/3 cup jelly

In a bowl, combine flour, baking powder, sugar, salt and cream of tartar. Cut in shortening until the mixture resembles coarse crumbs. Add milk; stir just until moistened. Drop by rounded tablespoonfuls onto a greased baking sheet. Make an indention in center of each biscuit; fill each with about 1 teaspoon of jelly. Bake at 450° for 10-12 minutes or until biscuits are lightly browned. **Yield:** 1 dozen.

Ham and Cheese Muffins

Doris Heath, Bryson City, North Carolina

(PICTURED AT RIGHT)

These savory biscuit-like muffins are delicious at breakfast or accompanying a bowl of soup.

> 2 cups self-rising flour*
> 1/2 teaspoon baking soda
> 1 cup milk
> 1/2 cup mayonnaise
> 1/2 cup finely chopped fully cooked ham
> 1/2 cup shredded cheddar cheese

In a large bowl, combine flour and baking soda. Combine milk and mayonnaise; add ham and cheese. Stir into dry ingredients just until moistened. Fill greased or paper-lined muffin cups two-thirds full. Bake at 425° for 16-18 minutes or until muffins test done. **Yield:** about 1 dozen. ***Editor's Note:** As a substitute for *each cup* of self-rising flour, place 1-1/2 teaspoons baking powder and 1/2 teaspoon salt in a measuring cup. Add all-purpose flour to equal 1 cup.

Buttery French Bread

Sally Holbrook, Pasadena, California

(PICTURED AT RIGHT)

The combination of paprika, celery seed and butter makes for a full-flavored bread.

> 1/2 cup butter *or* margarine, softened
> 1/4 teaspoon paprika
> 1/4 teaspoon celery seed
> 1 loaf French bread (1 pound), sliced

In a small bowl, combine butter, paprika and celery seed. Spread on both sides of bread and over top. Wrap in heavy-duty foil. Bake at 375° for 15 minutes. Unwrap foil and bake 5 minutes longer. **Yield:** 6-8 servings.

Favorite Corn Bread

Carol Allen, McLeansboro, Illinois

This corn bread is simple to make and a great addition to any meal.

> 1 cup all-purpose flour
> 1 cup yellow cornmeal
> 1/4 cup sugar
> 4 teaspoons baking powder
> 3/4 teaspoon salt
> 2 eggs
> 1 cup milk
> 1/4 cup shortening

In a mixing bowl, combine flour, cornmeal, sugar, baking powder and salt. Add eggs, milk and shortening; beat for 1 minute. Pour into a greased 9-in. square baking pan. Bake at 425° for 20-25 minutes or until bread tests done. **Yield:** 9 servings.

> **FRESH FROM THE OVEN.** *Pictured at right, top to bottom: Buttery French Bread, Ham and Cheese Muffins and Jellied Biscuits (all recipes on this page).*

BUTTERMILK OATMEAL MUFFINS

Robert Luebke, Appleton, Wisconsin

(PICTURED ABOVE)

These delicious muffins were part of the first dinner I had with my wife when we were courting. Now whenever she plans a menu, I ask her to put these muffins on it.

    1 cup quick-cooking oats
    1 cup buttermilk
    1 egg
    1/2 cup packed brown sugar
    1/4 cup vegetable oil
    1 cup all-purpose flour
    1 teaspoon baking powder
    1/2 teaspoon baking soda
    1/2 teaspoon salt

In a bowl, soak oats in buttermilk for 10 minutes. Stir in egg, brown sugar and oil. Combine flour, baking powder, baking soda and salt; stir into oat mixture just until moistened. Fill greased or paper-lined muffin cups three-fourths full. Bake at 400° for 16-18 minutes or until muffins test done. Cool in pan 5 minutes before removing to a wire rack. **Yield:** about 8 muffins.

> **MOIST MUFFINS.** For super-moist bran muffins, press a 1-inch cube of cream cheese into the batter of each muffin before baking.

FLUFFY WHOLE WHEAT BISCUITS

Ruth Ann Stelfox, Raymond, Alberta

Few foods taste homier than fresh biscuits still warm from the oven. These are just scrumptious —light and tasty!

    1 cup all-purpose flour
    1 cup whole wheat flour
    4 teaspoons baking powder
    1 tablespoon sugar
  3/4 teaspoon salt
  1/4 cup cold butter *or* margarine
    1 cup milk

In a bowl, combine dry ingredients. Cut in butter until mixture resembles coarse crumbs. Stir in milk just until moistened. Turn out onto a floured surface; knead gently 8-10 times. Roll to 3/4-in. thickness; cut with a 2-1/2-in. biscuit cutter and place on an ungreased baking sheet. Bake at 450° for 10-12 minutes or until lightly browned. Serve warm. **Yield:** 1 dozen.

CREAM CHEESE MUFFIN PUFFS

Diane Xavier, Hilmar, California

Family and friends are always thrilled to find the sweet cream cheese mixture tucked inside these tender puffs.

  1/2 cup sugar
    1 teaspoon ground cinnamon

1/4 cup butter *or* **margarine, melted**
1/2 teaspoon vanilla extract
  1 tube (10 ounces) refrigerated biscuits
  1 package (3 ounces) cream cheese, cut into 10 cubes

In a small bowl, combine the sugar and cinnamon. In another bowl, combine the butter and vanilla. Separate dough into 10 biscuits; press each into a 3-in. circle. Dip cream cheese cubes in butter and then in cinnamon-sugar. Place one in the center of each biscuit. Fold dough over cube; seal and shape into balls. Dip the balls in butter and then in cinnamon-sugar. Place with seam side down in greased muffin cups. Bake at 375° for 14-18 minutes or until golden brown. Serve warm. **Yield:** 10 muffins.

SOUR CREAM CORN BREAD

Linda Brown, Sinking Spring, Pennsylvania

(PICTURED AT RIGHT)

Mother's corn bread is a special treat she made often while I was growing up. My grandmother came up with this recipe years ago. True to tradition, I serve it frequently to my own family.

  1 cup all-purpose flour
  1 cup yellow cornmeal
  2 tablespoons sugar
  2 teaspoons baking powder
1/2 teaspoon salt
  1 egg, beaten
  1 cup (8 ounces) sour cream
1/3 cup milk
  2 tablespoons butter *or* **margarine, melted**
  2 tablespoons diced pimientos
  1 teaspoon minced dried onion

In a bowl, combine dry ingredients; mix well. Add remaining ingredients and stir just until moistened. Pour into a greased 8-in. square baking pan. Bake at 400° for 20-25 minutes or until bread tests done. **Yield:** 9 servings.

HONEY RAISIN MUFFINS

Joyce Reece, Mena, Arkansas

These melt-in-your-mouth muffins get their splendidly sweet flavor from honey.

1-1/4 cups all-purpose flour
  1 tablespoon baking powder
1/4 teaspoon salt
  2 cups bran flakes with raisins
  1 cup milk

1/4 cup honey
  1 egg
  3 tablespoons vegetable oil

Combine flour, baking powder and salt; set aside. In a large bowl, combine cereal, milk and honey; let stand until softened, about 2 minutes. Stir in egg and oil; mix well. Add dry ingredients; stir just until moistened. Fill greased or paper-lined muffin cups two-thirds full. Bake at 400° for 18-20 minutes or until muffins test done. Cool in pan 10 minutes before removing to a wire rack. **Yield:** about 10 muffins.

CORN MUFFINS WITH HONEY BUTTER

Marilyn Platner, Marion, Iowa

I especially like preparing these muffins for my family on a winter night—along with a big pot of chili, they make for a hearty meal!

2 cups all-purpose flour
2 cups yellow cornmeal
1 cup instant nonfat dry milk powder
1/4 cup sugar
2 tablespoons baking powder
1 teaspoon salt
1/2 teaspoon baking soda
2 eggs
2-2/3 cups water
1/2 cup butter *or* margarine, melted
1 tablespoon lemon juice
HONEY BUTTER:
1/2 cup butter (no substitutes), softened
2 tablespoons honey

In a bowl, combine flour, cornmeal, milk powder, sugar, baking powder, salt and baking soda. Add eggs, water, butter and lemon juice; stir just until dry ingredients are moistened. Spoon into greased or paper-lined muffin cups. Bake at 425° for 13-15 minutes. In a small mixing bowl, beat butter and honey. Serve with the muffins. **Yield:** 2 dozen.

CHOCOLATE CHIP OATMEAL MUFFINS

Cheryl Bohn, Dominion City, Manitoba

I saw this recipe in a newspaper years ago and have changed it quite a bit. I make these muffins at least once a month and get many requests for the recipe.

1/2 cup butter *or* margarine, softened
3/4 cup packed brown sugar
1 egg
1 cup all-purpose flour
1 teaspoon baking powder
1/4 teaspoon baking soda
1/4 teaspoon salt
3/4 cup applesauce
1 cup old-fashioned oats
1 cup (6 ounces) semisweet chocolate chips

In a large mixing bowl, cream butter and brown sugar. Beat in egg. Combine dry ingredients; add alternately with applesauce to the creamed mixture. Stir in oats and chocolate chips. Fill greased or paper-lined muffin cups three-fourths full. Bake

at 350° for 25 minutes or until muffins test done. **Yield:** 1 dozen.

ONION CHEESE MUFFINS

Judy Johnson, Mundelein, Illinois

(PICTURED BELOW)

When I don't have time to bake onion bread, I whip up a batch of these tasty muffins. They're simply wonderful!

1-1/2 cups biscuit/baking mix
3/4 cup shredded Colby *or* cheddar cheese, *divided*
1 egg
1/2 cup milk
1 small onion, finely chopped
1 tablespoon butter *or* margarine
1 tablespoon sesame seeds, toasted

Combine biscuit mix and 1/2 cup cheese in a large bowl. In a small bowl, beat egg and milk. In a small skillet, saute onion in butter until tender; add to milk mixture. Stir into cheese mixture just until moistened. Fill greased or paper-lined muffin cups three-fourths full. Top with sesame seeds and remaining cheese. Bake at 400° for 18-20 minutes or until muffins test done. Cool in pan 10 minutes. Serve warm. **Yield:** about 6 muffins.

NUTTY SWEET POTATO BISCUITS

Mrs. India Thacker, Clifford, Virginia

Back in the 1920's and '30's, Mom always had something good for us to eat when we got home from school. She often had a plate of these warm wonderful biscuits waiting for us.

2-3/4 cups all-purpose flour
    4 teaspoons baking powder
1-1/4 teaspoons salt
    1/2 teaspoon ground cinnamon
    1/2 teaspoon ground nutmeg
    3/4 cup chopped nuts
    2 cups mashed sweet potatoes (without added butter or milk)
    3/4 cup sugar
    1/2 cup butter *or* margarine, melted
    1 teaspoon vanilla extract

In a large mixing bowl, combine flour, baking powder, salt, cinnamon, nutmeg and nuts. In another bowl, combine sweet potatoes, sugar, butter and vanilla; add to flour mixture and mix well. Turn onto a floured surface; gently knead 3-4 times. Roll dough to 1/2-in. thickness. Cut with a 2-1/2-in. biscuit cutter and place on lightly greased baking sheets. Bake at 450° for 12 minutes or until golden brown. **Yield:** 1-1/2 to 2 dozen.

BLUEBERRY MUFFINS

Carolyn Gilman, Westbrook, Maine

I prepare these muffins with the blueberries that grow wild along the rocky coast of Maine. I have worked on this recipe for several years and finally feel that I have it perfected.

    2 cups all-purpose flour
3/4 cup sugar
    1 tablespoon baking powder
1/2 teaspoon ground cinnamon
1/2 teaspoon salt
3/4 cup milk
1/4 cup lemon juice
    1 egg
1/4 cup vegetable oil
    1 cup fresh *or* frozen blueberries

In a large bowl, combine flour, sugar, baking powder, cinnamon and salt. In a small bowl, mix milk and lemon juice. Add egg and oil; mix well. Stir into flour mixture just until moistened. Fold in blueberries. Fill greased or paper-lined muffin cups two-thirds full. Bake at 400° for 22-24 minutes or until center of muffin springs back when lightly touched. **Yield:** 1 dozen.

FEATHER-LIGHT BISCUITS

Eleanore Hill, Fresno, California

(PICTURED ABOVE)

I often bake these and share them with our kids. They like to split them and fill them with cheese or peanut butter and strawberry jam.

    6 cups biscuit/baking mix
1/4 cup sugar
    1 package (1/4 ounce) active dry yeast
1/3 cup shortening
    1 to 1-1/4 cups warm water (120° to 130°)
1/4 cup butter *or* margarine, melted

In a large bowl, combine the biscuit mix, sugar and yeast. Cut in shortening until mixture resembles coarse crumbs. Stir in enough warm water to make a soft and slightly sticky dough. Turn onto a floured surface; knead gently 3-4 times. Roll dough to 3/4-in. thickness; cut with a 2-1/2-in. biscuit cutter. Place on ungreased baking sheets. Brush tops with melted butter. Bake at 400° for 10-12 minutes or until lightly browned. **Yield:** about 2 dozen.

ITALIAN GARLIC TOAST

Cookie Curci-Wright, San Jose, California

(PICTURED BELOW)

I prepare this bread whenever we have an Italian meal. It's rich with cheese and butter and colorful with paprika.

- **1 unsliced loaf Italian *or* French bread (1-1/2 pounds)**
- **1/2 cup butter *or* margarine, melted**
- **1/4 cup grated Romano *or* Parmesan cheese**
- **2 garlic cloves, minced *or* 1/2 teaspoon garlic powder**
- **1/2 teaspoon dried oregano**

Paprika

Slice bread lengthwise; place with cut side up on a large baking sheet. In a small bowl, combine butter, cheese, garlic and oregano; brush onto the cut surfaces of the bread. Sprinkle with paprika. Broil about 4 in. from the heat for 2-3 minutes or until lightly toasted. Cut crosswise into 3-in. pieces. **Yield:** 8-10 servings.

BANANA CRUMB MUFFINS

Wendy Masters, Grand Valley, Ontario

This is one of my very favorite recipes—and it's the only kind of muffin our youngster will eat.

- **1-1/2 cups all-purpose flour**
- **1 teaspoon baking soda**
- **1 teaspoon baking powder**
- **1/2 teaspoon salt**
- **3 large ripe bananas, mashed**
- **1 egg**
- **3/4 cup sugar**
- **1/3 cup butter *or* margarine, melted**

TOPPING:
- **1/3 cup packed brown sugar**
- **1 tablespoon all-purpose flour**
- **1/8 teaspoon ground cinnamon**
- **1 tablespoon cold butter *or* margarine**

In a large bowl, combine the first four ingredients. Combine bananas, egg, sugar and butter; mix well. Stir into dry ingredients just until moistened. Fill greased or paper-lined muffin cups three-fourths full. Combine the first three topping ingredients;

cut in butter until crumbly. Sprinkle over muffins. Bake at 375° for 18-20 minutes or until muffins test done. Cool in pan 10 minutes before removing to a wire rack. **Yield:** about 1 dozen.

Mom's Muffins

Jane Jensen, Uma, Arizona

(PICTURED AT RIGHT)

These muffins were always a special treat when I was a child. Now I have lots of muffin recipes, but none are better than this.

- 2 cups all-purpose flour
- 2 tablespoons plus 1 teaspoon sugar
- 4 teaspoons baking powder
- 1 teaspoon salt
- 2 eggs
- 3/4 cup milk
- 1/4 cup vegetable oil

In a large bowl, combine flour, sugar, baking powder and salt; make a well in the center. In another bowl, beat eggs; add milk and oil. Stir into dry ingredients just until moistened. Spoon into greased or paper-lined muffin cups. Bake at 400° for 20-25 minutes or until golden brown. **Yield:** 1 dozen.

Orange Cream Cheese Muffins

Ed Toner, Howell, New Jersey

When you make these in the jumbo muffin pans, they certainly satisfy your hunger! They are very tasty muffins, and we really enjoy them.

- 1 package (3 ounces) cream cheese, softened
- 1/4 cup sugar
- 1 egg
- 1/2 cup orange juice
- 1-3/4 cups biscuit/baking mix
- 1/4 cup chopped pecans
- 6 teaspoons orange marmalade

In a mixing bowl, beat cream cheese and sugar. Add egg and orange juice; mix well. Stir in biscuit mix just until moistened. Fold in pecans. Grease six jumbo muffin cups generously. Spoon 1/4 cup into each muffin cup. Spoon 1 teaspoon marmalade into the center of each muffin. Divide remaining batter over marmalade. Bake at 400° for 20 minutes or until golden brown. Cool in pan for 5 minutes before removing to a wire rack. **Yield:** 6 jumbo muffins.

Poppy Seed Pound Cake Muffins

Shirley McCluskey, Colorado Springs, Colorado

I found this recipe in a cookbook published in our area. It's so good that I haven't done a single thing to change the original instructions!

- 2 cups all-purpose flour
- 1 tablespoon poppy seeds
- 1/2 teaspoon salt
- 1/4 teaspoon baking soda
- 1/2 cup butter *or* margarine, softened
- 1 cup sugar
- 2 eggs
- 1 carton (8 ounces) plain yogurt
- 1 teaspoon vanilla extract

Combine flour, poppy seeds, salt and baking soda; set aside. In a mixing bowl, cream butter and sugar. Beat in eggs, one at a time. Add yogurt and vanilla; mix well. Stir in flour mixture just until moistened. Spoon into greased or paper-lined muffin cups. Bake at 400° for 15-20 minutes or until muffins test done. Cool in pan for 5 minutes before removing to a wire rack. **Yield:** 1 dozen.

BISCUITS WITH HAM BUTTER

Andrea Bolden, Unionville, Tennessee

(PICTURED BELOW)

Whether as a finger food or brunch dish, these are a great way to use leftover ham.

1-1/2 cups all-purpose flour
   2 teaspoons baking powder
1/2 teaspoon salt
3/4 cup sour cream
   1 egg
   1 cup cubed fully cooked ham
1/2 cup butter *or* margarine, softened

In a bowl, combine the flour, baking powder and salt. Combine sour cream and egg; mix well. Stir into dry ingredients just until moistened. Turn onto a floured surface; knead gently 4-5 times. Roll to 1/2-in. thickness; cut with a 2-1/2-in. biscuit cutter. Place on a greased baking sheet. Bake at 425° for 10-12 minutes or until lightly browned. Meanwhile, in a blender or food processor, process ham until finely minced. Add butter and continue processing until well mixed. Serve with warm biscuits. **Yield:** 10 servings.

PEANUT MUFFINS

Ruby Williams, Bogalusa, Louisiana

I was tired of buying chips and candy for my many grandchildren and great-grandchildren. So I made these wholesome muffins. The kids loved them.

1-1/2 cups all-purpose flour
1/4 cup sugar
   1 tablespoon baking powder
1/4 teaspoon salt
   2 eggs
1/2 cup butter *or* margarine, melted
1/2 cup milk
3/4 cup chopped unsalted dry roasted peanuts

In a large bowl, combine flour, sugar, baking powder and salt. Combine eggs, butter and milk; add to the dry ingredients and stir just until moistened. Fold in peanuts. Fill greased or paper-lined muffin cups two-thirds full. Bake at 400° for 15 minutes or until muffins test done. **Yield:** 1 dozen.

APRICOT MUFFINS

Ann Chamberlain, Denver, Colorado

I tried apricots when I didn't have the usual muffin ingredients one time— and this recipe is the result! We enjoyed them, and I've made them often since.

   1 cup dried apricots, cut up
   1 cup boiling water
1/2 cup butter *or* margarine, softened
   1 cup sugar
3/4 cup sour cream
   2 cups all-purpose flour
   1 teaspoon baking soda
1/2 teaspoon salt
   1 tablespoon grated orange peel
1/2 cup chopped nuts
TOPPING:
1/4 cup sugar
1/4 cup orange juice

In a small bowl, combine apricots and water. Let stand for 5 minutes. Drain and discard liquid; set apricots aside. In a mixing bowl, cream butter and sugar until fluffy. Add sour cream and mix well. Combine dry ingredients; add to creamed mixture just until moistened. Fold in orange peel, nuts and apricots (batter will be very stiff). Fill greased or paper-lined muffin cups three-fourths full. Bake at 400° for 18-20 minutes or until muffins test done. Combine sugar and orange juice; dip tops of warm muffins. **Yield:** 1 dozen.

CORN HILL CORN BREAD

Ellen Burr, Truro, Massachusetts

I named this recipe after the wooded hill we can see from our house. It is said that Pilgrims discovered a cache of Indian corn here that enabled them to survive their first harsh winter in the New World.

1-1/4 cups all-purpose flour
3/4 cup yellow cornmeal
1/3 cup sugar
2 teaspoons baking powder
1/2 teaspoon salt
1/2 teaspoon ground coriander
1/2 teaspoon ground ginger
1/2 teaspoon dried thyme
1/8 teaspoon ground mace
1 egg
1 cup milk
1/4 cup vegetable oil
1 cup fresh corn, cooked
2 teaspoons cinnamon-sugar

In a large bowl, combine the first nine ingredients. Combine egg, milk and oil; stir into the dry ingredients just until moistened. Fold in corn. Pour into a greased 8-in. square baking pan. Sprinkle with cinnamon-sugar. Bake at 400° for 20-25 minutes or until bread tests done. **Yield:** 9 servings.

ORANGE PAN ROLLS

Jackie Riley, Holland, Michigan

(PICTURED BELOW)

A hint of orange in the dough makes these rolls refreshingly different. Similar in texture to biscuits, they bake to a beautiful golden brown.

1/2 cup all-purpose flour
3/4 teaspoon baking powder
1/8 teaspoon cream of tartar
1/8 teaspoon salt
1/2 teaspoon grated orange peel
2 tablespoons shortening
3 tablespoons milk
1 tablespoon butter *or* margarine, melted
1 tablespoon sugar
1/8 teaspoon ground nutmeg

In a bowl, combine flour, baking powder, cream of tartar and salt. Add orange peel; cut in shortening until the mixture resembles coarse crumbs. Stir in milk just until moistened. Divide dough into fourths. With floured hands, roll each piece of dough into a ball. Place butter in a small bowl. Combine sugar and nutmeg in another bowl. Dip balls in butter, then in sugar mixture. Evenly space in a greased 9-in. round baking pan. Bake at 450° for 10-12 minutes or until golden brown. **Yield:** 4 rolls.

SOUR CREAM 'N' CHIVE BISCUITS

Lucile Proctor, Panguitch, Utah

(PICTURED ABOVE)

I like to use my homegrown chives in these tender biscuits—they're delectable.

> 2 cups all-purpose flour
> 1 tablespoon baking powder
> 1/2 teaspoon salt
> 1/4 teaspoon baking soda
> 1/3 cup shortening
> 3/4 cup sour cream
> 1/4 cup milk
> 1/4 cup minced chives

In a bowl, combine dry ingredients. Cut in shortening until mixture resembles coarse crumbs. With a fork, stir in sour cream, milk and chives until the mixture forms a ball. Turn onto a floured surface and knead 5-6 times. Roll out to 3/4-in. thickness; cut with a 2-in. biscuit cutter. Place on an ungreased baking sheet. Bake at 350° for 12-15 minutes or until golden brown. **Yield:** 12-15 biscuits.

CHEESY CORN BREAD

Sandra Thorn, Sonora, California

What could be better for a Southwestern theme dinner than corn bread? Cheddar cheese mixed in makes it even more special.

> 4 cups all-purpose flour
> 2 cups yellow cornmeal
> 2/3 cup sugar
> 3 tablespoons baking powder
> 1 tablespoon salt
> 1 cup shortening
> 4 eggs
> 3 cups milk
> 1/2 cup finely shredded cheddar cheese

In a large bowl, combine the first five ingredients; cut in shortening until the mixture resembles coarse crumbs. Beat eggs and milk; stir into the dry ingredients just until blended. Pour into a greased 13-in. x 9-in. x 2-in. baking pan. Sprinkle with cheese. Bake at 400° for 25 minutes or until golden brown. **Yield:** 16-20 servings.

MORNING GLORY MUFFINS

Paddy Webber, Exeter, Ontario

I once took these muffins to a brunch. They soon disappeared, and everyone wanted the recipe!

> 2 cups all-purpose flour
> 1-1/4 cups sugar
> 2 teaspoons baking soda
> 2 teaspoons ground cinnamon
> 1/2 teaspoon salt
> 2 cups grated carrots
> 1/2 cup raisins
> 1/2 cup shredded coconut
> 1/2 cup chopped pecans
> 3 eggs
> 1 cup vegetable oil
> 1 medium tart apple, peeled and shredded
> 2 teaspoons vanilla extract

In a large bowl, combine flour, sugar, baking soda, cinnamon and salt. Stir in carrots, raisins, coconut and pecans. Combine eggs, oil, apple and vanilla; stir into dry ingredients just until moistened. Spoon into greased or paper-lined muffin cups. Bake at 350° for 15-18 minutes or until muffins test done. **Yield:** about 1-1/2 dozen.

SAGE CORN MUFFINS

Velma Martin, Stirum, North Dakota

These muffins are moist and flavorful—try them instead of rolls with most any meal.

1-1/2 cups yellow cornmeal
1/2 cup all-purpose flour
3 tablespoons sugar
1 tablespoon baking powder
1/2 teaspoon salt
2 eggs
1 cup buttermilk
1/4 cup butter *or* margarine, melted
1-1/2 cups cream-style corn
1/2 cup chopped fresh sage *or* 1-1/2 teaspoons rubbed sage
1/4 teaspoon pepper

In a mixing bowl, combine cornmeal, flour, sugar, baking powder and salt. Beat eggs, buttermilk and butter; stir into dry ingredients just until moistened. Fold in corn, sage and pepper. Fill greased or paper-lined muffin cups three-fourths full. Bake at 400° for 22-25 minutes or until muffins are golden brown and test done. **Yield:** 1 dozen.

CHEESE BISCUITS

Mary Lewis, Memphis, Tennessee

(PICTURED ON FRONT COVER)

The cheese gives these biscuits an unforgettable flavor, and buttermilk makes them especially light.

1-2/3 cups all-purpose flour
2 teaspoons baking powder
1/2 teaspoon salt
1/4 teaspoon baking soda
1/4 cup shortening
1 cup (4 ounces) shredded cheddar cheese
3/4 cup buttermilk

In a mixing bowl, combine flour, baking powder, salt and baking soda. Cut in shortening until the mixture resembles coarse crumbs. Stir in cheese. Add buttermilk; stir just until moistened. On a floured surface, gently knead dough until easy to handle. Roll into a 12-in. circle. Cut into eight wedges. Beginning at the wide end, roll up each wedge. Place biscuits with point side down on a greased baking sheet. Bake at 450° for 12-14 minutes or until golden brown. Serve warm. **Yield:** 8 biscuits.

BRAN MUFFINS

Betty Shaw, Weirton, West Virginia

(PICTURED BELOW)

I've experimented with many bran muffin recipes through the years, and my family ranks these as No. 1!

2 eggs
2 cups buttermilk
1/2 cup vegetable oil
1/2 cup sugar
3 cups bran flakes with raisins
1/4 to 1/2 cup raisins
2-1/2 cups all-purpose flour
2-1/2 teaspoons baking soda
1/2 teaspoon salt

In a mixing bowl, beat eggs, buttermilk, oil and sugar. Stir in cereal and raisins. Combine flour, baking soda and salt; add to egg mixture. Stir just until moistened. Fill greased or paper-lined muffin cups two-thirds full. Bake at 400° for 15-20 minutes or until golden brown. Serve warm. **Yield:** about 1-1/2 dozen.

Home-Style Sandwiches

MUSHROOM BACON BURGERS

Gail Kuntz, Dillon, Montana

(PICTURED AT RIGHT)

During summer, I use the grill often. Food just tastes better, and cleanup is easier. This recipe is a delicious way to dress up plain hamburgers.

> 1 pound ground beef
> 1 can (4 ounces) mushroom stems and pieces, drained
> 4 bacon strips, cooked and crumbled
> 2 tablespoons diced green onions
> 1 teaspoon Worcestershire sauce
> 1 teaspoon soy sauce
> 1/2 teaspoon salt
> 4 hamburger buns, split
> Lettuce leaves and tomato slices, optional

In a bowl, combine the first seven ingredients; mix well. Shape into four patties. Grill over medium-hot coals or fry in a skillet for 10-12 minutes or until meat is no longer pink, turning once. Serve on buns with lettuce and tomato if desired. **Yield:** 4 servings.

HOT ANTIPASTO POOR BOYS

Robyn Thompson, Culver City, California

(PICTURED AT RIGHT)

I like a simple sandwich recipe that eats like a meal. These zesty Italian sandwiches really hit the spot.

> 1/4 cup creamy Italian *or* Parmesan salad dressing
> 2 tablespoons grated Parmesan cheese
> 1 can (14 ounces) artichoke hearts in water, drained and quartered
> 1 cup quartered cherry tomatoes
> 1 package (5 ounces) thinly sliced pepperoni
> 1 can (2-1/4 ounces) sliced ripe olives, drained

> 2 submarine *or* hoagie rolls (about 10 inches)
> 1/2 cup shredded mozzarella cheese

In a medium bowl, combine dressing and Parmesan cheese. Add the artichokes, tomatoes, pepperoni and olives; toss to coat. Cut each roll in half horizontally; place with cut side up on an ungreased baking sheet. Broil 5 in. from the heat for 3-4 minutes or until golden brown. Spread filling over rolls; sprinkle with mozzarella. Broil 3-4 minutes longer or until the filling is hot and cheese is bubbly. **Yield:** 4 servings.

DOUBLE CHEESE AND HAM SANDWICHES

B.J. DeWitt, Lakeview, Oregon

This original recipe won me first prize in a local sandwich contest. Sometimes I'll use hazelnut bread instead to add to the nutty flavor.

> 1 package (3 ounces) cream cheese, softened
> 2 tablespoons chopped green chilies
> 1 tablespoon dry onion soup mix
> 1 cup (4 ounces) shredded cheddar cheese
> 1/4 cup chopped hazelnuts, toasted, optional
> 8 slices whole wheat bread
> 16 slices fully cooked ham
> 4 lettuce leaves

In a mixing bowl, beat cream cheese, chilies and soup mix until smooth. Add cheese and nuts if desired; mix well. Evenly spread on four slices of bread; layer each with four slices of ham and one lettuce leaf. Top with the remaining bread. **Yield:** 4 servings.

> **FAST FLAVORFUL FARE.** *Pictured at right, top to bottom: Mushroom Bacon Burgers and Hot Antipasto Poor Boys (both recipes on this page).*

NUTTY SHRIMP SALAD SANDWICHES

Delores Hicks, Kernersville, North Carolina

My daughter is a terrific cook and likes to come up with original adaptations of old favorites. As a matter of fact, she created this tropical-tasting shrimp salad.

  2 cups cooked salad shrimp
  3 kiwifruit, peeled, sliced and quartered
  3/4 cup shredded carrots
  1/2 cup mayonnaise
  1/2 cup chopped pecans
  1/8 teaspoon ground nutmeg
  3 pita breads, halved
Lettuce leaves

In a medium bowl, combine the first six ingredients. Line pita halves with lettuce; spoon about 1/2 cup of the shrimp mixture into each. **Yield:** 6 servings.

DEVILED CORNED BEEF BUNS

Helen Kennedy, Hudson, New York

(PICTURED BELOW)

This recipe's filling keeps for days in the refrigerator, so it's a good thing to have on hand for a quick-and-easy meal.

  1 cup crumbled canned corned beef
  1/2 cup shredded process American cheese
  1/3 cup chopped stuffed olives
  1/3 cup ketchup
  2 tablespoons finely chopped green onions
  1 tablespoon finely chopped green pepper
  1 tablespoon Worcestershire sauce
  1/4 teaspoon pepper
  4 submarine *or* hoagie rolls, split

In a bowl, combine the first eight ingredients. Spoon onto bottom of rolls. Replace tops; wrap each tightly in foil. Bake at 325° for 20 minutes or until heated through. **Yield:** 4 servings.

GRILLED HAMBURGERS

Marcille Meyer, Battle Creek, Nebraska

Even when I know we won't be eating all eight burgers, I make the whole recipe and freeze the leftovers already grilled for a quick meal later.

  2 pounds lean ground beef
  1/2 cup quick-cooking *or* old-fashioned oats
  1/2 cup diced onion
  1/4 cup milk
  1/4 cup ketchup
  1 egg
  1 tablespoon diced green pepper
  1 teaspoon salt
Dash pepper
  8 hamburger buns, split
Lettuce leaves and tomato slices, optional

In a large bowl, combine the first nine ingredients and mix well. Shape into eight patties. Grill over medium-hot coals or fry in a skillet for 10-12 minutes or until meat is no longer pink, turning once. Serve on buns with lettuce and tomato if desired. **Yield:** 8 servings.

CHALUPA JOES

Nancy Means, Moline, Illinois

Ordinary sloppy joes get a lift from extra seasonings and picante sauce. Try serving them with refried beans and tortilla chips.

- 1 pound ground beef
- 1 cup picante sauce
- 2 tablespoons soy sauce
- 1 tablespoon olive *or* vegetable oil
- 1 teaspoon Dijon mustard
- 1/2 teaspoon lemon-pepper seasoning
- 1/4 teaspoon garlic powder
- 1/8 teaspoon ground nutmeg
- 1/8 teaspoon ground cardamom
- 1 cup (4 ounces) shredded Monterey Jack cheese
- 6 Italian *or* hard rolls, split
- 1/4 cup sliced green onions

In a skillet, brown the beef; drain. Add picante sauce, soy sauce, oil, mustard, lemon pepper, garlic powder, nutmeg and cardamom; simmer, uncovered, for 3-4 minutes. Remove from the heat. Stir in cheese. Spoon onto bottom of rolls; sprinkle with onions. Replace tops. **Yield:** 6 servings.

CHICKEN SALAD SANDWICHES

Diane Hixon, Niceville, Florida

This salad gives kids two of their favorite foods—sunflower seeds and grapes.

- 2 cups cubed cooked chicken
- 1 cup cubed Monterey Jack cheese
- 1/2 cup green grapes, halved
- 1/2 cup mayonnaise
- 1/4 cup thinly sliced celery
- 1/4 cup sunflower seeds
- 1/4 teaspoon salt
- 1/4 teaspoon pepper

- 4 pita breads, halved *or* 8 slices bread
- Lettuce leaves

In a bowl, combine the first eight ingredients. Line pita or bread with lettuce and add 1/2 cup chicken salad to each. **Yield:** 4 servings.

GRILLED HAM AND EGG SALAD SANDWICHES

Beverly Stiger, Wolf Creek, Montana

(PICTURED ABOVE)

An aunt shared this wonderful recipe with me years ago. The ham and toasted bread make it a deliciously different kind of egg salad sandwich.

- 6 hard-cooked eggs, chopped
- 1 cup diced fully cooked ham
- 1/2 cup diced celery
- 1 tablespoon diced onion
- 1/2 cup mayonnaise
- 2 teaspoons prepared mustard
- 1/2 teaspoon salt
- 1/4 teaspoon pepper
- 12 slices whole wheat *or* white bread
- Cooking oil
- BATTER:
- 1/2 cup yellow cornmeal
- 1/2 cup all-purpose flour
- 1 teaspoon baking powder
- 1 teaspoon salt
- 2 cups milk
- 2 eggs

Combine eggs, ham, celery, onion, mayonnaise, mustard, salt and pepper; spread on six slices of bread. Top with remaining bread and set aside. In a bowl, whisk batter ingredients until well blended. Heat about 1/2 in. of oil in a large deep skillet. Dip sandwiches into batter. Fry in hot oil for 3 minutes on each side or until golden brown. Drain on paper towels. **Yield:** 6 servings.

PUMPKIN SLOPPY JOES

Eleanor McReynolds, Scott City, Kansas

(PICTURED ABOVE)

When my oldest granddaughter gave me eight of the 50 pumpkins she grew in her backyard, I didn't know how I'd use them all up! Then I remembered this recipe from a dear friend...I'm glad I tried it.

    1 pound ground beef
1/2 cup chopped onion
    1 garlic clove, minced
    1 cup canned *or* cooked pumpkin
    1 can (8 ounces) tomato sauce
    2 tablespoons brown sugar
    2 tablespoons prepared mustard
    2 teaspoons chili powder
1/2 teaspoon salt
American cheese slices
    8 hamburger buns, split

In a large skillet or saucepan, brown beef; drain. Add onion and garlic; cook until tender. Stir in the pumpkin, tomato sauce, brown sugar, mustard, chili powder and salt. Bring to a boil. Reduce heat; cover and simmer for 10 minutes. Meanwhile, if desired, cut cheese slices into shapes (triangles, half-circles, etc.) to make pumpkin faces. Spoon meat mixture onto buns; top with cheese shapes. Broil just until cheese melts. Serve with bun top off to side. **Yield:** 8 servings.

CURRIED TUNA MELT

Rose Maldet, Johnstown, Pennsylvania

An old-fashioned favorite is updated with curry powder and raisins.

    1 can (6 ounces) tuna, drained and flaked
1/4 cup thinly sliced celery
1/4 cup mayonnaise
    2 tablespoons thinly sliced green onions
    2 tablespoons raisins
    2 teaspoons lemon juice
1/4 teaspoon salt
1/4 teaspoon curry powder
    2 English muffins, split and toasted
    4 slices cheddar cheese

In a small bowl, combine tuna, celery, mayonnaise, onions, raisins, lemon juice, salt and curry powder. Spread about 1/4 cup on each muffin half; top with cheese. Broil 4 in. from the heat for 1-2 minutes or until cheese is melted. **Yield:** 4 servings.

TARRAGON CHICKEN SALAD SANDWICHES

Caroleah Johnson, Berry Creek, California

I became tired of traditional chicken sandwiches, so I came up with this recipe. Tarragon provides a nice subtle seasoning, while sunflower seeds add extra crunch.

1/2 cup mayonnaise
    1 tablespoon lemon juice
    1 teaspoon Dijon mustard
    3 cups cubed cooked chicken
3/4 cup chopped celery
    1 tablespoon minced fresh tarragon
      ***or* 1 teaspoon dried tarragon**
1/3 cup salted sunflower seeds
    8 croissants *or* rolls, split
Lettuce leaves

In a bowl, combine the first three ingredients. Stir in chicken, celery, tarragon and sunflower seeds. Line croissants or rolls with lettuce; top with 1/2 cup chicken salad. **Yield:** 8 servings.

TRIPLE TASTY SANDWICHES

Mickey Schnell, Myrtle Beach, South Carolina

An assortment of ham, salami and eggs makes this specially seasoned sandwich spread delicious. I'm sure your family will love the old-fashioned flavor as much as mine does.

 1/2 to 2/3 cup mayonnaise
 1 tablespoon Dijon mustard
 1 tablespoon finely chopped onion
 1 tablespoon minced jalapeno pepper
 1 teaspoon Worcestershire sauce
 1/2 pound fully cooked ham, ground
 1/2 pound Genoa salami, ground
 1/4 cup finely chopped sweet pickles
 3 hard-cooked eggs, chopped
 12 slices whole wheat bread, toasted

Combine the first five ingredients in a medium bowl. Stir in the ham, salami, pickles and eggs. Spoon about 1/2 cup between slices of toast. **Yield:** 6 servings.

DOUBLE-DECKER BURGERS

Marcy Schewe, Danube, Minnesota

These man-sized sandwiches look as delectable as they taste. We really enjoy the flavors in the special spread.

 2 pounds ground beef
 1/4 cup finely chopped onion
 2 eggs
 2 teaspoons Worcestershire sauce
 1 teaspoon salt
 1/4 teaspoon pepper
 1-1/2 cups (6 ounces) shredded cheddar cheese
 3 tablespoons mayonnaise
 4 teaspoons prepared mustard
 4 teaspoons dill pickle relish
Shredded lettuce
 6 onion slices
 6 hamburger buns, split
 6 tomato slices

In a large bowl, combine the first six ingredients; mix well. Shape into 12 thin patties. Broil 4 in. from the heat for 7-8 minutes on each side or until no longer pink. In a small bowl, combine the cheese, mayonnaise, mustard and relish; mix well. Spoon 2 tablespoons on each burger. Return to the broiler just until cheese softens. Place lettuce and onion onto bottom of buns; top each with two burgers, tomato and top of bun. **Yield:** 6 servings.

INDIANA-STYLE CORN DOGS

Sally Denney, Warsaw, Indiana

(PICTURED BELOW)

Among the best parts of the many fairs in Indiana are the corn dogs served there! My family loves corn dogs, so I fix them fairly often at home.

 1 cup all-purpose flour
 1/2 cup yellow cornmeal
 1 tablespoon baking powder
 1 tablespoon sugar
 1 teaspoon salt
 1/2 teaspoon ground mustard
 1/4 teaspoon paprika
Dash of pepper
 1 cup evaporated milk
 1 egg
 10 to 16 hot dogs
Cooking oil for deep-fat frying

In bowl, combine flour, cornmeal, baking powder, sugar, salt, mustard, paprika and pepper. Add milk and egg; stir until well blended. Pour mixture into a tall glass. Thread hot dogs onto wooden skewers; dip into the glass. In an electric skillet or deep-fat fryer, heat oil to 375°. Fry corn dogs until golden brown (about 2 minutes). Drain on paper towels. **Yield:** 10-16 corn dogs.

HEARTY MUFFALETA LOAF

Myra Innes, Auburn, Kansas

In the summer, we love to picnic outdoors as much as possible. Loaded with meat and flavor, this sandwich satisfies the heartiest of appetites.

    1 loaf (1 pound) French bread
  1/2 cup olive *or* vegetable oil
  1/3 cup cider *or* red wine vinegar
    1 teaspoon dried oregano
    2 garlic cloves, minced
    1 jar (6-1/2 ounces) marinated artichoke
      hearts, drained and chopped
    1 cup (4 ounces) shredded mozzarella
      cheese
  1/2 cup sliced stuffed olives
    1 can (2-1/4 ounces) sliced ripe olives,
      drained
  1/2 cup sliced fresh banana peppers
  1/4 cup chopped red onion
  1/4 pound sliced Genoa salami
  1/4 pound sliced Cotto salami
  1/4 pound sliced pepperoni
  1/4 pound sliced provolone cheese

Cut bread in half lengthwise; hollow out top and bottom, leaving a 1-in. shell. (Discard removed bread or save for another use.) Combine oil, vinegar, oregano and garlic; brush half on the inside of shell. Add the next six ingredients to the remaining oil mixture. Spoon into the bottom bread shell; layer with meats and cheese. Replace the bread top. **Yield:** 6-8 servings.

PIZZA JOES

Barbara Gorden, Hanover, Pennsylvania

This recipe is a creation of mine that resembles the traditional sloppy joe sandwich. I like to prepare it whenever I have a crowd to serve, because the recipe can easily be doubled or tripled.

    1 pound bulk Italian sausage
    1 medium green pepper, chopped
    1 small onion, chopped
  1/2 cup chopped fresh mushrooms
    2 teaspoons Italian seasoning
    1 garlic clove, minced
    1 can (8 ounces) tomato sauce
    6 English muffins, split and toasted
    2 cups (8 ounces) shredded mozzarella
      cheese

In a skillet, brown the sausage; drain. Add green pepper, onion, mushrooms, Italian seasoning and garlic; cook for 2 minutes. Stir in tomato sauce. Simmer, uncovered, for 10 minutes. Top each muffin half with 2 tablespoons meat sauce; sprinkle with cheese. Broil until cheese melts and filling is hot. **Yield:** 12 servings.

TACO CRESCENTS

Eleanor Lapen, Chicago, Illinois

These are easy to make—and they freeze well, too. Kids especially love 'em!

  3/4 pound ground beef
  1/4 cup chopped onion
    1 envelope taco seasoning mix
    1 can (4-1/4 ounces) chopped ripe olives,
      drained
    2 eggs, beaten
  1/2 cup shredded cheddar cheese
    2 tubes (8 ounces *each*) refrigerated
      crescent rolls

In a skillet, brown beef with onion; drain. Add taco seasoning and olives; mix well and set aside to cool. Add eggs and cheese; mix well. On an ungreased baking sheet, unroll crescent dough and separate into triangles. Place 2 tablespoons of meat mixture onto each triangle. Roll up and shape into crescents. Bake at 375° for 10-15 minutes or until lightly browned. **Yield:** 8 servings.

SPINACH BACON SANDWICHES

Jeanette Hios, Brooklyn, New York

Not only is this recipe quick and easy, it's a guaranteed crowd-pleaser.

      3 garlic cloves, minced
      3 tablespoons olive *or* vegetable oil
      2 packages (10 ounces *each*) frozen chopped
        spinach, thawed and squeezed dry
    3/4 teaspoon salt
    1/4 teaspoon pepper
      6 bacon strips, cooked and crumbled
  1-1/2 cups (6 ounces) shredded mozzarella
        cheese
      1 loaf (1 pound) Italian bread
    1/4 cup shredded Parmesan cheese, optional

In a large skillet over medium heat, saute garlic in oil. Add spinach, salt and pepper; cook, stirring occasionally, until heated through. Remove from the heat; cool for 5 minutes. Add the bacon and mozzarella; mix well. Slice bread in half lengthwise. Spread about 2-1/4 cups spinach mixture on each half. Sprinkle with Parmesan cheese if desired. Bake at 450° for 6-8 minutes or until cheese is melted. **Yield:** 8-10 servings.

Hawaiian Ham Sandwiches

Alice Lewis, Red Oak, Iowa

(PICTURED ABOVE)

I've made these sandwiches many times for family and friends. The pineapple is what gives them a Hawaiian flair—we think they're a real treat.

 8 submarine *or* hoagie rolls (8 inches)
 8 slices Swiss cheese, halved
 1/2 medium sweet red pepper, julienned
 1/2 medium green pepper, julienned
 6 to 8 green onions, sliced
 2 teaspoons cooking oil
 1 pound sliced fully cooked ham, julienned
 1 can (20 ounces) pineapple tidbits, drained
 1 cup (4 ounces) shredded mozzarella cheese

Cut thin slices off tops of rolls. Hollow out bread in the center, leaving 1/4-in. shells; set tops aside. (Discard removed bread or save for another use.) Place rolls on a baking sheet; line the inside of each with Swiss cheese. In a skillet, saute peppers and onions in oil for 3 minutes. Add ham and cook for 3 minutes. Add pineapple. Remove from the heat; drain. Spoon into rolls. Bake at 450° for 5 minutes. Sprinkle with mozzarella cheese; return to the oven until the cheese melts, about 1 minute. Replace tops of rolls. **Yield:** 8 servings.

Hot Tuna Buns

Mrs. Bob Keeley, Otter, Montana

You can mix the ingredients for these comforting sandwiches ahead of time and bake later.

 1 can (6 ounces) tuna, drained and flaked
 1 block (4 ounces) cheddar cheese, cut into 1/4-inch cubes
 3 hard-cooked eggs, chopped
 1/3 cup mayonnaise
 3 tablespoons sweet pickle relish
 2 tablespoons finely chopped onion
 1/4 teaspoon salt
 6 hot dog buns, split

In a medium bowl, combine the first seven ingredients. Spread about 1/3 cup on bottoms of buns; replace tops. Wrap each in foil. Bake at 400° for 10 minutes or until cheese is melted. **Yield:** 6 servings.

> **LEFTOVER BREAD** from sandwich recipes can be put to use as bread crumbs. Place bread in a single layer on a baking sheet; bake at 300° until completely dry and lightly browned. Cool; process until fine in a food processor or blender.

Beef 'n' Cheese Tortillas

Myra Innes, Auburn, Kansas

(PICTURED ABOVE)

You'll appreciate the convenience of these sandwiches, which can be made in advance and don't get soggy.

1/2 cup garlic-herb cheese spread
4 flour tortillas (10 inches)
3/4 pound thinly sliced cooked roast beef
20 to 25 whole spinach leaves
11 to 12 sweet banana peppers

Spread about 2 tablespoons cheese spread over each tortilla. Layer with roast beef and spinach. Remove seeds from peppers and slice into thin strips; arrange over spinach. Roll up each tortilla tightly. **Yield:** 4 servings.

Three Cheese Tomato Melt

Shirlee Medema, Grandville, Michigan

I love to make this open-faced sandwich for myself or unexpected guests...especially when homegrown tomatoes are ripe on the vine.

1/4 cup shredded cheddar cheese
2 tablespoons shredded mozzarella cheese
1 tablespoon grated Parmesan cheese
2 tablespoons mayonnaise
1/8 teaspoon garlic powder
4 tomato slices
2 bagels *or* English muffins, split and toasted

Combine cheeses, mayonnaise and garlic powder; set aside. Place a tomato slice on each bagel half; broil 5 in. from the heat for 1-2 minutes or until tomato is warm. Spread about 1 tablespoon cheese mixture over each tomato; broil 2-3 minutes longer or until cheese is melted. **Yield:** 2 servings.

Curried Chicken Pita Pockets

Vicky Whitehead, Norman, Oklahoma

I often prepare these sandwiches for special luncheons. Everyone who tries them raves about the refreshing combination of tender chicken, flavorful curry and cool grapes.

3/4 cup mayonnaise
1 teaspoon soy sauce
1 teaspoon lemon juice
1/2 teaspoon curry powder
2-1/2 cups cubed cooked chicken
1-1/2 cups halved green grapes
3/4 cup chopped celery
1 small onion, finely chopped
1/2 cup sliced almonds
6 pita breads, halved

In a large bowl, combine the first four ingredients. Stir in chicken, grapes, celery, onion and almonds. Spoon about 1/2 cup into each pita half. **Yield:** 6 servings.

Pizza Buns

Eleanor Martens, Rosenort, Manitoba

These taste especially good as a snack after an afternoon of cross-country skiing or snowmobiling. They really warm you up!

2 pounds ground beef
1 cup chopped onion

    1 garlic clove, minced
    1 cup ketchup
    1 tablespoon Worcestershire sauce
1/2 teaspoon dried oregano
1/4 teaspoon ground mustard
    2 cans (4 ounces *each*) mushroom stems
       and pieces, drained
  10 to 12 hamburger buns, split
Shredded mozzarella cheese

In a skillet, brown the beef with onion and garlic; drain. Combine ketchup, Worcestershire sauce, oregano and mustard; stir into beef mixture. Add mushrooms and mix well. Cover and simmer for 15 minutes or until heated through. Spoon onto buns; sprinkle with cheese. Place on a baking sheet; broil until the cheese melts. **Yield:** 10-12 servings.

GREEK BURGERS

Michelle Curtis, Baker City, Oregon

A friend served these lamb patties at a barbecue party. I wouldn't leave without the recipe!

    1 pound ground lamb
    1 tablespoon Dijon mustard
    1 tablespoon lemon juice
    1 tablespoon minced onion
    1 garlic clove, minced
1/2 teaspoon dried rosemary, crushed
1/2 teaspoon salt
1/4 teaspoon pepper
    4 hamburger buns *or* hard rolls, split

Sliced cucumbers and tomatoes, optional
Ranch salad dressing, optional

In a medium bowl, combine the first eight ingredients; mix well. Shape into four patties. Pan-fry, grill or broil until no longer pink. Serve on buns with cucumbers, tomatoes and ranch dressing if desired. **Yield:** 4 servings.

TURKEY SALAD SANDWICHES

Rose Bralowas, New Port Richey, Florida

(PICTURED BELOW)

When I first tried this recipe for leftover turkey, I knew it would be an instant hit. The cranberries and orange make it unique…it's a taste of Thanksgiving at any time of year!

    2 cups cubed cooked turkey
1/2 cup mayonnaise
1/2 cup finely chopped fresh *or* frozen
       cranberries
    1 medium orange, peeled and chopped
    1 teaspoon sugar
    1 teaspoon prepared mustard
1/2 teaspoon salt
1/4 cup chopped pecans
Lettuce leaves
    6 rolls *or* croissants, split

In a medium bowl, combine turkey, mayonnaise, cranberries, orange, sugar, mustard and salt. Stir in pecans. Place lettuce and 1/2 cup of turkey mixture on each roll. **Yield:** 6 servings.

SWISSCAMOLE BURGERS

Dlores DeWitt, Colorado Springs, Colorado

This recipe won the Chef Award at a contest sponsored by a major food company more than 20 years ago. Since then, it's been the burger recipe my husband and I like best.

> 1 pound lean ground beef
> 1-1/2 teaspoons salt, *divided*
> 1/4 teaspoon pepper
> 2 ripe avocados, pitted and peeled
> 1 tablespoon grated onion
> 1 tablespoon lemon juice
> 1/3 cup mayonnaise
> 4 bacon strips, cooked and crumbled
> 4 slices Swiss cheese
> 4 hamburger buns, split and toasted

Combine beef with 1/2 teaspoon salt and pepper; shape into eight patties. In a bowl, mash avocados with a fork; add onion, lemon juice, mayonnaise, bacon and remaining salt. Place a slice of cheese on four patties. Top with avocado mixture. Cover each with another patty; press edges to seal. Pan-fry, grill or broil until meat is no longer pink. Serve on buns. **Yield:** 4 servings.

GRILLED "PBJ" SANDWICHES

Barb Trautmann, Ham Lake, Minnesota

(PICTURED BELOW)

I was going to make grilled cheese sandwiches one day when I discovered I was out of cheese. So

I pulled out some peanut butter and jelly, and the result was this tasty variation of a popular classic.

> 4 tablespoons peanut butter
> 2 tablespoons strawberry jam
> 4 slices English muffin *or* white toasting bread
> 2 tablespoons butter *or* margarine, softened

Confectioners' sugar, optional

Spread peanut butter and jam on two slices of bread; top with remaining bread. Butter the outsides of sandwiches; grill in a large skillet over medium heat until golden brown on each side. Dust with confectioners' sugar if desired. **Yield:** 2 servings.

TURKEY BURRITOS

Chris Bakewell, Glendale, Arizona

When my husband and I were married almost 30 years ago, my biggest challenge was learning to cook. Now I struggle to find filling lunches for our son. He loves these burritos.

> 1 pound ground turkey
> 1/2 cup chopped onion
> 1 can (16 ounces) refried beans with green chilies
> 1 can (14-1/2 ounces) diced tomatoes, undrained
> 1 can (4 ounces) chopped green chilies
> 1 can (2-1/4 ounces) sliced ripe olives, drained

1 envelope taco seasoning mix
1/4 cup frozen corn
1/4 cup uncooked instant rice
10 to 12 flour tortillas (7 to 8 inches)
Shredded cheddar *or* Monterey Jack cheese,
  optional

In a large nonstick saucepan, brown turkey and onion; drain. Add the beans, tomatoes, chilies, olives, taco seasoning and corn; bring to a boil. Reduce heat; cover and simmer for 15 minutes. Return to a boil. Stir in rice; remove from the heat. Cover and let stand for 5 minutes. Place about 1/2 cup filling down the center of each tortilla; sprinkle with cheese if desired. Fold in sides of tortillas. **Yield:** 10-12 servings.

TUNA BURGERS

Nancy Selig, Lunenburg, Nova Scotia

(PICTURED ABOVE RIGHT)

I gave Mom's original recipe a boost by adding onion and green pepper to these delightfully different tuna sandwiches.

2 cans (6 ounces *each*) tuna, drained and
  flaked
6 hard-cooked eggs, chopped
1 cup (4 ounces) shredded sharp cheddar
  cheese
1/2 cup chopped green pepper
1/2 cup chopped onion
3/4 teaspoon garlic salt
3/4 teaspoon pepper
1 cup mayonnaise *or* salad dressing
8 kaiser rolls, split

In a bowl, combine tuna and eggs. Add cheese, green pepper, onion, garlic salt and pepper; mix well. Stir in the mayonnaise. Spoon about 1/2 cup onto each roll; wrap individually in foil. Bake at 400° for 15 minutes or until heated through. **Yield:** 8 servings.

BEEF STROGANOFF SANDWICH

Julie Terstriep, Industry, Illinois

This filling sandwich was a winner in our local beef cook-off several years ago. It's always been one of my favorites.

2 pounds ground beef
1/2 cup chopped onion
1 teaspoon salt
1/2 teaspoon pepper
1/2 teaspoon garlic powder

1 loaf (1 pound) French bread
Butter *or* margarine, softened
2 cups (16 ounces) sour cream
2 tomatoes, seeded and diced
1 large green pepper, diced
3 cups (12 ounces) shredded cheddar
  cheese

In a skillet, brown beef and onion; drain. Stir in salt, pepper and garlic powder. Cut bread in half lengthwise; butter cut sides of bread and place on a baking sheet. Add sour cream to meat mixture; spoon onto bread halves. Sprinkle with tomatoes, green pepper and cheese. Bake at 350° for 20 minutes or until cheese is melted (bake longer for crispier bread). **Yield:** 8-10 servings.

"ABC" SANDWICHES

Marilyn Dick, Centralia, Missouri

I just love the combination of apple, bacon and cheddar—that's how these sandwiches got their name.

2 cups (8 ounces) shredded cheddar cheese
1 medium apple, finely chopped
3/4 cup mayonnaise *or* salad dressing
1/2 cup finely chopped walnuts
12 slices bread, toasted and buttered
12 bacon strips, cooked and drained
6 hard-cooked eggs, sliced
6 tomato slices, optional

In a bowl, combine cheese, apple, mayonnaise and walnuts. Spread on six slices of bread; place two slices of bacon on each. Cover with egg slices. Top with tomatoes if desired and remaining slices of bread. **Yield:** 6 servings.

WALDORF SANDWICHES

Darlene Sutton, Arvada, Colorado

(PICTURED ABOVE)

The fresh fruity filling for this sandwich is a nice variation of a classic. My clan loves the cool and creamy combination.

- 1 can (20 ounces) crushed pineapple
- 3 cups cubed cooked chicken
- 1 medium red apple, chopped
- 1 medium green apple, chopped
- 1 cup chopped walnuts
- 1 cup sliced celery
- 1 cup mayonnaise
- 1 tablespoon poppy seeds
- 1 teaspoon sugar
- 1 teaspoon grated lemon peel
- 1/2 teaspoon vanilla extract
- 1/2 teaspoon salt

Rolls, croissants *or* pita bread

Drain pineapple, pressing out excess juice; reserve 1/4 cup juice. (Discard remaining juice or save for another use.) In a large bowl, combine pineapple, chicken, apples, walnuts and celery. In a small bowl, combine mayonnaise, poppy seeds, sugar, lemon peel, vanilla, salt and reserved pineapple juice. Pour over chicken mixture and toss well. Serve on rolls or croissants or in pita bread. **Yield:** 16 servings.

CREAMY TURKEY MELT

DeAnn Alleva, Columbus, Ohio

Cream cheese and sour cream make these sandwiches rich and irresistible. Using rye bread gives extra flavor and adds a nice contrast to the creamy white filling.

- 1/2 cup chopped red onion
- 5 tablespoons butter *or* margarine, softened, a
- 1 package (3 ounces) cream cheese, cubed
- 1/3 cup sour cream
- 2 cups cubed cooked turkey
- 8 slices dark rye *or* pumpernickel bread
- 4 slices Swiss cheese

In a saucepan over medium heat, saute onion in 1 tablespoon butter until tender. Reduce heat to low. Add cream cheese and sour cream; cook and stir until smooth. Add turkey and cook until heated through (do not boil). Spoon 1/2 cup filling onto four slices of bread; top with a slice of cheese and remaining bread. Spread outside of bread with remaining butter. In a skillet over medium heat, cook sandwiches until lightly browned on both sides. **Yield:** 4 servings.

TERIYAKI BURGERS

Rose Thusfield, Holcombe, Wisconsin

The teriyaki sauce takes these cheeseburgers from "ordinary" to "oh, boy"!

- 2 medium onions, sliced
- 1/2 cup teriyaki sauce
- 1 pound lean ground beef
- 4 slices mozzarella cheese
- 4 hamburger buns, split

In a skillet, saute onions in teriyaki sauce until tender. Shape beef into four patties; place on top of onion mixture. Cook on both sides until meat is no longer pink. Top with cheese. Serve burgers and onions on buns. **Yield:** 4 servings.

VEGGIE DELIGHTS

Barb Trautmann, Ham Lake, Minnesota

I started making these sandwiches after sampling a similar version in a local restaurant. They're particularly good for a quick summer meal.

- 1/2 cup thinly sliced onion rings
- 2 cups sliced fresh mushrooms
- 3 tablespoons butter *or* margarine, *divided*
- 1/4 teaspoon salt
- 1/4 teaspoon pepper
- 1/4 teaspoon garlic powder
- 1/8 teaspoon onion powder
- 1/8 teaspoon celery seed
- 4 French rolls, split
- 8 thin green pepper rings

8 thin slices Co-Jack ⬚⬚⬚⬚⬚ cheese,
   halved
8 thin tomato slices
20 thin zucchini slices
8 thin sweet red pepper rings
1/4 cup sliced stuffed ⬚⬚⬚

In a skillet over medium heat, saute onion rings and mushrooms in 1 tablespoon of butter until tender. Sprinkle with salt and pepper; set aside. Combine remaining butter with garlic powder, onion powder and celery seed; spread over cut sides of rolls. Broil 4-5 in. from the heat for 1-2 minutes or until lightly browned. Place about 1/4 cup mushroom mixture on the bottom of each roll. Layer with green pepper rings and two slices of cheese. On top halves, layer tomato, zucchini, red pepper, olives and remaining cheese. Broil 4 in. from the heat for 3-4 minutes or until cheese is bubbly. Put tops and bottoms of sandwiches together. **Yield:** 4 servings.

GRILLED SALMON SANDWICHES

June Formanek, Belle Plaine, Iowa

(PICTURED AT RIGHT)

This is a recipe I often used when our family was all home. These delicious sandwiches helped make Sunday meals special.

   1 can (8 ounces) salmon, drained, bones
      and skin removed
1/3 cup finely chopped celery
1/4 cup mayonnaise
   2 tablespoons sweet pickle relish, well
      drained
1/8 teaspoon ground pepper
   8 slices white *or* Italian bread
   1 egg
2/3 cup milk

In a small bowl, combine the first five ingredients. Spread on four slices of bread. Top with remaining bread. In a shallow bowl, beat egg and milk; dip the sandwiches. Cook on a well-greased griddle or skillet until browned on both sides. **Yield:** 4 servings.

GRILLED BLUE CHEESE SANDWICHES

Linda Zweifel, Beresford, South Dakota

Once they try these rich sandwiches, the blue cheese lovers in your family will never request a regular grilled cheese sandwich again!

1-1/2 cups sliced fresh mushrooms
   2 tablespoons chopped onion

1/2 cup mayonnaise, *divided*
   2 cups (8 ounces) shredded cheddar cheese
1/4 cup crumbled blue cheese
   1 teaspoon yellow *or* Dijon mustard
   1 teaspoon Worcestershire sauce
1/4 teaspoon salt
1/8 teaspoon cayenne pepper
   12 slices white *or* wheat bread
   2 to 4 tablespoons butter *or* margarine

In a skillet over medium heat, saute mushrooms and onion in 3 tablespoons mayonnaise for 5 minutes or until mushrooms are tender; cool. In a bowl, combine cheeses, mustard, Worcestershire sauce, salt, cayenne, mushroom mixture and remaining mayonnaise; mix well. Spread 1/3 cup on six slices of bread; top with remaining bread. Melt 2 tablespoons butter in a large skillet. Add sandwiches and grill until each side is golden brown and cheese is melted, adding additional butter if necessary. **Yield:** 6 servings.

FAVORITE SLOPPY JOES

Eleanor Mielke, Snohomish, Washington

I've prepared these sandwiches for years. I've tried many sloppy joe recipes, but this one is the best by far.

   2 pounds ground beef
   1/2 cup chopped onion
   3/4 cup chili sauce
   1/2 cup water
   1/4 cup prepared mustard
   2 teaspoons chili powder
   12 hamburger buns, split
   12 slices cheddar cheese

In a skillet, brown beef and onion; drain. Add chili sauce, water, mustard and chili powder. Simmer, uncovered, for 20 minutes, stirring occasionally. Spoon 1/2 cup onto each bun; top with a slice of cheese. **Yield:** 12 servings.

BAKED SOUTHWEST SANDWICHES

Holly Sorensen, Reedley, California

(PICTURED BELOW)

I like to serve these tasty sandwiches whenever I have a few friends over for an informal lunch. The combination of toppings is out of this world.

   1 can (4-1/4 ounces) chopped ripe olives,
     drained
   1/2 teaspoon chili powder
   1/2 teaspoon ground cumin
   1/4 teaspoon salt
   1/2 cup mayonnaise
   1/3 cup sour cream
   1/3 cup chopped green onions
   8 slices Italian bread
   3/4 to 1 pound thinly sliced cooked turkey
   2 medium tomatoes, thinly sliced
   2 ripe avocados, pitted, peeled and sliced
   3/4 cup shredded cheddar cheese
   3/4 cup shredded Monterey Jack cheese

In a bowl, combine olives, chili powder, cumin and salt; set aside 2 tablespoons. Add the mayonnaise, sour cream and onions to the remaining olive mixture. Place bread on an ungreased baking sheet; spread 1 tablespoon mayonnaise mixture on each slice. Top with turkey and tomatoes. Spread with another tablespoon of mayonnaise mixture; top with avocados and cheeses. Sprinkle with reserved olive mixture. Bake at 350° for 15 minutes or until heated through. **Yield:** 8 servings.

"LONG BOY" CHEESEBURGERS

Carolyn Griffin, Macon, Georgia

This flavorful sandwich is fast to prepare and makes a complete meal with a salad.

   1 pound uncooked lean ground beef
   1/2 cup crushed cornflakes
   1/2 cup whipping cream
   1/4 cup ketchup
   1/4 cup chopped onion
   1 tablespoon Worcestershire sauce
   1 teaspoon salt

1 teaspoon pepper
2 loaves brown 'n' serve French bread, halved lengthwise
1 cup (4 ounces) shredded cheddar cheese

In a large bowl, combine the first eight ingredients. Spread to the edges of the cut surface of the bread. Place on a baking sheet. Bake at 350° for about 20 minutes or until meat is no longer pink. Top with cheese; return to the oven for 5 minutes or until melted. Cut into slices to serve. **Yield:** 8 servings.

HOT CHICKEN HEROES

Holly Jean VeDepo, West Liberty, Iowa

My mom would make these sandwiches while I was growing up. Now I make them for my own children. For variety, I sometimes substitute tuna or ham for the chicken.

2 cups cubed cooked chicken
1/2 cup cubed process American cheese
1/2 cup chopped onion
1/2 cup mayonnaise
1/4 cup chopped green pepper
1/4 teaspoon salt
1/4 teaspoon pepper
4 submarine *or* hoagie rolls (6 inches), split

In a medium bowl, combine the first seven ingredients; mix well. Spread on rolls; wrap each in foil. Bake at 325° for 20 minutes. **Yield:** 4 servings.

STUFFED PIZZA SANDWICHES

Mary Clare, Dodge City, Kansas

I work outside the home, so time spent with my family is precious. These sandwiches take just minutes to put together before popping into the oven.

6 French rolls (6 inches)
2 cups spaghetti sauce
1 pound smoked fully cooked sausage, cubed
2 cups cubed mozzarella cheese

Cut 1 in. off the end of each roll; set ends aside. Hollow out the center of each roll, leaving a 1/2-in. shell. (Discard removed bread or save for another use.) In a saucepan over medium heat, warm spaghetti sauce and sausage. Remove from the heat; stir in cheese. Stuff about 3/4 cup filling into each roll. Replace ends of rolls; wrap each tightly in foil. Bake at 350° for 15 minutes or until heated through. **Yield:** 6 servings.

FIESTA LOAF

Kathleen Hooker, Toledo, Ohio

(PICTURED ABOVE)

When planning a camping trip a few years back, I looked for recipes that could be made ahead. This filling sandwich was the perfect solution.

1 round loaf (1 pound) sourdough bread
1/2 cup refried beans
4 ounces sliced Colby cheese
1 small sweet red pepper, sliced
4 ounces sliced Monterey Jack cheese
1 can (4 ounces) chopped green chilies
1 can (2-1/4 ounces) sliced ripe olives, drained
1 small tomato, seeded and diced
1 cup (4 ounces) shredded taco *or* cheddar cheese
2 tablespoons ranch salad dressing
1 ripe avocado, pitted, peeled and sliced
4 ounces sliced cheddar cheese

Cut the top fourth off loaf of bread. Carefully hollow out top and bottom of loaf, leaving a 1/2-in. shell. (Discard removed bread or save for another use.) Set top aside. Spread refried beans inside bottom of shell. Layer with Colby cheese, red pepper, Monterey Jack cheese, chilies, olives and tomato. Gently press layers together to flatten as needed. Combine taco cheese and ranch dressing; spoon over tomato. Top with avocado and cheddar cheese. Replace bread top. **Yield:** 6 servings. **Editor's Note:** Filled loaf may be tightly wrapped in plastic wrap and refrigerated before serving.

HAM BUNS

Esther Shank, Harrisonburg, Virginia

This recipe is a great way to use leftover ham. Friends with whom I've shared the recipe tell me these tasty sandwiches disappear fast at potlucks or parties.

    1/2 cup butter *or* margarine, softened
      1 small onion, grated
      1 tablespoon poppy seeds
      2 teaspoons Worcestershire sauce
      2 teaspoons prepared mustard
  1-1/4 cups finely chopped fully cooked ham
        (about 8 ounces)
      1 cup (4 ounces) shredded Swiss cheese
   6 to 8 hamburger buns, split

In a bowl, mix butter, onion, poppy seeds, Worcestershire sauce and mustard until well blended. Add ham and cheese; mix well. Divide evenly among buns. Place in a shallow baking pan and cover. Bake at 350° for 15-20 minutes or until hot. **Yield:** 6-8 servings.

CORNY TURKEY BURGERS

Audrey Thibodeau, Fountain Hills, Arizona

When I added the jalapeno pepper to my regular turkey burgers and served them with the sauce, they were a big hit.

SAUCE:
      1 cup fresh corn, cooked
      1 cup picante sauce
      1 tablespoon lime juice
BURGERS:
      1 pound ground turkey
    1/4 cup yellow cornmeal
      1 egg
 1/2 to 1 jalapeno pepper, seeded and
        chopped
      1 tablespoon lime juice
   2 to 4 drops hot pepper sauce
 1/2 to 1 teaspoon ground cumin
    1/4 teaspoon salt
    1/8 teaspoon pepper
      2 tablespoons cooking oil
      4 hamburger buns, split

In a small saucepan, combine sauce ingredients; heat through. Meanwhile, in a medium bowl, combine the first nine burger ingredients; mix well. Shape into four patties. In a skillet over medium heat, cook patties in oil for about 4 minutes on each side or until done. Serve with sauce on buns. **Yield:** 4 servings.

BEEF CRESCENT LOAF

Mabel Billington, Mayville, Wisconsin

I usually serve this family-pleasing recipe with a salad and raw vegetables.

  1-1/2 pounds ground beef
    1/2 cup chopped onion
    3/4 cup chopped green pepper
      2 cans (11 ounces *each*) condensed
        cheddar cheese soup, undiluted
      1 tablespoon Worcestershire sauce
    1/2 teaspoon salt
    1/4 teaspoon pepper
      1 tube (8 ounces) refrigerated crescent
        rolls
    1/2 cup shredded cheddar cheese

In a skillet, brown beef and onion; drain. Stir in green pepper, soup, Worcestershire sauce, salt and pepper; set aside. On an ungreased baking sheet, separate dough into two large rectangles. Join the longer sides together. Press edges and perforations together to form a 12-in. x 7-in. rectangle. Spread half of the meat mixture down the center of the rectangle to within 1 in. of edges. Set remaining meat mixture aside. Fold longer sides of dough over meat mixture to center; seal ends. Bake at 375° for 15 minutes. Remove from oven and spoon reserved meat mixture down center of loaf. Sprinkle with cheese; bake 10 minutes longer or until loaf is golden brown and cheese is melted. **Yield:** 6 servings.

CHICKEN BURGERS

Myrna Huebert, Tofield, Alberta

I love to cook and rarely work from any recipes. My family always wonders what's cooking in the kitchen! They really enjoy these herb-flavored chicken burgers.

    1/2 cup chopped onion
      3 tablespoons cooking oil, *divided*
  1-1/2 pounds cooked chicken, ground *or*
        finely chopped
  1-1/2 cups plain dry bread crumbs
    1/2 cup grated Parmesan cheese
      3 eggs
      2 tablespoons dried parsley flakes
      1 teaspoon *each* poultry seasoning, dried
        thyme, ground mustard and salt
    1/2 teaspoon rubbed sage
    1/2 teaspoon pepper
   3/4 to 1 cup milk
      8 hamburger buns, split
Lettuce leaves and tomato slices, optional

In a large skillet, saute onion in 1 tablespoon oil until tender. Place in a large bowl. Add chicken, crumbs, Parmesan cheese, eggs, herbs and seasonings; mix well. Stir in enough milk to be able to shape mixture into patties. Shape into eight patties. In the same skillet, cook patties in remaining oil for 5 minutes or until browned on both sides and heated through. Serve on buns with lettuce and tomato if desired. **Yield:** 8 servings.

CURRIED EGG SALAD SANDWICHES

Joyce McDowell, Winchester, Ohio

These open-faced sandwiches are quick and easy to assemble for supper when I get home after a full day of work.

1/2 cup mayonnaise
1/2 teaspoon honey
1/2 teaspoon curry powder
Dash ground ginger
6 hard-cooked eggs, chopped
3 green onions, sliced
6 slices whole wheat bread
Tomato slices, optional

In a bowl, blend mayonnaise, honey, curry and ginger. Stir in eggs and onions. Spread on each slice of bread; top with a tomato slice if desired. **Yield:** 6 servings.

REUBEN DELI SANDWICHES

Gigi LaFave Ryan, Longmont, Colorado

(PICTURED ABOVE)

Here's a new twist on the classic Reuben. The filling is easy to make and keeps well in the fridge.

3/4 cup mayonnaise
1 tablespoon chili sauce
1-1/2 teaspoons prepared mustard
1/4 teaspoon prepared horseradish
1 can (14 ounces) sauerkraut, rinsed and well drained
3/4 pound finely chopped corned beef (about 3 cups)
2 cups (8 ounces) shredded Swiss cheese
30 slices rye bread
1/2 cup butter *or* margarine, softened

In a large bowl, combine the mayonnaise, chili sauce, mustard and horseradish. Stir in sauerkraut, corned beef and cheese. Spread 1/3 cup each on 15 slices of bread; top with remaining bread. Lightly butter the outsides of sandwiches. Cook on a hot griddle for 4-5 minutes on each side or until golden brown. **Yield:** 15 servings.

> **SPECIAL SPREAD.** Combine your favorite chopped chutney and cream cheese for a unique ham and turkey sandwich spread.

Speedy Soups & Chili

TUSCAN SOUP

Rosemary Goetz, Hudson, New York

(PICTURED AT RIGHT)

I work full-time outside of the home, so I relish recipes like this that can be prepared in a flash.

- **1 small onion, chopped**
- **1 small carrot, sliced**
- **1 tablespoon olive *or* vegetable oil**
- **2 cans (14-1/2 ounces *each*) chicken broth**
- **1 cup water**
- **3/4 teaspoon salt**
- **1/4 teaspoon pepper**
- **1 can (15 to 16 ounces) white kidney *or* great northern beans, rinsed and drained**
- **2/3 cup uncooked small spiral pasta**
- **3 cups thinly sliced fresh escarole *or* spinach**

In a 2-qt. saucepan over medium-high heat, saute onion and carrot in oil until vegetables are tender. Add broth, water, salt and pepper; bring to a boil. Stir in beans and pasta; return to a boil. Reduce heat; cover and simmer for 15 minutes or until pasta is cooked, stirring occasionally. Add escarole; heat through. **Yield:** 4 servings.

30-MINUTE CHILI

Janice Westmoreland, Brooksville, Florida

(PICTURED AT RIGHT)

A dear neighbor gave me a pot of this delicious chili, and I asked for the recipe. The pork sausage is a nice change from the ground beef many chili recipes call for.

- **1 pound bulk pork sausage**
- **1 large onion, chopped**
- **2 cans (15-1/2 ounces *each*) chili beans**
- **1 can (28 ounces) crushed tomatoes**
- **3 cups water**
- **1 can (4 ounces) chopped green chilies**
- **1 envelope chili seasoning mix**
- **2 tablespoons sugar**
- **Additional chopped onion, optional**

In a Dutch oven or soup kettle, brown sausage and onion; drain. Add the next six ingredients; cover and simmer for 20 minutes, stirring often. Garnish with chopped onion if desired. **Yield:** 12 servings (3 quarts).

TURKEY WILD RICE SOUP

Terri Holmgren, Swanville, Minnesota

(PICTURED AT RIGHT)

An area turkey grower shared this recipe with me. A rich and smooth soup, it makes great use of two Minnesota resources—turkey and wild rice. Be prepared to serve seconds!

- **1 medium onion, chopped**
- **2 celery ribs, diced**
- **2 medium carrots, diced**
- **1/2 cup butter *or* margarine**
- **1/2 cup all-purpose flour**
- **4 cups chicken *or* turkey broth**
- **2 cups cooked wild rice**
- **2 cups half-and-half cream**
- **2 cups diced cooked turkey**
- **1 teaspoon dried parsley flakes**
- **1/2 teaspoon salt**
- **1/4 teaspoon pepper**

In a Dutch oven or soup kettle over medium heat, saute onion, celery and carrots in butter until onion is transparent. Reduce heat. Blend in flour; cook and stir for 2 minutes. Gradually add broth, stirring constantly. Bring to a boil; cook for 1 minute. Reduce heat. Add remaining ingredients; simmer for 20 minutes. **Yield:** 8-10 servings (about 2-1/2 quarts).

> **MOUTH-WATERING WARM-UPS.** *Pictured at right, top to bottom: Tuscan Soup, 30-Minute Chili and Turkey Wild Rice Soup (all recipes on this page).*

Swiss 'n' Cheddar Broccoli Soup

Ada Lee Cook, Vernon, Texas

(PICTURED ABOVE)

With two varieties of cheese—Swiss and cheddar—this soup is doubly delicious! I'm sure it will become a favorite in your home.

        4 cups water, *divided*
        4 teaspoons chicken bouillon granules
        2 packages (10 ounces *each*) frozen
            chopped broccoli
        4 cups milk
    1/2 teaspoon salt
    1/4 teaspoon pepper
    1/8 teaspoon ground nutmeg
    1/2 cup all-purpose flour
1-1/4 cups (5 ounces) shredded Swiss cheese
    3/4 cup shredded cheddar cheese

In a 3-qt. saucepan, combine 3 cups water and bouillon; heat until bouillon is dissolved. Add broccoli; cover and cook over low heat until tender, about 8 minutes. Stir in milk, salt, pepper and nutmeg. Combine flour and remaining water; stir into soup. Cook and stir over medium heat for 3 minutes or until thick and bubbly. Remove from the heat. Add cheeses; stir until melted. **Yield:** 6-8 servings (2 quarts).

Ham, Beef and Bacon Soup

Mrs. J.C. Mantel, Orange City, Iowa

I invented this recipe one evening by using whatever I had on hand. When my husband said, "Please make it again", I hurriedly wrote down the ingredient list!

        2 cans (15 ounces *each*) butter beans,
            rinsed and drained
        1 package (20 ounces) frozen mixed
            vegetables, thawed
        1 medium onion, chopped
    1/2 pound ground beef, browned and
            drained
    1/2 pound bacon, diced, cooked and
            drained
    1/2 pound fully cooked ham, cubed
        1 can (10-1/2 ounces) condensed beef
            broth, undiluted
        1 can (10-3/4 ounces) condensed tomato
            soup, undiluted
        1 teaspoon sugar
    3/4 teaspoon salt
    1/4 teaspoon pepper
        1 to 2 cups tomato juice, optional

In a Dutch oven or soup kettle, combine the first 11 ingredients; bring to a boil. Reduce heat and simmer for 25 minutes or until vegetables are tender. If a thinner soup is preferred, stir in tomato juice. **Yield:** 10-12 servings (3 quarts).

cream; stir to mix. Gradually add to soup, stirring constantly; heat through (do not boil). Sprinkle with parsley and chives. **Yield:** 4-6 servings.

TOMATO LEEK SOUP

Lois McAtee, Oceanside, California

A friend in Australia gave me this recipe years ago. Of all the soups we've ever tried, it remains one of the best.

  5 cups chicken broth
  3 leeks (white part only), finely sliced
  2 pounds tomatoes (about 6 medium),
    peeled and chopped
  1 teaspoon minced fresh basil *or* 1/4
    teaspoon dried basil
  1/2 teaspoon lemon-pepper seasoning
  1/4 teaspoon salt

In a 3-qt. saucepan, bring broth and leeks to a boil. Cook and stir occasionally for 5 minutes. Add tomatoes. Reduce heat; simmer, uncovered, for 10 minutes. Stir in basil, lemon pepper and salt. **Yield:** 6-8 servings (2 quarts).

CHUNKY POTATO SOUP

Betty Ann Walery, Joplin, Montana

This special soup is a true family favorite. I received the recipe from my sister and then passed it on to my daughters.

  2 cups water
  2 chicken bouillon cubes
  3 cups cubed peeled potatoes
  1/2 cup chopped onion
  1/2 cup thinly sliced celery
  3/4 teaspoon salt
  1/2 teaspoon pepper
  2 cups milk, *divided*
  2 tablespoons all-purpose flour
  1 cup (8 ounces) sour cream
  2 tablespoons chopped fresh parsley
  1 tablespoon chopped chives

In a 3-qt. saucepan, combine water, bouillon, potatoes, onion, celery, salt and pepper; bring to a boil over medium heat. Reduce heat; cover and simmer for 15-20 minutes or until potatoes are tender. Add 1-3/4 cups milk. Combine flour with remaining milk; stir to form a smooth paste. Add to soup, stirring constantly. Bring to a boil; cook and stir for 2 minutes or until thickened and bubbly. Add a small amount of hot liquid to sour

ITALIAN VEGETABLE SOUP

Janet Frieman, Kenosha, Wisconsin

(PICTURED BELOW)

This swift soup cooks up in only minutes more than the time it takes to heat the store-bought kind.

  1 pound bulk Italian sausage
  1 medium onion, sliced
  1 can (15 ounces) garbanzo beans,
    rinsed and drained
  1 can (14-1/2 ounces) diced tomatoes,
    undrained
  1 can (14-1/2 ounces) beef broth
1-1/2 cups water
  2 medium zucchini, cut into 1/4-inch
    slices
  1/2 teaspoon dried basil
Grated Parmesan cheese

In a 3-qt. saucepan, brown sausage and onion; drain. Stir in beans, tomatoes, broth, water, zucchini and basil; bring to a boil. Reduce heat and simmer for 5 minutes or until the zucchini is tender. Sprinkle each serving with cheese. **Yield:** 6-8 servings (2 quarts).

GREEN BEAN SOUP

Elvira Beckenhauer, Omaha, Nebraska

(PICTURED BELOW)

This soup has been passed down for generations beginning with my great-grandmother. I make it often, especially when I can use homegrown ingredients.

✓ This tasty dish uses less sugar, salt and fat. Recipe includes *Diabetic Exchanges*.

    4 cups water
    2 cups fresh green beans, cut into 2-inch
      pieces
1-1/2 cups cubed peeled potatoes
    1 cup cubed fully cooked ham
  1/2 cup thinly sliced carrot
    1 medium onion, diced
    1 bay leaf
    1 sprig fresh parsley
    1 sprig fresh savory *or* 1/4 teaspoon dried
      savory
    1 beef bouillon cube
  1/4 teaspoon pepper
  1/2 teaspoon salt, optional

In a 2-qt. saucepan, combine all ingredients; bring to a boil. Reduce heat; cover and simmer for 20 minutes or until vegetables are tender. Before serving, remove bay leaf and parsley and savory sprigs. **Yield:** 6 servings. **Diabetic Exchanges:** One 1-cup serving (prepared with low-fat ham and low-sodium bouillon and without salt) equals 1 lean meat, 1 vegetable, 1/2 starch; also, 107 calories, 175 mg sodium, 19 mg cholesterol, 12 gm carbohydrate, 9 gm protein, 2 gm fat.

CABBAGE SOUP

Nancy Stevens, Morrison, Illinois

My husband was never too fond of cabbage...until he tried this recipe from my aunt. Now he even asks me to make this soup!

    8 cups water
    1 medium head cabbage, chopped
    1 cup chopped celery
    1 cup chopped onion
1-1/2 pounds ground beef, browned and
      drained
    2 cans (15 ounces *each*) tomato sauce
    1 beef bouillon cube
    1 tablespoon salt
    2 teaspoons pepper
  1/4 cup ketchup
    1 tablespoon brown sugar

In a Dutch oven or soup kettle, bring water, cabbage, celery and onion to a boil; reduce heat and simmer until vegetables are tender. Add beef, tomato sauce, bouillon, salt and pepper; bring to a boil. Reduce heat and simmer for 10 minutes. Stir in ketchup and brown sugar; simmer 10 minutes longer or until heated through. **Yield:** 16-20 servings (5 quarts).

GARDEN HARVEST CHILI

Judy Sloter, Charles City, Iowa

(PICTURED ABOVE)

I started making this chili recipe back when we lived near a huge farmer's market that sold all sorts of vegetables.

✔ This tasty dish uses less sugar, salt and fat. Recipe includes *Diabetic Exchanges*.

 1 medium green pepper, chopped
 1 medium sweet red pepper, chopped
 1-1/2 cups sliced fresh mushrooms
 1/2 cup chopped onion
 2 garlic cloves, minced
 2 tablespoons cooking oil
 1 can (28 ounces) diced tomatoes, undrained
 1 can (15 ounces) tomato sauce
 2 tablespoons chili powder
 2 teaspoons sugar
 1 teaspoon ground cumin
 1 can (16 ounces) kidney beans, rinsed and drained
 2 cups sliced zucchini
 1 package (10 ounces) frozen corn, thawed
 1-1/2 cups (6 ounces) shredded cheddar cheese, optional

In a large skillet, saute peppers, mushrooms, onion and garlic in oil until tender. Add tomatoes, tomato sauce, chili powder, sugar and cumin; bring to a boil. Reduce heat; add the beans, zucchini and corn. Simmer, uncovered, for 10 minutes or until zucchini is tender. Garnish individual servings with cheese if desired. **Yield:** 6 servings (2-1/2 quarts). **Diabetic Exchanges:** One serving (prepared with low-salt tomato sauce and without cheese) equals 2 starch, 2 vegetable, 1 fat; also, 252 calories, 675 mg sodium, 0 cholesterol, 44 gm carbohydrate, 10 gm protein, 7 gm fat.

CAULIFLOWER AND WILD RICE SOUP

Judy Schield, Merrill, Wisconsin

This recipe is versatile because it makes a fine complement to a main meal or can be a meal all by itself.

 1 medium onion, chopped
 1 cup thinly sliced celery
 1 cup sliced fresh mushrooms
 1/2 cup butter *or* margarine
 1/2 cup all-purpose flour
 4 cups chicken broth
 2 cups cooked wild rice
 2 cups cauliflowerets, cooked and drained
 1 cup half-and-half cream

In a 3-qt. saucepan, saute the onion, celery and mushrooms in butter until tender. Sprinkle with flour; stir to coat well. Gradually add broth. Cook and stir for 1-2 minutes or until thickened. Stir in rice, cauliflower and cream. Simmer until heated through (do not boil). **Yield:** 6-8 servings (about 2 quarts).

TOMATO DILL SOUP

Patty Kile, Greentown, Pennsylvania

(PICTURED ABOVE)

Most often, I make this soup ahead and keep it in the fridge. It's particularly good to take out and heat up with tuna or grilled cheese sandwiches, hard rolls or a salad.

        1 medium onion, thinly sliced
        1 garlic clove, minced
        2 tablespoons cooking oil
        1 tablespoon butter *or* margarine
        3 large tomatoes, sliced
    1/2 teaspoon salt
Pinch pepper
        1 can (6 ounces) tomato paste
    1/4 cup all-purpose flour
        2 cups water, *divided*
    3/4 cup whipping cream, whipped
        1 to 2 tablespoons minced fresh dill
        or 1 to 2 teaspoons dill weed

In a 3-qt. saucepan over low heat, saute onion and garlic in oil and butter until tender. Add tomatoes, salt and pepper; cook over medium-high heat for 3 minutes. Remove from the heat and add tomato paste. In a small bowl, stir flour and 1/2 cup of water until smooth; add to soup. Gradually stir in remaining water until smooth; bring to a boil over medium heat. Cook and stir for 2 minutes. Place mixture in a sieve over a bowl. With the back of a spoon, press vegetables through the sieve to remove seeds and skin; return puree to pan. Add cream and dill; simmer just until heated through (do not boil). **Yield:** 4 servings.

BROCCOLI CRAB BISQUE

Dorothy Child, Malone, New York

Since our son is a broccoli grower, our friends keep supplying us with recipes using broccoli. To this family favorite, I add a tossed salad and rolls for an easy but delicious supper.

        1 cup sliced leeks (white part only)
        1 cup sliced fresh mushrooms
        1 cup fresh broccoli florets
        1 garlic clove, minced
    1/4 cup butter *or* margarine
    1/4 cup all-purpose flour
    1/4 teaspoon dried thyme
    1/8 teaspoon pepper
        1 bay leaf
        2 cans (10-1/2 ounces *each*) chicken broth
        1 cup half-and-half cream
        1 package (6 ounces) frozen crabmeat, thawed, drained and cartilage removed
    3/4 cup shredded Swiss cheese

In a 3-qt. saucepan, saute leeks, mushrooms, broccoli and garlic in butter over medium heat until broccoli is crisp-tender. Remove from the heat; blend in flour and seasonings. Stir in broth and cream; cook and stir for 2 minutes or until thickened. Add crab and heat through. Add cheese and stir until melted (do not boil). Remove bay leaf before serving. **Yield:** 4-5 servings.

VEGETABLE BEEF SOUP

June Formanek, Belle Plaine, Iowa

I send my husband off to the farm every day with lunch. It's hard to have a variety of meals, especially hot ones. But a thermos full of this speedy soup keeps him smiling till he returns home!

    1-1/2 pounds ground beef
    1/3 cup dried minced onion
        1 can (46 ounces) tomato juice
        1 package (20 ounces) frozen mixed vegetables, thawed
        2 beef bouillon cubes

1 teaspoon sugar
1/2 teaspoon pepper

In a Dutch oven or soup kettle, brown beef and onion; drain. Add remaining ingredients; bring to a boil. Reduce heat and simmer for 20 minutes or until the vegetables are tender. **Yield:** 8-10 servings (2-1/2 quarts).

FAVORITE FISH CHOWDER

Fran Gustafson, Bethesda, Maryland

(PICTURED AT RIGHT)

Money may have been scarce during the Depression, but fish was plentiful and affordable, so that's how we began eating this dish.

   1 large onion, chopped
 1/2 cup butter *or* margarine
   4 cups water
   6 cups diced peeled potatoes
   2 pounds fresh *or* frozen cod fillets, cut into large chunks
   3 tablespoons lemon juice
   2 cans (12 ounces *each*) evaporated milk
   2 cups milk
2-1/2 teaspoons salt
   2 teaspoons pepper
Chopped fresh parsley, optional

In a Dutch oven or soup kettle, saute onion in butter. Add water and bring to a boil. Add potatoes; cover and cook for 10 minutes. Add fish and lemon juice; reduce heat and simmer for 10 minutes. Add evaporated milk, milk, salt and pepper. Garnish with parsley if desired. **Yield:** 14-16 servings (4 quarts).

QUICK TURKEY-BEAN SOUP

Debbie Schermerhorn, Colorado Springs, Colorado

This recipe calls for canned beans, so cooking time is minimal. I make this soup mild and allow guests to add as much "heat" as they want with hot pepper sauce.

   1 pound ground turkey
   1 medium onion, chopped
   2 garlic cloves, minced
   1 tablespoon cooking oil
1-1/2 cups chopped celery
   1 medium green pepper, chopped
   1 medium sweet red pepper, chopped
   2 cans (14-1/2 ounces *each*) beef broth
   1 can (28 ounces) stewed tomatoes
   3 tablespoons tomato paste
 1/2 teaspoon cayenne pepper
 1/4 teaspoon dried basil
 1/4 teaspoon dried oregano
   2 cans (16 ounces *each*) kidney beans, rinsed and drained
   1 can (15 ounces) black beans, rinsed and drained
   1 can (15 ounces) pinto beans, rinsed and drained
   1 can (15-1/4 ounces) whole kernel corn, drained

In a Dutch oven or soup kettle over medium heat, brown turkey, onion and garlic in oil; drain. Add celery and peppers; cook and stir for 2 minutes. Add broth, tomatoes, tomato paste, cayenne, basil and oregano; mix well. Bring to a boil. Add beans and corn. Reduce heat; cover and simmer for 15 minutes. **Yield:** 14-16 servings (4 quarts).

TACO SOUP

Roxanne Barone, Billings, Montana

(PICTURED BELOW)

I can put dinner on the table in record time with this extra-speedy creation. Friends and family will savor every bite.

- 2 pounds ground beef
- 1 medium onion, finely chopped
- 1 can (28 ounces) crushed tomatoes
- 1 can (15 ounces) tomato sauce
- 1 cup water
- 1 can (15-1/4 ounces) whole kernel corn, drained
- 1 can (15 ounces) pinto beans, rinsed and drained
- 1 envelope taco seasoning mix
- Shredded cheddar cheese, sliced avocado, chopped tomato and corn chips, optional

In a Dutch oven or soup kettle, brown beef and onion; drain. Add tomatoes, tomato sauce, water, corn, beans and taco seasoning. Bring to a boil. Reduce heat and simmer for 5 minutes. If de-sired, top each serving with cheese, avocado and tomato and serve with chips. **Yield:** 10 servings (2-1/2 quarts).

SOUTHERN GARDEN SOUP

Leslie Owens, Poplar Bluff, Missouri

I created this recipe as a way to combine all of my family's favorite produce into one dish. No matter how much I make, this soup never lasts too long around our house.

- 6 cups water
- 5 chicken bouillon cubes
- 2 cups cauliflowerets
- 1/2 cup pearl onions
- 2 pounds fresh asparagus, trimmed and cut into 1/2-inch pieces
- 1 can (8 ounces) sliced water chestnuts, drained
- 1 cup chopped fresh spinach
- 1/2 cup chopped chives
- 1/2 teaspoon dried marjoram
- 1/2 teaspoon salt
- 1/8 to 1/4 teaspoon pepper
- 1/8 teaspoon ground nutmeg
- 3 tablespoons cornstarch
- 1/4 cup cold water

In a 3-qt. saucepan, bring water and bouillon to a boil. Add cauliflower and onions; cover and simmer for 5 minutes. Add the next eight ingredients. Bring to a boil. Reduce heat; cover and simmer for 5 minutes or until asparagus is tender. Dissolve cornstarch in cold water; stir into soup. Bring to a boil; boil for 2 minutes, stirring constantly. **Yield:** 8 servings (2-1/4 quarts).

EASY CHICKEN CHILI

Nancy Maxey, Rogue River, Oregon

We have lots of visitors on our 10-acre farm, so I like to make down-home dishes. Whenever I serve this chili, I'm asked for the recipe.

- 1/2 cup chopped onion
- 1 tablespoon cooking oil
- 2 cans (15-1/2 ounces *each*) great northern beans, rinsed and drained
- 2 cans (14-1/2 ounces *each*) chicken broth
- 2 cups cubed cooked chicken
- 1 can (4 ounces) chopped green chilies
- 2 garlic cloves, minced
- 2 tablespoons minced fresh cilantro *or* parsley

1 teaspoon salt
1 teaspoon dried oregano
1 teaspoon ground cumin
1/8 to 1/4 teaspoon cayenne pepper

In a 3-qt. saucepan over medium heat, saute onion in oil until tender. Add remaining ingredients; bring to a boil. Reduce heat; cover and simmer for 10-15 minutes or until heated through. **Yield:** 6-8 servings.

PIZZA SOUP

Janet Beldman, London, Ontario

This family favorite is done in no time at all. I like to serve it with a crusty bread or garlic bread, and I'll sometimes substitute bacon or salami for the pepperoni.

1 pound ground beef
1 small onion, chopped
1 cup sliced fresh mushrooms
1 medium green pepper, julienned
1 can (28 ounces) diced tomatoes, undrained
1 cup beef broth
1 cup sliced pepperoni
1 teaspoon dried basil
Shredded mozzarella cheese

In a 3-qt. saucepan, cook the beef, onion, mushrooms and green pepper until meat is no longer pink and vegetables are tender; drain. Stir in tomatoes, broth, pepperoni and basil; heat through. Ladle into ovenproof bowls; top with cheese. Broil or microwave until cheese is bubbly. **Yield:** 4-6 servings.

ZUCCHINI POTATO SOUP

Christine Gibson, Fontana, Wisconsin

(PICTURED ABOVE)

When my husband and I planted our first garden, we overdid it with the zucchini plants. By the end of harvest, I was at my wit's end wondering what I could do with the rest of the zucchini. This recipe saved the day.

5 cups chicken broth
4 small zucchini (about 1 pound), thinly sliced
1 large potato, peeled, halved and thinly sliced
1 large onion, thinly sliced
3 eggs
2 tablespoons lemon juice
2 teaspoons dill weed
Salt and pepper to taste

In a 3-qt. saucepan, bring broth to a boil. Stir in zucchini, potato and onion. Reduce heat; cover and simmer for 15 minutes or until vegetables are tender. In a small bowl, beat eggs; blend in lemon juice and 1/2 cup hot broth. Return all to pan. Cook over medium heat for 1 minute, stirring constantly (do not boil). Add dill, salt and pepper. **Yield:** 6-8 servings (about 2 quarts).

TEXAS CORN CHOWDER

Mildred Sherrer, Bay City, Texas

(PICTURED ABOVE)

Now that we have an empty nest, I cut this recipe down to serve two so we can still enjoy it. The jalapeno adds a little zip and color!

1/4 cup chopped onion
1 tablespoon butter *or* margarine
1 tablespoon all-purpose flour
1 cup water
1 cup diced peeled potato
1 chicken bouillon cube
2 cups milk
1 cup fresh *or* frozen corn
1 to 2 teaspoons finely chopped jalapeno *or* green chilies
1/4 teaspoon garlic salt
1/8 teaspoon pepper
Dash paprika

In a medium saucepan, saute onion in butter until tender. Stir in flour. Add the water, potato and bouillon; bring to a boil. Reduce heat; cover and simmer for 7-10 minutes or until potato is tender. Add milk, corn, jalapeno and seasonings. Cover and simmer for 15 minutes. **Yield:** 2 servings.

> **HOT HINT.** Once you cut open a jalapeno, don't touch your mouth, nose or eyes—the oils can be severely irritating. Wash hands thoroughly after chopping. Removing the seeds and membranes makes jalapenos less hot.

SPINACH BISQUE

Mary Lou Allaman, Kirkwood, Illinois

When my grandchildren were young, they tried this "yummy" soup at a local restaurant and fell in love with it, so I immediately asked for the recipe. They still call it "Yummy Soup".

5 packages (10 ounces *each*) frozen chopped spinach, thawed and well drained
3 cups half-and-half cream
3 packages (8 ounces *each*) cream cheese, cubed
1 can (14-1/2 ounces) chicken broth
1 cup (4 ounces) shredded cheddar cheese
3/4 cup grated Parmesan cheese
2 garlic cloves, minced
1 teaspoon salt
1/2 teaspoon pepper

In a Dutch oven or soup kettle, combine spinach and cream. Cover and cook over medium-low heat until heated through. Add remaining ingredients. Cook, uncovered, stirring constantly, until cheese is melted and soup is heated through **Yield:** 12-14 servings (3-1/2 quarts).

ZESTY TURKEY CHILI

Margareta Thorner, Carlsbad, California

Cooked turkey breast makes this chili a welcome change from the traditional variety.

✓ This tasty dish uses less sugar, salt and fat. Recipe includes *Diabetic Exchanges*.

1 large onion, chopped
3 garlic cloves, minced
1 teaspoon cooking oil
1 can (4 ounces) chopped green chilies
2 teaspoons ground cumin
1-1/2 teaspoons dried oregano
1/4 teaspoon ground cloves
1/8 teaspoon hot pepper sauce
1/8 teaspoon cayenne pepper
2 cans (15-1/2 ounces *each*) great northern beans, rinsed and drained
3 cups chicken broth
3 cups cubed cooked turkey breast

In a 3-qt. saucepan, saute onion and garlic in oil for 5 minutes. Add chilies and seasonings; cook and stir for 3 minutes. Stir in beans, broth and turkey; simmer for 15 minutes. **Yield:** 8 servings (2 quarts). **Diabetic Exchanges:** One 1-cup serving (prepared with low-sodium broth) equals 2 starch, 1 lean meat, 1 vegetable; also, 219 calories, 554 mg sodium, 32 mg cholesterol, 31 gm carbohydrate, 17 gm protein, 3 gm fat.

Swiss-Barley Mushroom Soup

Germaine Stank, Pound, Wisconsin

Hearty barley and rich Swiss cheese add a flavorful twist to traditional mushroom soup. You'll find a serving of this filling soup goes a long way.

- 1/2 pound fresh mushrooms, sliced
- 1/2 cup chopped onion
- 1/2 cup butter *or* margarine, melted
- 1/2 cup all-purpose flour
- 3 cups water
- 1/2 cup quick-cooking barley
- 3 chicken bouillon cubes
- 3 cups milk
- 2 cups (8 ounces) shredded Swiss cheese
- 2 tablespoons Worcestershire sauce
- 1 tablespoon dried parsley flakes
- 1/4 teaspoon pepper

In a 3-qt. saucepan, saute mushrooms and onion in butter until tender. Remove vegetables with a slotted spoon and set aside. Stir flour into pan drippings; cook over medium heat until lightly browned. Stir in water until smooth. Add barley and bring to a boil. Reduce heat; simmer, uncovered, stirring constantly, for 15 minutes or until the barley is tender. Add bouillon, milk, cheese, Worcestershire sauce, parsley and pepper; cook and stir until bouillon is dissolved and cheese is melted. Add the mushroom mixture and heat through. **Yield:** 6 servings.

Pasta Sausage Soup

Alice Rabe, Beemer, Nebraska

(PICTURED BELOW)

This is a good soup for our area since we have many good sausage makers. The soup has a rich flavor and is even tastier the next day. If you are unable to find bow tie pasta, you can substitute another macaroni product.

- 1-1/2 pounds hot *or* sweet Italian sausage links
- 1 medium onion, chopped
- 1 medium green pepper, julienned
- 1 garlic clove, minced
- 6 cups water
- 1 can (28 ounces) diced tomatoes, undrained
- 2 to 2-1/2 cups uncooked bow tie pasta
- 1 tablespoon sugar
- 1 tablespoon Worcestershire sauce
- 2 chicken bouillon cubes
- 1 teaspoon dried basil
- 1 teaspoon dried thyme
- 1 teaspoon salt

Remove casings from the sausage and cut into 1-in. pieces; brown in a Dutch oven over medium heat. Remove sausage, reserving 2 tablespoons drippings. Saute onion, green pepper and garlic in drippings until tender. Add sausage and remaining ingredients. Simmer, uncovered, stirring occasionally, until pasta is tender, about 15-20 minutes. **Yield:** 10-12 servings (3 quarts).

SPEEDY CHILI

Betty Ruenholl, Syracuse, Nebraska

(PICTURED BELOW)

A pot of chili slowly simmering on the stove makes a mighty appetizing image. But on the days that my schedule's hotter than the spiciest of varieties, I turn to this fast favorite.

> 1 pound ground beef
> 1 large onion, chopped
> 1 garlic clove, minced
> 2 cans (8 ounces *each*) tomato sauce
> 1 tablespoon chili powder
> 1 tablespoon cider *or* red wine vinegar
> 2 teaspoons baking cocoa
> 1/4 teaspoon ground cinnamon
> Dash ground allspice
> 1 can (16 ounces) kidney beans, rinsed
>   and drained
> Hot cooked macaroni, shredded cheddar cheese
>   and sliced green onions, optional

In a 2-qt. microwave-safe bowl, place beef, onion and garlic. Cover and cook on high for 3 minutes; stir to crumble meat. Cover and cook for 3 minutes; drain. Add the next six ingredients; cover and cook on high for 6 minutes. Stir in beans. Cover and cook 4 minutes more. Let stand for 3-5 minutes. If desired, serve over macaroni and top with cheese and onions. **Yield:** 4 servings. **Editor's Note:** This recipe was tested in a 700-watt microwave.

HEARTY STEAK SOUP

Waldeane Logan, Butler, Missouri

Our granddaughters love to come and help me cook—especially when the result is this soup. We like it with toasted French bread and a crisp salad for a complete meal.

> 1/2 cup butter *or* margarine
> 1 cup all-purpose flour
> 6 cups water
> 2 pounds ground round steak *or* ground
>   beef, browned and drained
> 1 can (28 ounces) diced tomatoes,
>   undrained
> 1 package (20 ounces) frozen mixed
>   vegetables, thawed
> 1 cup chopped onion
> 1 cup chopped celery
> 2 tablespoons browning sauce
> 1 tablespoon seasoned salt
> 1 teaspoon salt
> 1 teaspoon pepper

In a Dutch oven or soup kettle, melt butter. Stir in flour to form a smooth paste. Gradually add water, stirring constantly. Bring to a boil; cook and stir for 2 minutes or until thickened. Add remaining ingredients; bring to a boil. Reduce heat; cover and simmer for 20-25 minutes or until the vegetables are tender. **Yield:** 12-16 servings (4 quarts).

EASY BEAN SOUP

Kathleen Drott, Pineville, Louisiana

Making homemade soup is a quick trick when you start with canned soup and beans.

> 3 cans (15-1/2 ounces *each*) great
>   northern *or* navy beans, undrained
> 2 cans (11-1/2 ounces *each*) condensed
>   bean and bacon soup, undiluted
> 1 can (15 ounces) jalapeno pinto beans,
>   undrained

1-1/3 cups water
    1 medium onion, finely chopped
    1 teaspoon salt
1/2 teaspoon garlic powder
1/4 teaspoon pepper

In a large Dutch oven or soup kettle, combine all ingredients. Cover and simmer for 20 minutes or until heated through. **Yield:** 10-12 servings (3 quarts).

CREAM OF CRAB SOUP

Wanda Weller, Westminster, Maryland

(PICTURED AT RIGHT)

One of our Chesapeake Bay delicacies is the Maryland Blue Crab. It's abundant from May through October and used in a variety of dishes, like this rich soup.

1/2 cup butter *or* margarine
1/2 cup all-purpose flour
    1 to 2 tablespoons seafood seasoning
    1 teaspoon salt
1/2 teaspoon curry powder
    4 cups milk
    1 pound cooked crabmeat *or* 3 cans
       (6 ounces *each*) crabmeat, drained and
       cartilage removed
    2 tablespoons minced fresh parsley
Additional milk and parsley, optional

Melt butter in a 3-qt. saucepan; stir in the flour, seafood seasoning, salt and curry powder to form a smooth paste. Gradually add milk; cook and stir until mixture is hot and thickened. Add crab and parsley; cook and stir just until crab is heated. If desired, thin soup with additional milk; garnish with parsley. **Yield:** 6-8 servings (2 quarts).

CONFETTI CHOWDER

Rose Bomba, Lisbon, New Hampshire

This delightful golden chowder was one of Grandma's favorite recipes. The broccoli, carrots and zucchini in it add flavor as well as color.

    1 cup diced carrots
    1 cup diced zucchini
    1 cup broccoli florets
1/2 cup chopped onion
1/2 cup chopped celery
    3 tablespoons butter *or* margarine
1/4 cup all-purpose flour
1/2 teaspoon salt

1/2 teaspoon pepper
1/4 teaspoon sugar
    3 cups milk
    1 cup chicken broth
    1 cup whole kernel corn
    1 cup diced fully cooked ham
1/2 cup peas
    1 jar (2 ounces) diced pimientos, drained
    1 cup (4 ounces) shredded cheddar cheese

In a Dutch oven, saute carrots, zucchini, broccoli, onion and celery in butter for 5 minutes or until crisp-tender. Sprinkle with flour, salt, pepper and sugar; mix well. Gradually add milk and broth. Bring to a boil; cook and stir for 2 minutes or until thickened and bubbly. Add corn, ham, peas and pimientos; heat through. Remove from the heat; add cheese and stir until melted. **Yield:** 6-8 servings (2 quarts).

CHEESEBURGER SOUP

Joanie Shawhan, Madison, Wisconsin

(PICTURED ABOVE)

I created this recipe by modifying one for potato soup. I was really pleased at how good this "all-American" soup turned out.

- 1/2 pound ground beef
- 3/4 cup chopped onion
- 3/4 cup shredded carrots
- 3/4 cup diced celery
- 1 teaspoon dried basil
- 1 teaspoon dried parsley flakes
- 4 tablespoons butter *or* margarine, *divided*
- 3 cups chicken broth
- 4 cups diced peeled potatoes (1-3/4 pounds)
- 1/4 cup all-purpose flour
- 1/2 pound process American cheese, cubed
- 1-1/2 cups milk
- 3/4 teaspoon salt
- 1/4 to 1/2 teaspoon pepper
- 1/4 cup sour cream

In a 3-qt. saucepan, brown beef; drain and set aside. In the same pan, saute onion, carrots, celery, basil and parsley in 1 tablespoon of butter until vegetables are tender, about 10 minutes. Add broth, potatoes and beef; bring to a boil. Reduce heat; cover and simmer for 10-12 minutes or until potatoes are tender. Meanwhile, in a small skillet, melt the remaining butter. Add flour; cook and stir for 2 minutes or until bubbly. Add to soup; bring to a boil. Cook and stir for 2 minutes. Reduce heat to low. Add cheese, milk, salt and pepper; cook and stir until cheese melts (do not boil). Remove from the heat; blend in sour cream. **Yield:** 8 servings (2-1/4 quarts).

CHILI-CHEESE SOUP

Janne Rowe, Wichita, Kansas

With green chilies, corn and cheese, this slightly spicy soup has a Mexican flair. You're sure to like the extra "zip" it brings to your dinner table.

- 1 cup chopped onion
- 2 tablespoons cooking oil
- 2 tablespoons butter *or* margarine
- 3 garlic cloves, minced
- 2 tablespoons all-purpose flour
- 3 cups chicken broth
- 3 cups frozen corn
- 2 cans (4 ounces *each*) chopped green chilies
- 1 cup chopped seeded tomatoes
- 1 can (12 ounces) evaporated milk
- 3 cups (12 ounces) shredded sharp cheddar *or* Monterey Jack cheese
- 1 teaspoon ground cumin

In a Dutch oven or soup kettle over medium heat, saute onion in oil and butter until tender. Add garlic and saute for 1 minute. Add flour; cook and stir for 2 minutes. Stir in broth, corn, chilies and tomatoes; bring to a boil. Reduce heat and simmer, uncovered, for 15 minutes, stirring occasionally. Add remaining ingredients; heat, stirring frequently, until the cheese is melted (do not boil). **Yield:** 6-8 servings (about 2 quarts).

CHICKEN BISQUE

Mary Wagner, Woodburn, Oregon

When the weather starts turning cooler, we like to sit down to dinner with this colorful rich bisque. Add hot rolls and a salad, and you have a hearty meal.

    2 quarts chicken broth
    2 cups cubed cooked chicken
    1 jar (4 ounces) diced pimientos,
       undrained
1/4 cup chopped green onions
    2 chicken bouillon cubes
    1 teaspoon dried tarragon
1/2 teaspoon salt
1/2 teaspoon pepper
1/2 cup butter *or* margarine
    1 cup all-purpose flour

In a Dutch oven or soup kettle, combine the first eight ingredients; bring to a simmer. In a small saucepan, melt butter. Stir in flour to form a smooth paste. Cook and stir for 2 minutes. Gradually add to the soup, stirring constantly until smooth. Bring to a boil. Reduce heat; simmer, uncovered, for 15 minutes. **Yield:** 8-10 servings (2-1/2 quarts).

QUICK ZESTY CHILI

Laura Whitcomb, Wauseon, Ohio

This chili always has everyone coming back for seconds—that's because I use fresh tomatoes in the recipe.

    1 pound ground beef
    2 cans (16 ounces *each*) kidney beans,
       rinsed and drained
    2 cups chopped tomatoes
    1 can (8 ounces) tomato sauce
    1 cup water
    2 tablespoons chili powder
    1 tablespoon dried minced onion
    1 to 2 teaspoons hot pepper sauce
    1 teaspoon ground cumin
1/4 teaspoon ground cinnamon

In a 3-qt. saucepan, brown beef; drain. Add remaining ingredients. Bring to a boil; reduce heat and simmer for 15 minutes. **Yield:** 6-8 servings (2 quarts).

WINTER VEGETABLE SOUP

Mavis Diment, Marcus, Iowa

(PICTURED BELOW)

I've enjoyed this soup for years because it tastes good, is simple to make and doesn't leave a lot of leftovers.

✓ This tasty dish uses less sugar, salt and fat. Recipe includes *Diabetic Exchanges.*

1/2 cup sliced green onions
    1 tablespoon cooking oil
    1 can (14-1/2 ounces) chicken broth
    1 small potato, peeled and cubed
    1 large carrot, sliced
1/4 teaspoon dried thyme
    1 cup broccoli florets
1/4 teaspoon salt, optional
1/8 teaspoon pepper

In a 2-qt. saucepan, saute onions in oil until tender. Add the next four ingredients; bring to a boil. Reduce heat; simmer, uncovered, for 5 minutes. Add the broccoli, salt if desired and pepper; simmer, uncovered, for 7 minutes or until vegetables are tender. **Yield:** 2 servings **Diabetic Exchanges:** One 1-1/3-cup serving (prepared with low-sodium broth and without salt) equals 1-1/2 fat, 1 starch, 1 vegetable; also, 168 calories, 125 mg sodium, 5 mg cholesterol, 19 gm carbohydrate, 5 gm protein, 8 gm fat.

Chicken & Turkey

TURKEY DRESSING PIE

De De Boekelheide, Northville, South Dakota

(PICTURED AT RIGHT)

I fix turkey all year long, and I purposely make too much just so we can have this pie later on. People tell me it's almost better than the original dinner!

3-1/2 to 4 cups cooked turkey dressing
1/2 cup turkey *or* chicken broth
   2 tablespoons butter *or* margarine, melted
   1 egg
1/2 cup chopped onion
   1 tablespoon cooking oil
   3 cups diced cooked turkey
   1 cup turkey gravy
   2 tablespoons dried parsley flakes
   2 tablespoons diced pimientos
   1 teaspoon Worcestershire sauce
1/2 teaspoon dried thyme
   1 cup frozen peas

In a large bowl, combine dressing, broth, butter and egg; mix well. Press onto the bottom and up the sides of an ungreased 10-in. pie plate; set aside. In a large skillet, saute onion in oil until tender. Stir in turkey, gravy, parsley, pimientos, Worcestershire sauce, thyme and peas; heat through. Pour into crust. Bake at 375° for 20 minutes or until golden. **Yield:** 6 servings.

HONEY LIME CHICKEN

Faye Hoffman, Dubuque, Iowa

(PICTURED AT RIGHT)

Everyone in the family enjoys the delightful flavors of this tart, sweet chicken. I usually round out the meal with rice, salad and dessert.

   4 boneless skinless chicken breast halves
1-1/2 teaspoons garlic salt
   1 tablespoon cooking oil
   1 can (20 ounces) sliced pineapple
1/4 cup honey
   3 tablespoons lime juice
   2 tablespoons soy sauce
   2 teaspoons cornstarch
Lime wedges, optional

Sprinkle chicken with garlic salt. In a large skillet over medium-high heat, brown chicken in oil. Drain pineapple, reserving juice. Add 1/4 cup juice to skillet; set remaining juice aside. Reduce heat; cover and simmer for 6-8 minutes or until juices run clear. Remove chicken and keep warm. Combine honey, lime juice, soy sauce, cornstarch and reserved pineapple juice; pour into skillet. Bring to a boil over medium heat, stirring for 1-2 minutes. Add pineapple; heat through. Pour over chicken; garnish with lime wedges if desired. **Yield:** 4 servings.

CRANBERRY APPLE RELISH

Mary Guengerich, High River, Alberta

I first served this tangy fruit relish at Thanksgiving. Now my family requests it whenever I fix turkey.

   4 cups fresh *or* frozen cranberries
   2 tart apples, peeled and cored
   2 unpeeled oranges, quartered and seeded
   1 unpeeled lemon, quartered and seeded
2-1/2 cups sugar *or* 1-1/2 cups honey
Hot cooked chicken *or* turkey

In a blender or food processor, process the first four ingredients until coarsely chopped. Stir in sugar or honey. Refrigerate. Serve with chicken or turkey. **Yield:** about 6 cups.

PLEASING POULTRY. *Pictured at right, top to bottom: Turkey Dressing Pie and Honey Lime Chicken (both recipes on this page).*

Recipe for: Honey Lime Chicken
4 boneless chicken breast h...

Recipes

PEPPER

SALT

CAZUELA

Louise Schmid, Marshall, Minnesota

(PICTURED BELOW)

I learned to make Cazuela while we were living in Chile for a few months. We grow extra butternut squash in our garden just for this favorite recipe.

6 chicken drumsticks *or* thighs
Butternut squash, peeled and cut into 24
  1-inch cubes
  6 small potatoes, peeled
  6 pieces of corn on the cob (2 inches)
  3 carrots, cut into 1-inch chunks
  4 cans (14-1/2 ounces *each*) chicken broth
Hot cooked rice
Hot pepper sauce to taste
Salt and pepper to taste
Minced fresh cilantro *or* parsley

In a large soup kettle or Dutch oven, place chicken, squash, potatoes, corn, carrots and broth; bring to a boil. Reduce heat; cover and simmer for 25 minutes or until meat juices run clear and vegetables are tender. Serve over rice in a shallow soup bowl. Season to taste with hot pepper sauce, salt, pepper and cilantro. **Yield:** 6-8 servings.

DILLY CHICKEN BREASTS

Lori Rodman, Ostrander, Ohio

I consider this to be one of my "safe" recipes. No matter how many times I make it, the chicken turns out moist and delicious. It's a guaranteed hit with family and friends.

1/2 cup lemon juice
1/4 cup butter *or* margarine, melted
  1 teaspoon salt
  1 teaspoon dill weed
  1 teaspoon dried minced onion
1/4 teaspoon pepper
  4 boneless skinless chicken breast halves

In a small bowl, combine the first six ingredients. Reserve 1/4 cup for basting; cover. Place chicken in a shallow glass baking dish. Pour remaining sauce over chicken. Marinate for 10 minutes. Drain, discarding marinade. Grill chicken, covered, over medium-low coals, turning and basting with reserved marinade, for 10-15 minutes or until juices run clear. **Yield:** 4 servings.

TROPICAL CHICKEN BAKE

Jane Bower, Normal, Illinois

Cooking is a wonderful way to let your creativity come through. I start with basic recipes, then add my own personal touches to create meals like this one that my family loves.

    4 boneless skinless chicken breast halves
    1 tablespoon butter *or* margarine
    3 medium sweet potatoes, cooked, peeled
       and quartered
    2 medium firm bananas, cut into 1/2-inch
       slices
    1 can (11 ounces) mandarin oranges,
       drained
    1 can (8 ounces) crushed pineapple,
       drained
 1/2 cup sweet-and-sour sauce
 1/3 cup chopped almonds *or* pecans

In a skillet over medium heat, brown chicken in butter. In an ungreased 2-qt. baking dish, combine sweet potatoes, bananas, oranges and pineapple. Top with chicken; pour sweet-and-sour sauce over all. Sprinkle with nuts. Bake, uncovered, at 350° for 20-25 minutes or until meat juices run clear. **Yield:** 4 servings.

CHICKEN 'N' NOODLES FOR TWO

Verna Keinath, Millington, Michigan

I discovered this recipe quite a few years ago. It's a fast and flavorful supper that's just the right size for us "empty nesters". But it can be easily doubled for guests.

 1/2 cup cottage cheese
 1/4 cup mayonnaise *or* salad dressing
 1/4 cup chopped onion
    2 tablespoons chopped green pepper
    1 tablespoon chopped pimientos
    1 teaspoon Dijon mustard
 1/2 teaspoon Worcestershire sauce
 1/2 teaspoon snipped chives
    2 drops hot pepper sauce

    1 cup cubed cooked chicken
    1 cup cooked wide egg noodles
 1/2 cup frozen peas
 1/8 teaspoon paprika

In a bowl, combine the first nine ingredients. Toss with chicken, noodles and peas. Spoon into a greased 1-qt. casserole; sprinkle with paprika. Bake, uncovered, at 375° for 20-25 minutes or until bubbly. **Yield:** 2 servings.

CHICKEN AND HAM ROLL-UPS

Karen Mawhinney, Teeswater, Ontario

I first started making these easy roll-ups as a way to use leftover chicken. My family raved about them so much that I now frequently serve them when entertaining.

    3 cups cooked rice
 1-1/2 cups chopped cooked chicken
    1 can (10-3/4 ounces) condensed cream of
       chicken soup, undiluted, *divided*
 1/4 cup finely chopped celery
    1 green onion, thinly sliced
 1/4 teaspoon pepper, *divided*
    6 slices fully cooked ham
 1/4 cup sour cream *or* plain yogurt
 1/4 cup milk
 1/4 teaspoon dried thyme
 1/2 cup shredded Swiss *or* mozzarella
       cheese
Paprika *or* additional chopped green onion

Spread rice in a greased 11-in. x 7-in. x 2-in. microwave-safe baking dish; set aside. In a medium bowl, combine chicken, 1/3 cup soup, celery, onion and 1/8 teaspoon pepper. Place 1/4 cup on each ham slice and roll up; secure with a toothpick if necessary. Place, seam side down, over rice. Combine sour cream, milk, thyme and remaining soup and pepper; spoon over roll-ups. Cover and microwave on high, turning dish halfway through cooking time, for 10-14 minutes or until heated through. Sprinkle with cheese and paprika or onion; cover and let stand for 5 minutes. Remove toothpicks before serving. **Yield:** 4-6 servings. **Editor's Note:** This recipe was tested in a 700-watt microwave. Roll-ups may be baked in a conventional oven at 375° for 20-25 minutes or until heated through.

FAST AND FRUITY. For a quick barbecue sauce, add ground ginger and teriyaki sauce to cherry pie filling; blend until smooth. Brush on chicken or turkey during the last 5 minutes of grilling.

CHICKEN TAMALE PIE

Diane Thayer, Iowa City, Iowa

This pie's zesty filling satisfies our craving for Mexican food. And the kids like the crust, which tastes like corn muffins.

- 1 package (8-1/2 ounces) corn bread/ muffin mix
- 1 egg
- 1/3 cup milk
- 1/2 cup shredded cheddar cheese
- 1 can (10-3/4 ounces) condensed cream of chicken soup, undiluted
- 2 cups cubed cooked chicken
- 1 cup frozen corn
- 1/2 cup chopped green onions
- 1 can (4 ounces) chopped green chilies
- 1 garlic clove, minced
- 1/2 to 3/4 teaspoon chili powder

In a mixing bowl, combine muffin mix, egg and milk; add cheese. Spread onto the bottom and up the sides of a greased 9-in. pie plate. In a saucepan, combine remaining ingredients; heat through. Pour into crust. Bake at 400° for 20-25 minutes or until crust is golden and filling is hot. **Yield:** 6 servings.

CHEESY CHICKEN ROLL-UPS

Sally Uhrmacher, Nelson, Nebraska

Until I served my family these slightly spicy chicken breasts, they never cared for white meat. Now they prefer them to dark meat...and to just about anything else I make!

- 8 boneless skinless chicken breast halves
- 1 block (6 ounces) cheddar cheese
- 1 cup cheese-flavored cracker crumbs
- 4-1/2 teaspoons taco seasoning mix
- 1/4 cup butter *or* margarine, melted

Flatten chicken breasts to 1/4-in. thickness. Cut cheese into eight 3-1/2-in. x 3/4-in. strips. Place one cheese strip in the center of each chicken breast. Fold long sides over cheese; fold ends up and secure with a toothpick if necessary. In a bowl, combine crumbs and taco seasoning. Dip chicken in butter, then roll in crumb mixture. Place, seam side down, in a greased 13-in. x 9-in. x 2-in. baking dish. Cover and bake at 400° for 20-25 minutes or until chicken is no longer pink. **Microwave Directions:** Place chicken rolls in a greased 13-in. x 9-in. x 2-in. microwave-safe baking dish. Cover with waxed paper and microwave on high for 5 minutes. Turn each roll; cover and microwave on high for 4-5 minutes or until chicken is no longer pink. **Yield:** 8 servings. **Editor's Note:** This recipe was tested in a 700-watt microwave.

SOUTH SEAS SKILLET

Carol Mead, Los Alamos, New Mexico

This skillet meal is tasty and easy to prepare. It gets a tropical touch from a freshly squeezed orange.

- 4 boneless skinless chicken breast halves, cut into thin strips
- 1/4 cup butter *or* margarine
- 1/3 cup sliced green onions
- 3 garlic cloves, minced
- 1 cup water
- 1/3 cup raisins
- 3 tablespoons chopped fresh parsley, *divided*
- 2 teaspoons brown sugar
- 1 teaspoon chicken bouillon granules
- 1/8 teaspoon salt
- 1 orange, cut into 8 wedges

Hot cooked rice

In a large skillet over medium heat, saute chicken in butter for 6-8 minutes or until juices run clear. Remove and keep warm. Saute onions and garlic in drippings until tender. Add water, raisins, 2 tablespoons parsley, brown sugar, bouillon and salt. Reduce heat; simmer, uncovered, for 15 minutes or until liquid is reduced by half. Add chicken and heat through. Sprinkle with remaining parsley. Squeeze orange wedges over chicken. Serve over rice. **Yield:** 4 servings.

CHICKEN AND TOMATO SCAMPI

Jan Gridley, Elverson, Pennsylvania

I try to turn ordinary ingredients into "lively" meals. For example, garlic and onions enhance the Italian flavor of this winning combination.

✓ This tasty dish uses less sugar, salt and fat. Recipe includes *Diabetic Exchanges.*

- 1/4 cup chopped green onions
- 2 to 3 garlic cloves, minced
- 2 tablespoons butter *or* margarine
- 1 tablespoon olive *or* vegetable oil
- 1 pound boneless skinless chicken breasts, cut into 1-inch pieces
- 1 teaspoon salt, optional
- 1/2 teaspoon pepper
- 1 can (14-1/2 ounces) Italian stewed tomatoes

1/4 cup lemon juice
1/2 teaspoon sugar
  2 teaspoons cornstarch
  2 teaspoons cold water
1/4 cup chopped fresh parsley
Hot cooked rice, optional

In a skillet over medium heat, saute onions and garlic in butter and oil until onions are tender. Add chicken, salt if desired and pepper. Cook for 6-8 minutes or until meat juices run clear. Add the tomatoes, lemon juice and sugar; heat through. Combine cornstarch and water; stir into chicken mixture. Bring to a boil; cook and stir for 1 minute or until thickened. Add parsley. Serve over rice if desired. **Yield:** 4 servings. **Diabetic Exchanges:** One serving (prepared with margarine and without salt and rice) equals 3 lean meat, 1-1/2 vegetable, 1 fat; also, 255 calories, 356 mg sodium, 73 mg cholesterol, 8 gm carbohydrate, 28 gm protein, 13 gm fat.

Citrus Glazed Chicken

Mary Hogarth, Lynden, Ontario

(PICTURED ABOVE)

I don't make very many main dishes with fruit in them, but my two children and I love this recipe. The chicken's very tender and the sauce is absolutely wonderful.

  1 tablespoon lemon juice
  1 tablespoon orange juice
1/2 teaspoon grated lemon peel
1/2 teaspoon grated orange peel
  4 boneless skinless chicken breast halves
  1 tablespoon cooking oil
  2 green onions, thinly sliced

  1 garlic clove, minced
1/4 teaspoon ground ginger
  1 tablespoon butter *or* margarine
  1 tablespoon all-purpose flour
1/2 teaspoon salt
3/4 cup milk
  1 tablespoon chopped fresh parsley

In a shallow bowl, combine the first four ingredients. Flatten the chicken to 1/4-in. thickness; dip into citrus mixture. In a large skillet over medium heat, brown the chicken in oil for about 2 minutes per side. Remove and set aside. In the same skillet, cook onions, garlic and ginger in butter for 1 minute. Add flour and salt; cook and stir for 1 minute. Gradually stir in milk; bring to a boil. Cook and stir for 2 minutes. Return chicken to pan; sprinkle with parsley. Reduce heat; simmer for 8-10 minutes, turning occasionally, or until chicken juices run clear. **Yield:** 4 servings.

Mexican Grilled Chicken

Lisa Ousley, Willard, Ohio

As a full-time homemaker and mother of two, I'm thrilled to find dishes that can be assembled and cooked in no time—like this chicken.

1/2 cup mayonnaise
  3 tablespoons lime juice
  1 envelope taco seasoning
  8 boneless skinless chicken breast halves

In a small bowl, mix together mayonnaise, lime juice and taco seasoning until smooth. Place chicken on grill over medium coals. Sear one side; turn and brush with sauce. Grill, uncovered, for 6 minutes; turn and brush with sauce. Grill 6 minutes longer or until chicken juices run clear. **Yield:** 8 servings.

EGGPLANT PROVENCALE

Sharon Skildum, Maple Grove, Minnesota

This hearty one-dish meal is sure to please. The classic combination of chicken, eggplant and pasta is unbeatable.

    3 cups peeled eggplant strips
  1/4 cup butter *or* margarine
  1/2 cup chopped onion
  1/2 cup sliced celery
    1 garlic clove, minced
    2 cups cubed cooked chicken
    1 can (8 ounces) tomato sauce
    1 tablespoon dried parsley flakes
    1 teaspoon dried basil
    1 teaspoon dried oregano
    1 teaspoon salt
  1/8 teaspoon pepper
    2 cups cooked pasta
  1/2 cup shredded mozzarella cheese

In a large skillet over medium heat, saute eggplant in butter for 10 minutes. Add the onion, celery and garlic; saute until vegetables are tender. Add chicken, tomato sauce and seasonings. Reduce heat; simmer for 10 minutes. Stir in pasta; sprinkle with mozzarella cheese. **Yield:** 4-6 servings.

CURRIED TURKEY

Evelyn Gunn, Andrews, Texas

(PICTURED ABOVE)

You'll like how the apple and curry flavors accent the meat. With a tossed green salad and fresh hot rolls, this dish makes an easy delicious meal!

    2 cups milk
    2 chicken bouillon cubes
    2 cups diced peeled apples
    1 cup chopped onion
  1/4 cup cooking oil
    2 tablespoons all-purpose flour
    2 teaspoons curry powder
  1/2 teaspoon salt
  1/4 teaspoon pepper
    1 tablespoon lemon juice
    4 cups diced cooked turkey
  Hot cooked rice

In a small saucepan, heat the milk and bouillon until bouillon is dissolved; set aside. In a large saucepan, saute apples and onion in oil until tender. Add flour, curry powder, salt and pepper; cook and stir for 1 minute or until thickened and bubbly. Gradually add milk mixture and lemon juice; mix well. Add turkey and heat through. Serve over rice. **Yield:** 4-6 servings.

ASPARAGUS-LOVER'S STIR-FRY

Nancy Street, Dublin, California

After tasting this special stir-fry, even folks who don't like vegetables learn to love asparagus in no time.

    1 cup sliced celery
    4 tablespoons cooking oil, *divided*
    4 cups cut fresh asparagus (1-inch pieces)
  1/2 cup sliced green onions
    1 pound boneless skinless chicken breasts,
       cut into 1-inch strips
    2 teaspoons grated orange peel
    1 garlic clove, minced
  1/2 cup water
  1/4 cup orange juice
    2 tablespoons orange juice concentrate
    2 tablespoons soy sauce
    4 teaspoons cornstarch
  1/2 cup sliced almonds
  Hot cooked rice

In a large skillet or wok over medium-high heat, stir-fry celery in 2 tablespoons oil for 1 minute. Add asparagus and onions; stir-fry for 3-5 minutes or until asparagus is crisp-tender. Remove and set aside. Add remaining oil to the skillet.

Stir-fry chicken, orange peel and garlic for 3-4 minutes or until chicken is no longer pink. Meanwhile, in a small bowl, combine water, orange juice, concentrate, soy sauce and cornstarch; add to skillet along with reserved vegetables. Cook and stir for 3 minutes or until sauce is thickened and vegetables are heated through. Stir in almonds. Serve over rice. **Yield:** 6 servings.

ONION-BAKED CHICKEN

Barbara Erwin, Shipman, Illinois

Toasted onion is the deliciously different ingredient in the coating for this chicken.

- **1/2 cup spicy brown mustard**
- **1/4 cup soy sauce**
- **2 tablespoons dried minced onion**
- **1 cup dry bread crumbs *or* crushed cornflakes**
- **1/2 teaspoon chicken bouillon granules**
- **4 boneless skinless chicken breast halves**

Combine mustard and soy sauce in a shallow bowl; set aside. In a small skillet over medium heat, toast onion until lightly browned, about 3 minutes. Pour into a shallow bowl. Add crumbs and bouillon; mix well. Dip chicken in mustard mixture, then coat with crumb mixture. Place on a rack over a greased baking sheet. Bake, uncovered, at 350° for 25 minutes or until juices run clear. **Yield:** 4 servings.

CHICKEN PICCATA

Linda Carver, Cedar Rapids, Iowa

I first fixed this chicken for guests during the Christmas season. It was a refreshing change from turkey and ham.

- **1/2 cup all-purpose flour**
- **1/2 teaspoon garlic powder**
- **1/2 teaspoon paprika**
- **2 eggs**
- **6 tablespoons lemon juice, *divided***
- **4 boneless skinless chicken breast halves**
- **1/2 cup butter *or* margarine**
- **1 cup water**
- **2 teaspoons chicken bouillon granules**

In a shallow bowl or resealable plastic bag, combine flour, garlic powder and paprika; set aside. In another shallow bowl, beat eggs and 2 tablespoons lemon juice. Dip chicken in egg mixture, then coat with flour mixture. In a large skillet over medium-high heat, brown chicken in butter. Combine water, bouillon and remaining lemon juice; pour over chicken. Reduce heat; cover and

simmer for 20 minutes or until juices run clear. **Yield:** 4 servings.

CHICKEN 'N' PEPPERS

Cathy Zoller, Lovell, Wyoming

(PICTURED BELOW)

With garden-fresh peppers and tender chicken, this dish is perfect when your family is craving a lighter dinner. Serve it with rice and a green salad.

✓ This tasty dish uses less sugar, salt and fat. Recipe includes *Diabetic Exchanges*.

- **3/4 cup chicken broth**
- **1/4 cup soy sauce**
- **2 garlic cloves, minced**
- **2 tablespoons cornstarch**
- **3/4 teaspoon ground ginger**
- **1/4 teaspoon cayenne pepper**
- **1-1/2 pounds boneless skinless chicken breasts, cut into 1-inch pieces**
- **1 tablespoon cooking oil**
- **1 *each* medium green, sweet red and yellow peppers, cut into 1-inch pieces**
- **1/4 cup water**

In a bowl, combine broth, soy sauce, garlic, cornstarch, ginger and cayenne pepper; mix well. Add chicken; stir to coat. In a large skillet over medium-high heat, stir-fry chicken in oil for 7 minutes. Reduce heat to medium. Add peppers and water; cook and stir for 5-8 minutes or until peppers are tender. **Yield:** 6 servings. **Diabetic Exchanges:** One serving (prepared with low-sodium broth and light soy sauce) equals 3 lean meat, 1 vegetable; also, 200 calories, 207 mg sodium, 73 mg cholesterol, 8 gm carbohydrate, 29 gm protein, 7 gm fat.

HERB CHICKEN WITH MUSTARD SAUCE

Sue Broyles, Cherokee, Texas

A wonderful blend of herbs gives this chicken its appealing flavor. And the mustard sauce adds a little "zip".

>   1/2 cup crushed cornflakes
>   1/4 cup yellow cornmeal
>   2 teaspoons dried basil
>   2 teaspoons salt
>   1 teaspoon dried tarragon
>   1/2 teaspoon pepper
>   4 boneless skinless chicken breast halves
>   1/2 cup buttermilk
> MUSTARD SAUCE:
>   1 cup chicken broth
>   2 teaspoons cornstarch
>   1/4 cup Dijon mustard
>   1/4 cup sour cream

In a shallow bowl or large resealable plastic bag, combine the first six ingredients. Dip chicken in buttermilk, then coat with crumb mixture. Place in a single layer in a greased 13-in. x 9-in. x 2-in. baking dish. Sprinkle with remaining crumbs. Bake, uncovered, at 375° for 25 minutes or until juices run clear. Meanwhile, for the sauce, bring broth and cornstarch to a boil in a small saucepan. Stir in mustard; reduce heat and simmer for 3 minutes. Add sour cream; heat through, stirring constantly (do not boil). Serve over chicken. **Yield:** 4 servings.

TURKEY STIR-FRY

Julianne Johnson, Grove City, Minnesota

Here's a tasty way to prepare turkey anytime of year. My family loves the tender turkey strips, colorful vegetables and crunchy cashews.

✓ This tasty dish uses less sugar, salt and fat. Recipe includes *Diabetic Exchanges*.

> 1-1/2 pounds boneless turkey, cut into thin strips
>   1 tablespoon cooking oil
>   2 cups sliced fresh mushrooms
>   1 small onion, chopped
>   1 carrot, julienned
>   1/2 medium green pepper, sliced
>   1 cup chicken broth
>   3 tablespoons cornstarch
>   3 tablespoons soy sauce
>   1/2 teaspoon ground ginger
>   2 cups fresh *or* frozen snow peas, trimmed
> Hot cooked rice, optional
>   1/3 cup cashews, optional

In a large skillet or wok over medium-high heat, stir-fry turkey in oil until no longer pink, about 5-6 minutes. Remove turkey and keep warm. Stir-fry mushrooms, onion, carrot and green pepper until crisp-tender, about 5 minutes. Meanwhile, in a small bowl, combine broth, cornstarch, soy sauce and ginger. Add to the skillet; cook and stir until thickened and bubbly. Return turkey to skillet with peas; cook and stir until peas are crisp-tender. If desired, serve over rice and top with cashews. **Yield:** 6 servings. **Diabetic Exchanges:** One serving (prepared with low-sodium broth and light soy sauce and served without rice or cashews) equals 4 lean meat, 1 vegetable, 1/2 starch; also, 277 calories, 200 mg sodium, 84 mg cholesterol, 11 gm carbohydrate, 40 gm protein, 7 gm fat.

CHICKEN AND APRICOT SAUTE

Carolyn Griffin, Macon, Georgia

This stir-fry dish is popular in our home because it's quick, healthy and tastes great, too!

✓ This tasty dish uses less sugar, salt and fat. Recipe includes *Diabetic Exchanges*.

>   1 cup chicken broth
>   1 tablespoon cornstarch
> Pepper to taste
>   1 pound boneless skinless chicken breasts, cut into thin strips
>   1 tablespoon cooking oil
>   3 cups sliced celery
>   2 garlic cloves, minced
>   1 can (16 ounces) apricot halves, drained
>   6 ounces fresh *or* frozen snow peas, trimmed
> Hot cooked rice, optional

Combine broth, cornstarch and pepper; set aside. In a large skillet or wok over high heat, stir-fry chicken in oil until no longer pink. Remove and set aside. Add celery and garlic; stir-fry until the celery is crisp-tender, about 3 minutes. Stir broth mixture and add to skillet; cook, stirring constantly, until thickened and bubbly, about 1 minute. Add apricots, peas and chicken. Stir-fry until heated through, about 1-2 minutes. Serve over rice if desired. **Yield:** 6 servings. **Diabetic Exchanges:** One serving (served without rice) equals 2-1/2 lean meat, 1-1/2 vegetable, 1/2 fruit; also, 204 calories, 114 mg sodium, 64 mg cholesterol, 14 gm carbohydrate, 25 gm protein, 5 gm fat.

POULTRY POINTER. After working with raw poultry, always be sure to thoroughly wash your hands, the utensils used and the surface with hot soapy water.

QUICK SKILLET CHICKEN

LaVonne Elsbernd, Fortuna, North Dakota

Our teenagers' many activities keep me going right up until dinnertime. So I welcome recipes like this that can be made in a hurry. Plus it's a great way to use leftover chicken.

       3 **cups diced cooked chicken**
       1 **egg**
     1/2 **cup crushed saltines**
     1/2 **cup ground almonds**
     1/2 **teaspoon salt**
       3 **tablespoons butter *or* margarine**
       1 **cup sliced celery**
       2 **medium tomatoes, cut into thin wedges**
     1/2 **medium green pepper, julienned**
     1/2 **cup sugar**
       3 **tablespoons cornstarch**
     1/2 **cup water**
       1 **can (6 ounces) pineapple juice**
     1/2 **cup lemon juice**
       2 **tablespoons soy sauce**
**Hot cooked rice and chow mein noodles,
  optional**

In a bowl, combine chicken and egg. Add saltines, almonds and salt; toss well. In a skillet, saute chicken mixture in butter over medium heat for 10 minutes, stirring occasionally. Add vegetables; saute for 2-3 minutes or until crisp-tender. Remove from the heat and set aside. In a saucepan, combine sugar and cornstarch; add water, juices and soy sauce. Stir until smooth. Bring to a boil over medium heat; boil and stir for 1 minute or until thickened. Pour over chicken and vegetables; heat through. If desired, serve over rice and top with chow mein noodles. **Yield:** 6 servings.

CHICKEN AND PEPPERONI PIZZA

Diana Messner, Livonia, Michigan

(PICTURED ABOVE)

My husband is the supreme pizza maker in the family. He'll try new ingredient combinations and stick with the winners. This palate-pleasing pizza is one of his "masterpieces"!

       1 **package (16 ounces) prebaked Italian
         bread shell crust**
     3/4 **cup pizza sauce**
       1 **cup frozen cut broccoli, cooked and
         drained**
       1 **cup cubed cooked chicken**
       1 **can (4 ounces) mushroom stems and
         pieces, drained**
     1/4 **cup sliced pepperoni**
       8 **small cherry tomatoes, halved**
   1-1/2 **cups (6 ounces) shredded mozzarella
         cheese**

Place crust on an ungreased pizza pan. Spread with pizza sauce. Top with the broccoli, chicken, mushrooms, pepperoni and tomatoes. Sprinkle with cheese. Bake at 400° for 15-20 minutes or until heated through. **Yield:** 6-8 servings.

COUNTRY CHICKEN CASSEROLE

Frances Gleichmann, Baltimore, Maryland

(PICTURED BELOW)

Have leftover chicken? This recipe makes good use of it. The potatoes in this casserole also make it a dish that will appeal to any hearty "country" appetite. It's simple to prepare and delicious served with a salad and rolls.

1/2 pound fresh mushrooms, quartered
2 medium onions, chopped
5 tablespoons butter *or* margarine, *divided*
2 cups cubed cooked chicken
2 cups diced peeled potatoes, cooked
1 cup half-and-half cream
1 jar (2 ounces) diced pimientos, drained
1/4 cup chopped fresh parsley
1 teaspoon chicken bouillon granules
1 teaspoon salt
1/2 teaspoon dried rosemary, crushed
1/8 teaspoon pepper
1 cup soft bread crumbs
Additional parsley, optional

In a skillet over medium heat, saute the mushrooms and onions in 3 tablespoons butter until tender. Add chicken, potatoes, cream, pimientos, parsley, bouillon, salt, rosemary and pepper; heat through. Spoon into a greased 2-qt. casserole. Melt remaining butter; combine with the bread crumbs and sprinkle over casserole. Bake, uncovered, at 350° for 20-25 minutes or until crumbs are toasted. Garnish with parsley if desired. **Yield:** 6 servings.

CHICKEN CREOLE

Dolly Hall, Wheelwright, Kentucky

I like food with a little "zip" to it, and this recipe fills the bill. It's especially good served over rice.

✓ This tasty dish uses less sugar, salt and fat. Recipe includes *Diabetic Exchanges*.

1 pound boneless skinless chicken breasts, cut into 1-inch cubes
1/4 teaspoon pepper
1 teaspoon salt, *divided*, optional
1 tablespoon cooking oil
1 cup diced onion
1/2 cup diced celery

1/2 cup diced green pepper
2 garlic cloves, minced
1 can (14-1/2 ounces) diced tomatoes, undrained
1/2 cup water
1-1/2 teaspoons paprika
Dash cayenne pepper
1 bay leaf
1 tablespoon cold water
2 teaspoons cornstarch

Sprinkle chicken with pepper and 1/2 teaspoon salt if desired. In a large skillet over medium heat, brown chicken in oil; remove and set aside. In the same skillet, saute the onion, celery, green pepper and garlic until crisp-tender. Stir in tomatoes, water, paprika, cayenne pepper, bay leaf and remaining salt if desired; bring to a boil. Reduce heat; cover and simmer for 10 minutes. Add chicken. Combine cold water and cornstarch; stir into chicken mixture and bring to a boil. Reduce heat; simmer, uncovered, for 10-15 minutes or until chicken is tender. Remove bay leaf before serving. **Yield:** 4 servings. **Diabetic Exchanges:** One 1-1/4-cup serving (prepared without salt) equals 3 lean meat, 2-1/2 vegetable; also, 223 calories, 410 mg sodium, 73 mg cholesterol, 12 gm carbohydrate, 29 gm protein, 7 gm fat.

TURKEY MUSHROOM SUPREME

Jeanie Beers, Montgomery, New York

This recipe was served at a thank-you luncheon for me and my co-workers. It was so good I asked for the recipe. I've made it many times since and it always gets rave reviews.

1 cup diced green pepper
1 cup sliced fresh mushrooms
1/4 cup butter *or* margarine
1/3 cup all-purpose flour
1/2 teaspoon salt
1/4 teaspoon pepper
1/8 to 1/4 teaspoon curry powder
1/8 to 1/4 teaspoon dried tarragon
1/8 teaspoon ground coriander
1 cup chicken broth
1/2 cup milk
2 cups diced cooked turkey *or* chicken
1/2 cup frozen peas, thawed
1 jar (4 ounces) diced pimientos, drained
6 puff-pastry patty shells, baked

In a saucepan over medium heat, saute green pepper and mushrooms in butter until peppers are crisp-tender. Meanwhile, mix together flour and seasonings; stir into vegetables. Stir in broth

and milk. Cook, stirring constantly, for 2 minutes. Add turkey and peas; heat through. Gently stir in pimientos. Spoon into shells. **Yield:** 6 servings.

CHICKEN-MUSHROOM GRAVY

Mary Fry, Cedar Rapids, Iowa

Don't pass on the gravy...say, "Please pass the gravy!" This low-fat version is a flavorful accompaniment to chicken or turkey.

✓ This tasty dish uses less sugar, salt and fat. Recipe includes *Diabetic Exchanges*.

1/2 cup finely chopped onion
1/2 cup finely chopped fresh mushrooms
2 tablespoons chopped fresh parsley
2 cups chicken broth, *divided*
2 tablespoons cornstarch
Pinch pepper

In a saucepan, saute onion, mushrooms and parsley in 1/4 cup broth until vegetables are tender. Combine cornstarch, pepper and 1/2 cup of broth; stir until smooth. Add to vegetable mixture along with the remaining broth. Bring to a boil; cook and stir for 2 minutes. **Yield:** 2 cups. **Diabetic Exchanges:** One 1/4-cup serving (prepared with low-sodium chicken broth) equals a free food; also, 19 calories, 28 mg sodium, 2 mg cholesterol, 3 gm carbohydrate, 1 gm protein, 1 gm fat.

SESAME CHICKEN

Mrs. Wilson Irey, Rochester Hills, Michigan

Cornflake crumbs and sesame seeds give these moist chicken breasts a crunchy golden coating.

1/2 cup dry bread crumbs
1/2 cup crushed cornflakes
3 tablespoons sesame seeds
1/2 teaspoon onion powder
1/4 teaspoon salt
1/8 teaspoon pepper
1/8 teaspoon garlic powder
4 boneless skinless chicken breast halves
1/2 cup buttermilk
3 tablespoons cooking oil

In a shallow bowl or large resealable plastic bag, combine the first seven ingredients. Flatten the chicken breasts to 1/4-in. thickness. Dip in buttermilk, then coat with crumb mixture. In an electric skillet, heat oil to 350°. Fry chicken for 3-4 minutes per side or until browned and juices run clear. **Yield:** 4 servings.

Quick & Easy Beef

MUSTARD GRILLED STEAKS AND ONION

Sharon Kraeger, Plattsmouth, Nebraska

(PICTURED AT RIGHT)

The delicious mustard sauce really adds zing to this easy-to-grill dinner for two.

1/3 cup Dijon mustard
2 tablespoons honey
1 tablespoon cider vinegar
1 tablespoon water
1 tablespoon minced fresh parsley
1/4 teaspoon hot pepper sauce
1/8 teaspoon pepper
2 New York strip *or* T-bone steaks (1 inch thick)
1 large onion, cut into 4 thick slices

Combine the first seven ingredients; set aside. Grill steaks and onion slices, uncovered, over hot coals for 3 minutes on each side. Brush with mustard sauce. Continue grilling for 10-15 minutes or until steaks reach desired doneness and onion is tender, basting with sauce and turning occasionally. **Yield:** 2 servings.

SWEET-SOUR MEATBALLS

Janis Plourde, Smooth Rock Falls, Ontario

(PICTURED AT RIGHT)

Our family eats a lot of ground beef, so I was glad to find this tasty recipe. The combination of meatballs, green pepper and pineapple covered in a tangy sauce is a real change of pace.

1 pound ground beef
1 egg, beaten
4 tablespoons cornstarch, *divided*
2 tablespoons chopped onion
1 teaspoon salt
1/4 teaspoon pepper
1 tablespoon cooking oil
3 tablespoons vinegar

1 can (8 ounces) pineapple chunks
1/2 cup sugar
1 tablespoon soy sauce
1 medium green pepper, cut into strips
Hot cooked wide egg noodles

In a bowl, combine beef, egg, 1 tablespoon cornstarch, onion, salt and pepper. Shape into 1-1/2-in. balls. In a large skillet over medium heat, brown meatballs in oil. Reduce heat to low; cover and cook for 10 minutes or until no longer pink. Meanwhile, in a saucepan, stir vinegar and remaining cornstarch until smooth. Drain pineapple, reserving juice. Set pineapple aside. Add water to juice to measure 1-1/2 cups; stir into vinegar mixture. Add sugar and soy sauce; cook and stir over medium heat until thickened. Add the meatballs, pineapple and green pepper; cook until meatballs are heated through and the green pepper is tender. Serve over noodles. **Yield:** 3-4 servings.

BEEF 'N' CHEDDAR BISCUITS

Della Jackson, Loomis, California

This was a winning recipe at the county fair when I was a child. It remains a family favorite—and great picnic fare.

2 tubes (4-1/2 ounces *each*) refrigerated biscuits
1 pound ground beef, cooked and drained
1/4 cup barbecue sauce
1 cup (4 ounces) shredded cheddar cheese

Place one biscuit each in 12 greased muffin cups; press firmly onto the bottom and up the sides. Combine beef and barbecue sauce; spoon 1-2 tablespoons into each cup. Sprinkle with cheese. Bake at 350° for 15-18 minutes or until biscuits are golden and cheese is melted. **Yield:** 1 dozen.

HEARTY BEEF. *Pictured at right, from top to bottom: Sweet-Sour Meatballs and Mustard Grilled Steaks and Onion (both recipes on this page).*

POACHED MEATBALLS IN LEMON SAUCE

Taj Renee Brown, San Antonio, Texas

I discovered this among my collection of Southern recipes, and when I fixed these meatballs for my husband, there wasn't one left!

- 1/2 **cup seasoned dry bread crumbs**
- 1 **egg**
- 1/2 **teaspoon salt**
- 1 **teaspoon grated lemon peel**
- 1 **pound ground beef**
- 2-1/4 **cups water**, *divided*
- 2 **beef bouillon cubes**
- 2 **teaspoons cornstarch**
- 2 **tablespoons lemon juice**
- 2 **egg yolks, beaten**

Hot cooked rice

In a bowl, combine bread crumbs, egg, salt and lemon peel. Add ground beef; mix well. Shape into 12 meatballs, about 1-1/2 in. in diameter; set aside. In a saucepan, bring 2 cups water to a boil; add bouillon and stir to dissolve. Gently drop the meatballs into broth. Reduce heat and simmer for 10 minutes or until the meatballs are no longer pink; remove to a bowl and keep warm. Combine cornstarch and remaining water; stir into broth. Add lemon juice; cook and stir until thickened. Stir a small amount of broth into egg yolks. Return to saucepan and cook for 2 minutes, stirring frequently. Serve sauce over meatballs and rice. **Yield:** 4 servings.

MOCK FILET MIGNON

Cheri Legaard, Fortuna, North Dakota

(PICTURED BELOW)

I get rave reviews—and plenty of requests for the recipe—whenever I serve this to friends and family.

- 1-1/2 **pounds lean ground beef**
- 2 **cups cooked rice**
- 1 **cup diced onion**
- 1 **tablespoon Worcestershire sauce**
- 1-1/2 **teaspoons salt**
- 1/4 **teaspoon pepper**
- 1/4 **teaspoon garlic powder**
- 6 **bacon strips**

In a large bowl, combine beef, rice, onion, Worcestershire sauce, salt, pepper and garlic powder; mix well. Shape into six patties. Wrap a strip of bacon around each patty; fasten with a toothpick. Place in an ungreased shallow baking dish. Bake at 450° for 20 minutes or until meat is no longer pink. **Yield:** 6 servings.

MAPLE ALMOND BEEF

Valerie Witt, Centralia, Washington

(PICTURED AT RIGHT)

This recipe mixes the country goodness of beef and pure maple syrup with Oriental flavors. The result is delicious!

> 3 garlic cloves, minced
> 2 tablespoons cooking oil
> 2 pounds boneless round *or* sirloin steak, cut into thin strips
> 1/2 medium onion, thinly sliced
> 1 medium sweet red pepper, cut into strips
> 1/2 cup maple syrup
> 1/3 cup cider *or* red wine vinegar
> 2 tablespoons soy sauce
> 2 tablespoons cornstarch
> 3/4 cup frozen tiny peas, thawed
> 1/2 cup slivered almonds

Hot cooked rice

In large skillet or wok over high heat, saute garlic in oil for 1 minute. Add beef and stir-fry until browned. Stir in onion and pepper. Cover and steam until vegetables are crisp-tender, about 7 minutes. Meanwhile, combine syrup, vinegar, soy sauce and cornstarch; stir into beef mixture. Heat and stir until thickened. Add peas and almonds; heat through. Serve over rice. **Yield:** 6-8 servings.

MICROWAVE PIZZA CASSEROLE

Susan Slagel, Ashkum, Illinois

Who doesn't like pizza? With this one, just toss a salad, set the table…and fill up your family—fast.

> 1 pound ground beef
> 1 can (16 ounces) pizza sauce
> 2 cups uncooked noodles
> 1-1/2 cups water
> 1/2 cup chopped onion
> 1/2 cup chopped green pepper
> 1 can (4 ounces) sliced mushrooms, drained
> 4 ounces sliced pepperoni
> 1/2 teaspoon dried oregano
> 1/2 teaspoon garlic powder
> 1/2 teaspoon dried basil
> 1/2 teaspoon salt
> 3/4 cup shredded mozzarella cheese

In a 2-qt. microwave-safe casserole, microwave beef on high for 3-1/2 minutes; stir. Cook 2-1/2 minutes longer or until no longer pink. Drain well. Add the next 11 ingredients; mix well. Microwave on high for 17 minutes, stirring twice. Top with cheese; microwave for 1 minute or until cheese is melted. **Yield:** 6-8 servings. **Editor's Note:** This recipe was tested in a 700-watt microwave.

CLASSIC GERMAN BEEF PATTIES

Virginia Biehler, Fremont, Ohio

The hint of nutmeg in the meat mixture adds a subtle Old World flavor to these patties. Serve them with your favorite potato recipe.

> 2 pounds lean ground beef
> 1 medium onion, minced
> 2 eggs, beaten
> 3 tablespoons minced fresh parsley
> 2 tablespoons all-purpose flour
> 1/2 to 1 teaspoon salt
> 1/8 teaspoon pepper
> 1/8 teaspoon ground nutmeg
> 2 tablespoons butter *or* margarine
> 2 large onions, thinly sliced into rings

In a large bowl, combine beef, onion, eggs, parsley, flour and seasonings; mix well. Shape into six patties. In a skillet over medium heat, cook patties in butter until no longer pink. Remove to a serving platter and keep warm. Cook onion rings in pan juices until soft and golden. Spoon onions and pan juices over patties. **Yield:** 6 servings.

2 tablespoons chopped green pepper
1 egg, beaten
1/4 teaspoon salt
1 tablespoon cooking oil
1 cup tomato juice
1 tablespoon all-purpose flour
1/4 cup water

In a bowl, combine beef, potatoes, onion, green pepper, egg and salt. Shape into four patties. In a skillet over medium heat, brown the patties in oil; drain. Add tomato juice. Reduce heat; simmer 20-25 minutes or until meat is no longer pink. Remove patties to a serving platter; keep warm. Combine flour and water; gradually add to juice in the skillet. Cook over medium-low heat, stirring constantly until thickened. Spoon over patties. Serve immediately. **Yield:** 4 servings.

PIZZA POTATO TOPPERS

Sheila Friedrich, Antelope, Montana

(PICTURED ABOVE)

Not only is this recipe easy to make, it's an economical treat as well.

  1/2 **pound ground beef**
  1/2 **cup chopped green pepper**
    1 **small onion, chopped**
    1 **tomato, chopped**
  1/2 **to 3/4 cup pizza sauce**
    4 **hot baked potatoes**
    1 **cup (4 ounces) shredded mozzarella cheese**
Chopped fresh oregano, basil *or* parsley, optional

In a skillet over medium heat, cook beef, green pepper and onion until the meat is browned and the vegetables are tender; drain. Stir in tomato and pizza sauce; heat through. Slice baked potatoes lengthwise; fluff potato pulp with a fork. Spoon meat mixture into each; top with cheese. Sprinkle with oregano, basil or parsley if desired. **Yield:** 4 servings.

MEAT-AND-POTATO PATTIES

Gladys Klein, Burlington, Wisconsin

Whenever I want something different from regular hamburgers, I make these. Children really like them, just as I did when I was a child!

  3/4 **pound lean ground beef**
  3/4 **cup coarsely ground peeled potatoes**
  1/4 **cup finely chopped onion**

SALISBURY STEAK

Faye Hintz, Springfield, Missouri

(PICTURED ON FRONT COVER)

I remember enjoying Salisbury Steak often when I was growing up. I came up with these ingredients and experimented until it tasted like I recalled.

    2 **eggs**
    6 **tablespoons butter-flavored cracker crumbs**
    2 **tablespoons diced onion**
    1 **teaspoon salt**
  1/2 **teaspoon pepper**
  1/2 **teaspoon rubbed sage**
 1-1/2 **pounds ground beef**
    2 **cans (4 ounces *each*) mushroom stems and pieces, drained**
  1/4 **cup butter *or* margarine**
    6 **tablespoons all-purpose flour**
 3-1/2 **cups water**
    4 **beef bouillon cubes**
  1/2 **teaspoon browning sauce, optional**
Hot cooked noodles

In a bowl, beat eggs; add cracker crumbs, onion, salt, pepper and sage. Add beef and mix well. Shape into four patties. In a skillet over medium heat, cook patties for 4-5 minutes on each side or until browned; drain. Remove to a platter and keep warm. In the same skillet, saute mushrooms in butter for 2 minutes. Stir in flour until smooth. Add water and bouillon; cook and stir until smooth and thickened. Stir in browning sauce if desired. Return patties to gravy. Reduce heat to low; cook, uncovered, for 10 minutes or until no longer pink, stirring occasionally. Serve over noodles. **Yield:** 4 servings.

CARROT MEAT LOAF

Irene Knodel, Golden Prairie, Saskatchewan

(PICTURED BELOW)

We love to take slices of this tasty meat loaf to the field during harvest season. It cooks up quickly in the microwave, so it's a real blessing during our busiest time of year.

- **2 cups shredded carrots**
- **1 cup dry bread crumbs**
- **3 eggs, beaten**
- **1/2 cup milk**
- **1 envelope dry onion soup mix**
- **2 pounds lean ground beef**
- **1/2 pound ground pork**

GLAZE:
- **1/2 cup ketchup**
- **1/4 cup packed brown sugar**
- **2 teaspoons prepared mustard**

In a bowl, combine carrots, bread crumbs, eggs, milk and soup mix. Add beef and pork; mix well. On a microwave-safe platter, shape mixture into a circle with a 9-in. diameter; form a 3-in. hole in the center of the circle. Cover with waxed paper. Microwave on high for 16-18 minutes or until no longer pink, rotating the platter a quarter turn every 3 minutes. Drain. Let stand for 5 minutes. Meanwhile, in a custard cup, combine glaze in-gredients. Spread half the glaze over meat loaf. Microwave on medium for 1 minute; remove. Cover remaining glaze with waxed paper and heat in the microwave on medium for 1 minute. Serve glaze in center of meat loaf. **Yield:** 10 servings. **Editor's Note:** This recipe was tested in a 700-watt microwave.

CAMPER'S SPECIAL

Marie Hart, Fombell, Pennsylvania

When you're on the road, this dish comes in handy. Since my husband and I often enjoy travel-ing by ourselves, we can usually enjoy any left-overs the next day.

- **1 pound ground beef**
- **1 medium onion, chopped**
- **1 can (16 ounces) baked beans**
- **3/4 cup ketchup**
- **2 teaspoons prepared mustard**
- **3 cups cubed cooked peeled potatoes**

Salt and pepper to taste

In a skillet over medium heat, cook beef and on-ion until the beef is browned and the onion is ten-der; drain. Stir in beans, ketchup and mustard; cook over medium heat until hot and bubbly. Gently stir in potatoes and heat through. Season with salt and pepper. **Yield:** 4 servings.

BEEF AND BROCCOLI CASSEROLE

Dorothy Buttrill, Fairfield, Texas

I came up with this recipe on one of those "what in the world can I fix for dinner" days. I usually have the ingredients in the freezer and pantry, so it's handy when I need to make a meal in a hurry.

> **1 pound ground beef**
> **1/2 cup chopped onion**
> **1 tablespoon olive *or* vegetable oil**
> **1 can (10-3/4 ounces) condensed cream of mushroom soup, undiluted**
> **1 cup uncooked instant rice**
> **1/2 cup water**
> **1 tablespoon Worcestershire sauce**
> **1 teaspoon garlic salt**
> **1 teaspoon Italian seasoning**
> **2 pounds fresh broccoli, chopped *or* 2 packages (10 ounces *each*) frozen chopped broccoli, cooked and drained**
> **6 ounces sliced mozzarella cheese**

Chopped fresh parsley, optional

In a skillet over medium heat, brown beef and onion in oil until beef is browned and onion is tender; drain. Stir in the next six ingredients. Place broccoli in a greased 11-in. x 7-in. x 2-in. baking dish; top with meat mixture and mozzarella cheese. Bake, uncovered, at 400° for 15-20 minutes. Garnish with parsley if desired. **Yield:** 6 servings.

MEAT LOAVES WITH PESTO SAUCE

Lou Ganser, Grafton, Wisconsin

The pesto sauce adds an herb and cheese flavor that makes this recipe unique. If there's just two of you, prepare the whole recipe and use the leftovers for sandwiches.

PESTO SAUCE:
> **1 cup olive *or* vegetable oil**
> **2 cups fresh spinach *or* parsley**
> **2 garlic cloves**
> **1/2 cup walnuts**
> **1 tablespoon dried basil**
> **1/2 cup grated Parmesan cheese**

Salt and pepper to taste
MEAT LOAVES:
> **1 can (8 ounces) tomato sauce, *divided***
> **1/2 cup seasoned dry bread crumbs**
> **1/4 cup diced onion**
> **1 egg, beaten**
> **1/2 teaspoon salt**
> **1/4 teaspoon pepper**
> **1 pound lean ground beef**

> **1 tablespoon cooking oil**
> **1/4 cup water**

In a blender or food processor, combine pesto ingredients; cover and process until smooth. Set aside. In a bowl, combine 2 tablespoons tomato sauce, bread crumbs, onion, egg, salt, pepper and 3 tablespoons pesto sauce; add beef and mix well. Shape into four loaves. In a skillet over medium heat, brown meat loaves in oil. Meanwhile, combine 1 tablespoon pesto sauce, remaining tomato sauce and water; pour over meat. Reduce heat; cover and simmer for 20 minutes or until meat is no longer pink. Serve the loaves topped with tomato-pesto sauce. Refrigerate or freeze remaining pesto sauce for future use. **Yield:** 4 servings.

HAYSTACKS WITH CHEESE SAUCE

Dorothy Krauss, Halstead, Kansas

This recipe from my daughter is simple to toss together with ingredients I usually have on hand …and it's fun at the table, too, because everyone gets to build their own "haystack"!

> **1-1/2 pounds ground beef**
> **2 tablespoons chopped onion**
> **1 can (10-3/4 ounces) condensed tomato soup, undiluted**
> **1-1/2 teaspoons ground cumin**
> **1 teaspoon chili powder**
> **1 teaspoon dried oregano**
> **1 teaspoon salt**
> **1/2 teaspoon pepper**
> **1/4 teaspoon garlic powder**

CHEESE SAUCE:
> **1/4 cup butter *or* margarine**
> **1/4 cup all-purpose flour**
> **1 cup milk**
> **1 can (11 ounces) condensed cheddar cheese soup, undiluted**
> **1/2 pound process American cheese, cubed**

Corn chips
Hot cooked rice
Shredded lettuce
Picante sauce, optional

In a skillet over medium heat, cook beef and onion until the beef is browned and the onion is tender; drain. Stir in tomato soup, cumin, chili powder, oregano, salt, pepper and garlic powder. Reduce heat and simmer until heated through. For cheese sauce, melt butter in a saucepan. Stir in flour. Gradually add milk; cook and stir for 2 minutes or until thickened and bubbly. Stir in soup. Add cheese; heat only until cheese melts.

To serve, prepare individual corn chip "nests"; layer each with meat mixture, rice and lettuce. Top with cheese sauce and picante sauce if desired. **Yield:** 6-8 servings.

GREEN PEPPER STEAK

Emmalee Thomas, Laddonia, Missouri

(PICTURED ABOVE)

For a delicious fast meal, try this flavorful beef dinner loaded with tomatoes and peppers. It's a perfect recipe to use garden vegetables.

- 1/4 cup soy sauce
- 1/4 cup water
- 1 tablespoon cornstarch
- 1 pound boneless sirloin steak, cut into thin strips
- 2 to 3 tablespoons cooking oil, *divided*
- 2 small onions, thinly sliced into rings
- 2 celery ribs, sliced
- 1 green pepper, cut into 1-inch pieces
- 2 tomatoes, cut into wedges

Hot cooked rice

Combine soy sauce, water and cornstarch; set aside. In a large skillet or wok over high heat, stir-fry half of the beef in 1 tablespoon of oil until browned. Remove and repeat with remaining beef, adding additional oil as needed. Remove beef and keep warm. Add onions, celery and green pepper to pan; stir-fry until crisp-tender, about 3-4 minutes. Return beef to pan. Stir soy sauce mixture and add to pan. Cook and stir for 2 minutes or until sauce is thickened and bubbly.

Add tomatoes; cook just until heated through. Serve over rice. **Yield:** 4 servings.

SOUTHWEST ZUCCHINI SKILLET

Cathy Barkley, De Beque, Colorado

I like to serve this dish with corn bread. I also make sure to have extra salsa on hand to add a bit more spice!

- 1 pound ground beef
- 1/2 cup chopped onion
- 1/2 teaspoon salt
- 4-1/2 cups chopped zucchini
- 1 can (16 ounces) diced tomatoes, drained
- 1 cup salsa
- 1 can (16 ounces) chili beans
- 1 can (15-1/4 ounces) corn, drained
- 1 cup (8 ounces) sour cream
- 1-1/2 cups (6 ounces) shredded cheddar cheese

In a large skillet over medium heat, brown beef, onion and salt; drain. Add zucchini, tomatoes and salsa. Reduce heat; cover and simmer for 20 minutes or until zucchini is crisp-tender. Add the beans and corn; heat through. Remove from the heat. Gradually stir in sour cream; sprinkle with cheese. Cover and let stand until cheese melts. **Yield:** 6-8 servings.

LOOK FOR ZUCCHINI that's nicely green and firm. One pound of zucchini will yield about 2-1/2 cups chopped.

AUNT FRAN'S GOULASH

LaVergne Krones, Matteson, Illinois

(PICTURED BELOW)

When I was a young girl, Aunt Fran always made this when we went to visit her...my brother and I would have been disappointed if she didn't because it was our favorite. It's quick to make on busy days and also freezes well.

1-1/2 pounds ground beef
1 medium onion, diced
1 can (10-3/4 ounces) condensed tomato soup, undiluted
1 can (8 ounces) tomato sauce
1 can (15 ounces) kidney beans, rinsed and drained
1-1/2 cups water
1 beef bouillon cube
Dash pepper
8 ounces spiral noodles, cooked and drained
Grated Parmesan cheese, optional

In a skillet over medium heat, cook beef and onion until beef is browned and onion is tender; drain and set aside. In a large saucepan, combine the soup and tomato sauce. Stir in beans, water, bouillon and pepper. Add the noodles and beef mixture; heat through. Sprinkle with Parmesan cheese if desired. **Yield:** 4-6 servings.

HEARTY BEEF CASSEROLE

Joan Govier, Victoria Harbour, Ontario

If my family and friends gave out blue ribbons for their favorite casserole dish, this one would win a fistful!

1 pound ground beef
2 medium onions, diced
1 green pepper, diced
1 tablespoon butter *or* margarine
4 medium potatoes, peeled, cut into 1/2-inch cubes and cooked
2 medium tomatoes, seeded and chopped
1 can (10-3/4 ounces) condensed cream of chicken soup, undiluted
1/4 cup chili sauce
3/4 teaspoon salt
1/4 teaspoon pepper
1/4 cup grated Parmesan cheese

In a skillet over medium heat, cook beef, onion and green pepper in butter until beef is browned

and vegetables are tender; drain. Add potatoes and tomatoes. Stir in soup and chili sauce; mix well. Pour into a greased 13-in. x 9-in. x 2-in. baking dish. Sprinkle with salt, pepper and Parmesan cheese. Bake, uncovered, at 350° for 15 minutes or until lightly browned and bubbly. **Yield:** 4 servings.

CHEESY STUFFED PEPPERS

Betty DeRaad, Sioux Falls, South Dakota

(PICTURED AT RIGHT)

This is my favorite summertime supper because I can use green peppers and tomatoes fresh from my garden.

> **6 medium green peppers**
> **1-1/2 pounds ground beef**
> **1 medium onion, chopped**
> **1/2 teaspoon salt**
> **2-1/2 cups chopped tomatoes**
> **2 cups (8 ounces) shredded cheddar cheese**

Cut tops from peppers and remove seeds. Place in a saucepan and cover with water; bring to a boil and cook for 6-8 minutes. Meanwhile, brown beef, onion and salt in a skillet over medium heat; drain. Cool slightly; add tomatoes and cheese. Drain peppers and stuff with meat mixture. Place in an ungreased baking dish. Bake, uncovered, at 350° for 20 minutes. **Yield:** 6 servings.

oil for 5 minutes or until meat reaches desired doneness. Serve over rice or noodles. **Yield:** 4 servings.

SESAME BEEF

Kim Champlin, Miami, Florida

A simple marinade turns this beef stir-fry into a special meal the whole family loves.

> **3 tablespoons cooking oil, *divided***
> **2 tablespoons sugar**
> **2 tablespoons soy sauce**
> **3 green onions, thinly sliced**
> **2 garlic cloves, minced**
> **1 tablespoon sesame seeds**
> **1/4 teaspoon pepper**
> **1 pound boneless sirloin steak, cut into thin strips**
> **Hot cooked rice *or* chow mein noodles**

In a large resealable plastic bag or shallow glass container, combine 2 tablespoons oil, sugar, soy sauce, onions, garlic, sesame seeds and pepper. Add beef; seal bag or cover container and let stand 15 minutes. In a skillet or wok over high heat, stir-fry the beef and marinade in remaining

BEEF 'N' RICE HOT DISH

Elma Katainen, Menahga, Minnesota

When I want something that I know will stick to my family's ribs, I make this hearty dish. It never fails to please.

> **1 pound ground beef**
> **1 medium onion, chopped**
> **1/2 cup chopped green pepper**
> **1/2 teaspoon salt**
> **Pinch pepper**
> **1 can (14-1/2 ounces) stewed tomatoes**
> **1-1/2 cups uncooked instant rice**
> **1-1/2 cups hot water**
> **1 can (8 ounces) tomato sauce**
> **1 teaspoon prepared mustard**

In a skillet over medium heat, brown beef; drain. Add onion, green pepper, salt and pepper; cook and stir until vegetables are tender. Add remaining ingredients; bring to a boil. Reduce heat; cover and simmer for 10 minutes. **Yield:** 4 servings.

Spaghetti Con Carne

Carol Ice, Burlingham, New York

This is a hearty recipe that belonged to my grand-parents, who homesteaded in Wyoming.

SAUCE:
- 1 small onion, chopped
- 1 garlic clove, minced
- 1 teaspoon cooking oil
- 3 cups tomato juice
- 1 to 2 tablespoons chili powder
- 1 teaspoon salt

MEATBALLS:
- 1 pound ground beef
- 1 egg, beaten
- 1 small onion, minced
- 1 garlic clove, minced
- 1/4 cup cornmeal
- 1 teaspoon salt
- 1/2 teaspoon pepper
- 1/2 teaspoon dried oregano
- 1 tablespoon cooking oil

Hot cooked spaghetti

For sauce, in a large saucepan over medium heat, saute onion and garlic in oil; add tomato juice, chili powder and salt. Reduce heat; simmer for 10 minutes. In a bowl, mix the first eight meatball ingredients. Shape into 3/4-in. meatballs. In a skillet over medium heat, brown meatballs in oil. Add meatballs to sauce. Cover and simmer for 10 minutes or until the meatballs are cooked through. Serve over spaghetti. **Yield:** 4-6 servings.

Taco-Stuffed Potatoes

Beverly Hockel, Odin, Minnesota

Here's a tasty, different way to serve up the flavor of tacos without having to make a trip to the grocery store for taco shells. And if you bake the potatoes in a microwave oven, the whole entree takes even less time to prepare.

- 1 pound ground beef
- 3/4 cup water
- 1/2 cup chopped onion
- 1 envelope taco seasoning
- 1 teaspoon chili powder
- 1 can (15 ounces) refried beans
- 6 hot baked potatoes
- 1 cup (4 ounces) shredded cheddar cheese

Sour cream

In a skillet over medium heat, brown beef; drain. Add water, onion, taco seasoning and chili powder. Simmer for 5-10 minutes. Heat refried beans in a small saucepan. Slice baked potatoes lengthwise. Spoon taco filling into each; top with 1-2 tablespoons beans and cheese. Microwave for 1 minute. Top with sour cream. **Yield:** 6 servings. **Editor's Note:** This recipe was tested in a 700-watt microwave.

Unstuffed Cabbage

Diana Filban, Cut Bank, Montana

If you like stuffed cabbage but want to save time, this recipe fills the bill—deliciously!

- 1 pound ground beef
- 1 cup chopped onion
- 4 cups shredded cabbage
- 1 can (28 ounces) Mexican-style tomatoes, undrained
- 1 tablespoon brown sugar
- 1 tablespoon vinegar
- 1/4 teaspoon salt
- 1/8 teaspoon pepper

Hot cooked rice

In a Dutch oven over medium heat, brown beef and onion; drain. Stir in cabbage. Cover and cook for 5 minutes or until cabbage is crisp-tender. Stir in tomatoes, brown sugar, vinegar, salt and pepper. Cook 10 minutes longer, stirring occasionally. Serve over rice. **Yield:** 4-6 servings.

Chop Suey

Debra Weihert, Waterloo, Wisconsin

This recipe is my children's all-time favorite meal. How much do they like it? Even more than they like pizza...and that's a lot!

- 1 pound ground beef
- 2 cups water, *divided*
- 2 beef bouillon cubes
- 2 tablespoons cornstarch
- 1 can (28 ounces) chop suey vegetables, drained
- 2 tablespoons soy sauce

Hot cooked rice
Chow mein noodles

In a skillet over medium heat, brown beef; drain. Heat 1-1/2 cups water to boiling; add bouillon and stir to dissolve. Add to skillet. Combine remaining water with cornstarch; stir into beef mixture. Bring to a boil; reduce heat and simmer until thickened. Add vegetables and soy sauce; cook and stir until heated through, about 15 minutes. Serve over rice; sprinkle with chow mein noodles. **Yield:** 4-6 servings.

LIVER SKILLET SUPPER

Karen Ann Bland, Gove, Kansas

(PICTURED BELOW)

Whenever I serve this to people for the first time, someone exclaims, "I can't believe it's liver!" Around here, that's what we call this recipe, which we've enjoyed for many years.

  1/2 pound sliced bacon
  3/4 cup all-purpose flour
    1 teaspoon garlic salt, *divided*
    1 teaspoon onion salt, *divided*
    1 teaspoon pepper, *divided*
    1 pound beef liver
    6 large potatoes, peeled and thinly sliced
    1 large onion, thinly sliced
Green pepper rings, optional

In a large skillet, cook bacon until crisp. Remove to a paper towel to drain; reserve drippings in the skillet. Combine flour and half of the garlic salt, onion salt and pepper. Cut liver into 2-in. x 1/2-in. strips; dredge in the flour mixture, coating well. Brown liver in drippings. Add potatoes and onion. Sprinkle with remaining seasonings; cook until the potatoes are browned and tender, stirring occasionally. Crumble bacon over top. Garnish with green pepper rings if desired. **Yield:** 4-6 servings.

BAKED POTATOES...FAST! Pierce similar-sized baking potatoes with a fork. Microwave, uncovered, on high for 6-12 minutes, rotating once, or until potatoes are tender.

SOUTHWEST STEW

Lois McAtee, Oceanside, California

My whole family loves foods spiced with picante sauce, so I developed this recipe.

    2 pounds ground beef
1-1/2 cups diced onion
    1 can (28 ounces) diced tomatoes, undrained
    1 can (15-1/4 ounces) corn, drained
    1 can (15 ounces) pinto beans, rinsed and drained
    1 cup picante sauce
  3/4 cup water
    1 teaspoon ground cumin
  1/2 teaspoon garlic powder
  1/2 teaspoon pepper
Salt to taste
Shredded cheddar cheese, optional

In a large skillet over medium heat, brown beef and onion; drain. Add the next nine ingredients; bring to a boil. Reduce heat; cover and simmer for 15-20 minutes. Garnish with cheese if desired. **Yield:** 8 servings.

SKILLET BEEF AND MACARONI

Maxine Neuhauser, Arcadia, California

(PICTURED ABOVE)

I found this recipe 30 years ago on a can label. My family loves it, and I always receive compliments when I take the dish to potluck suppers.

1-1/2 pounds ground beef
1/2 cup chopped onion
2 cans (8 ounces *each*) tomato sauce
1 cup water
1 package (7 ounces) macaroni
1/2 cup chopped green pepper
2 tablespoons Worcestershire sauce
1 teaspoon salt
1/4 teaspoon pepper

In a skillet over medium heat, cook beef and onion until the meat is browned and onion is tender; drain. Stir in the remaining ingredients; bring to a boil. Reduce heat; cover and simmer until macaroni is tender, about 20 minutes. Stir occasionally, adding additional water if needed. **Yield:** 4-6 servings.

HAMBURGER STROGANOFF

Jutta Doering, Kelowna, British Columbia

I just love cooking with ground beef, especially when the result is an economical dish like this. I serve it over poppy seed noodles for extra flavor.

1-1/2 pounds ground beef
1/2 cup chopped onion

2 tablespoons butter *or* margarine
1 can (4 ounces) mushroom stems and pieces, drained
2 tablespoons all-purpose flour
1/2 teaspoon salt
1 garlic clove, minced
1/4 teaspoon pepper
1 can (10-3/4 ounces) condensed cream of chicken soup, undiluted
1 cup (8 ounces) sour cream
POPPY SEED NOODLES:
8 ounces wide noodles, cooked and drained
2 teaspoons poppy seeds
1 tablespoon butter *or* margarine, melted
Chopped fresh parsley

In a skillet over medium heat, cook beef and onion in butter until the beef is browned and the onion is tender; drain. Stir in mushrooms, flour, salt, garlic and pepper. Cook for 5 minutes, stirring constantly. Stir in soup; bring to a boil, stirring constantly. Reduce heat; simmer, uncovered, for 10 minutes, stirring occasionally. Stir in sour cream; heat through, but do not boil. Meanwhile, combine noodles, poppy seeds and butter; toss lightly. Spoon stroganoff over noodles. Garnish with parsley. **Yield:** 6 servings.

BEEF FRIED RICE

Cathy Wadden, Hamilton, Ontario

I came up with this recipe by experimenting—and it's become a family favorite. I often add whatever vegetables and seasonings I have on hand.

1 tablespoon cooking oil
2 eggs, lightly beaten
1-1/2 pounds ground beef
1 cup diced carrots
1 cup diced celery
1/2 cup diced onion
2 garlic cloves, minced
3/4 cup chopped fresh mushrooms
1/2 cup frozen peas, thawed
5 cups cooked long grain rice
1 tablespoon dried parsley flakes
1 teaspoon dried basil
1/4 teaspoon ground ginger
Salt and pepper to taste
1/4 to 1/2 cup soy sauce

In a large skillet over medium-high heat, heat oil. Pour eggs into skillet. As eggs set, lift edges, allowing uncooked eggs to flow underneath. Cook until eggs are firmly set. Remove eggs to a plate; chop into small pieces and set aside. In the same skillet, brown beef; drain, reserving 2 tablespoons drippings. Set meat aside. In the same skillet, stir-fry carrots, celery, onion and garlic in drippings. Add mushrooms and peas; cook until tender. Add rice, parsley, basil, ginger, salt, pepper, beef and eggs; mix well. Add soy sauce; heat through. **Yield:** 8-10 servings.

QUICK BEEF STEW

Valerie Cook, Hubbard, Iowa

This flavorful stew is ready so quick, you'll have to call the family to dinner!

  2 cups cubed cooked roast beef
  1 can (16 ounces) mixed vegetables, drained
  1 can (10-3/4 ounces) cream of celery soup, undiluted
  1 can (10-3/4 ounces) cream of mushroom soup, undiluted
  1/2 teaspoon dried thyme
  1/4 teaspoon dried rosemary, crushed
Pepper to taste

In a saucepan, combine all of the ingredients; heat through. Add water as needed if stew is too thick. **Yield:** 4 servings.

NORWEGIAN MEATBALLS

Karen Hoylo, Duluth, Minnesota

(PICTURED BELOW RIGHT)

I can still see Grandmother making dozens of these little meatballs! The hint of spices gives them a savory taste that's authentically Norwegian.

  1 medium onion, diced
  1/2 cup milk
  1 egg, beaten
  1 tablespoon cornstarch
  1 teaspoon salt
  1/4 teaspoon ground nutmeg
  1/4 teaspoon ground allspice
  1/4 teaspoon ground ginger
Dash pepper
1-1/2 pounds lean ground beef
  3 to 4 tablespoons butter *or* margarine
GRAVY:
  1 tablespoon butter *or* margarine
  2 tablespoons all-purpose flour
  1 cup beef broth
  1/2 cup half-and-half cream

Salt and pepper to taste
Minced fresh parsley, optional

In a bowl, combine the first nine ingredients. Add beef; mix well. Shape into 1-1/2-in. meatballs. (Mixture will be very soft. For easier shaping, rinse hands in cold water frequently.) In a large skillet over medium heat, brown the meatballs in butter, half at a time, for 10 minutes or until no longer pink. Turn to brown evenly. Remove to paper towels to drain, reserving 1 tablespoon drippings in skillet. For gravy, add butter to drippings. Stir in flour. Add broth and cream; cook and stir for 2 minutes or until thickened and bubbly. Season with salt and pepper. Reduce heat to low. Return meatballs to skillet; heat through. Garnish with parsley if desired. **Yield:** 6 servings.

MEAT LOAF PARMESAN

Laddie Nichols, Lakeside, Arizona

Meat loaf slices get a face-lift with this crunchy coating that's a breeze to prepare.

  1 cup crushed saltines
  1/4 cup grated Parmesan cheese
  1 egg
  3 tablespoons water
  4 cooked meat loaf slices (about 3/8 inch thick)
Cooking oil
Ketchup, optional

Combine the saltine crumbs and Parmesan cheese in a shallow bowl; set aside. In another bowl, beat egg with water. Dip meat loaf slices in egg mixture, then in crumb mixture. Heat oil in a skillet. Brown meat loaf slices on each side. Serve with ketchup if desired. **Yield:** 2-4 servings.

Down-Home Pork

VEGETABLE PORK STIR-FRY

Marilyn Platner, Marion, Iowa

(PICTURED AT RIGHT)

Hearty meals in a hurry are as near as my skillet when I use this quick recipe.

    1 pound boneless pork loin, cut into thin
        strips
1-1/2 teaspoons ground ginger
    1/4 to 1/2 teaspoon garlic powder
    2 tablespoons cooking oil
    1 package (16 ounces) frozen vegetables
        (broccoli, mushrooms, green beans,
        onions and red pepper), thawed
    1 package (6 ounces) frozen pea pods,
        thawed
    1 large tomato, cut into wedges
    1/2 cup water
    1/4 cup soy sauce
    1 tablespoon cornstarch
Hot cooked rice *or* chow mein noodles

In a wok or skillet over high heat, stir-fry pork, ginger and garlic powder in oil until meat is no longer pink. Add vegetables; cook until heated through. Mix water, soy sauce and cornstarch until smooth; add to skillet. Cook and stir until sauce is thickened. Serve over rice or chow mein noodles. **Yield:** 4 servings.

PORK TENDERLOIN DIANE

Janie Thorpe, Tullahoma, Tennessee

(PICTURED AT RIGHT)

Pork medallions are served in a savory sauce.

✓ This tasty dish uses less sugar, salt and fat. Recipe includes *Diabetic Exchanges*.

    1 pork tenderloin (1 pound)
    1 tablespoon lemon-pepper seasoning
    2 tablespoons butter *or* margarine
    2 tablespoons lemon juice
    1 tablespoon Worcestershire sauce
    1 teaspoon Dijon mustard

Fresh parsley and lemon slices, optional

Cut tenderloin into eight pieces; flatten to 1/2-in. thickness. Sprinkle with lemon pepper. In a large skillet over medium heat, cook pork in butter for 3-4 minutes on each side or until juices run clear. Remove to a serving platter and keep warm. To the pan juices, add lemon juice, Worcestershire sauce and mustard; heat through, stirring occasionally. Pour over the pork. Garnish with parsley and lemon if desired. Serve immediately. **Yield:** 4 servings. **Diabetic Exchanges:** One serving (prepared with margarine) equals 3 meat; also, 214 calories, 491 mg sodium, 6 mg cholesterol, 1 gm carbohydrate, 18 gm protein, 14 gm fat.

HAM AND ASPARAGUS ROLL-UPS

Grace Andres, Grand Rapids, Michigan

My family is always delighted when I turn leftover holiday ham into this lively dish.

    1 pound fresh asparagus
   10 slices fully cooked ham (1/8 inch thick)
    1 can (10-3/4 ounces) condensed cream of
        celery soup, undiluted
    1/4 cup milk
    3 tablespoons sliced almonds

In a skillet, cook asparagus in a small amount of water for 6-8 minutes or until crisp-tender; drain well. Roll each slice of ham around two to three asparagus spears. Place ham rolls, seam side down, in a greased 11-in. x 7-in. x 2-in. microwave-safe baking dish. Combine soup and milk; pour over ham rolls. Top with almonds. Cover and microwave on high for 3-5 minutes or until bubbly. **Yield:** 5 servings. **Editor's Note:** This recipe was tested in a 700-watt microwave.

EASY ENTREES. *Pictured at right, top to bottom: Vegetable Pork Stir-Fry (recipe on this page), Orange Ham Kabobs (recipe on page 152) and Pork Tenderloin Diane (recipe on this page).*

ORANGE HAM KABOBS

Robbyn Stephen, Jenkintown, Pennsylvania

(PICTURED ON PAGE 151)

On the first warm day of spring, I plan on preparing these kabobs. The orange basting sauce nicely pairs with ham.

1-1/2 pounds fully cooked ham, cut into 24
    cubes (1-inch pieces)
2 medium oranges, peeled and cut into
    eighths
1 large green pepper, cut into 16 pieces
1 large sweet red pepper, cut into 16 pieces
1/2 cup orange juice
2 tablespoons tomato paste
1/4 teaspoon ground ginger

On eight metal or soaked bamboo skewers, alternately thread three ham cubes, two orange pieces, two green pepper pieces and two red pepper pieces. Broil 4-5 in. from the heat for 8 minutes, turning occasionally. Meanwhile, in a small bowl, combine orange juice, tomato paste and ginger; mix well. Brush half over kabobs; broil 2-3 minutes longer. Turn kabobs and brush with remaining sauce; broil 2 minutes more or until the vegetables are tender. **Yield:** 8 servings.

SAUSAGE 'N' NOODLE DINNER

Phyllis Dennewitz, Frankfort, Ohio

I adapted this dish from a recipe my German grandmother gave me. It reminds me of my heritage whenever I make it.

1 pound bulk pork sausage
1 medium head cabbage (about 1-1/2
    pounds), thinly sliced
1 large onion, thinly sliced
1 large carrot, shredded
2 teaspoons chicken bouillon granules
1/4 cup boiling water
2 cups (16 ounces) sour cream
3/4 teaspoon salt
1/2 teaspoon pepper
8 ounces noodles, cooked and drained
Chopped fresh parsley, optional

In a skillet over medium-high heat, brown sausage; drain. Add cabbage, onion and carrot; mix well. Dissolve bouillon in water; pour over vegetables.

> **STORAGE TIPS.** Tightly wrap fresh pork and store in your refrigerator's meat compartment for 2 to 3 days or in the freezer for up to 6 months.

Cover and cook for 10-15 minutes or until the vegetables are tender. Reduce heat; stir in sour cream, salt and pepper. Heat through. Transfer to a serving bowl; add hot noodles and toss. Garnish with parsley if desired. **Yield:** 4-6 servings.

CHOPS WITH PRUNES

Margaret Pache, Mesa, Arizona

The wonderful orange juice-based sauce is simple to prepare, and its hint of spices enhances the flavor of the meat.

4 pork chops *or* 8 lamb chops (1 inch thick)
1 tablespoon cooking oil
Salt and pepper to taste
3/4 cup orange juice, *divided*
2 tablespoons maple syrup
1/2 teaspoon ground ginger
1/4 teaspoon ground allspice
8 ounces pitted prunes
1-1/2 teaspoons cornstarch

In a skillet over medium heat, brown chops in oil; sprinkle with salt and pepper. Drain. Set aside 1 tablespoon of orange juice; pour remaining juice over chops. Add syrup, ginger and allspice; cover and cook for 10 minutes, turning chops once. Add prunes. Cover and simmer until meat is tender. Remove the chops to a serving platter and keep warm. Combine cornstarch and reserved orange juice; add to skillet. Bring to a boil over medium heat; cook and stir for 2 minutes. Spoon over chops. **Yield:** 4 servings.

HAM AND BROCCOLI STUFFED POTATOES

Dia Steele, Comanche, Texas

This is one of my favorite light suppers...an easy spur-of-the-moment meal that satisfies even the heartiest appetites.

2 tablespoons butter *or* margarine
2 tablespoons all-purpose flour
1 cup milk
1/4 teaspoon ground mustard
1/4 teaspoon salt
1/4 teaspoon pepper
1/2 cup shredded cheddar cheese
3 cups chopped fresh broccoli, cooked
1 cup chopped fully cooked ham
4 to 6 hot baked potatoes

In a small saucepan over low heat, melt butter. Add flour and stir until smooth. Stir in milk;

cook and stir until thickened and bubbly. Add mustard, salt and pepper. Stir in the cheese until melted. Fold in broccoli and ham; heat through. Serve over baked potatoes. **Yield:** 4-6 servings.

CRANBERRY CHUTNEY

Joyce Vivian, Mitchell, Ontario

I've served this at holiday dinners for years. It also makes a great gift.

    3 cups fresh *or* frozen cranberries
    1 cup chopped dried apricots
    3/4 cup packed brown sugar
    3/4 cup orange juice
    1/2 cup chopped dates
    1/2 cup chopped onion
    1/2 cup cider vinegar
    1/2 cup light corn syrup
    1 tablespoon grated orange peel
    1/2 teaspoon ground mustard
    1/2 teaspoon salt
    1/4 teaspoon ground ginger
Hot cooked ham, pork *or* turkey

In a large heavy saucepan, combine the first 12 ingredients. Bring to a boil. Reduce heat and simmer, uncovered, for 15-20 minutes or until thickened and cranberries have popped. Serve with ham, pork or turkey. **Yield:** about 3-1/2 cups.

RASPBERRY VINEGAR PORK CHOPS

Maurita Merrill, Lac la Hache, British Columbia

(PICTURED ABOVE)

We often entertain out-of-town guests, and I like to serve this main dish when we do. It makes a pretty presentation and it's delicious.

    8 pork chops *or* 3 pounds pork tenderloin (1 inch thick)
    1 tablespoon butter *or* margarine
    1 tablespoon olive *or* vegetable oil
  1/2 cup raspberry vinegar, *divided*
    3 garlic cloves, thinly sliced
    2 tomatoes, seeded and chopped
  1/2 cup chicken broth
    1 tablespoon chopped fresh parsley
    1 teaspoon dried sage, thyme, tarragon *or* basil
Salt and pepper to taste

In a large skillet over high heat, brown pork in butter and oil; drain. Reduce heat to medium-low; add 2 tablespoons vinegar and garlic. Cover and simmer for 10 minutes or until meat juices run clear. Remove pork and keep warm. Add remaining vinegar to the skillet; stir to loosen browned bits. Increase heat and boil until the vinegar is reduced to a thick glaze. Add tomatoes, broth, parsley and sage. Boil until liquid is reduced by half. Strain; season with salt and pepper. Spoon over pork. **Yield:** 8 servings.

HORSERADISH SAUCE FOR HAM

Edna Duffield, Lineville, Iowa

Tangy horseradish is what stands out in this delicious, unique sauce for your next meal with ham.

1/4 cup prepared horseradish
1 tablespoon prepared mustard
1-1/2 teaspoons vinegar
1/2 teaspoon salt
1/2 teaspoon Worcestershire sauce
4 drops hot pepper sauce
1 cup whipping cream, whipped
Hot cooked ham, ham loaf *or* ham balls

In a small bowl, combine the first six ingredients; mix well. Gently fold in whipped cream. Serve with ham, ham loaf or ham balls. **Yield:** about 2 cups.

PEACHY HAM SLICE

Erika Klop, Agassiz, British Columbia

(PICTURED BELOW)

The delightful flavor of peaches gives this ham an extra-special taste.

1 can (16 ounces) sliced peaches
1 fully cooked ham slice (about 1-1/2 pounds)
1 tablespoon butter *or* margarine
1 tablespoon sugar
2 teaspoons cornstarch

1/8 teaspoon ground nutmeg
1/2 cup orange juice
1 tablespoon lemon juice
Hot cooked rice

Drain peaches, reserving 1/2 cup syrup; set peaches and syrup aside. In a large skillet over medium heat, brown ham in butter. Remove to a platter and keep warm, reserving drippings in skillet. In a small bowl, mix sugar, cornstarch and nutmeg. Add juices and reserved peach syrup; stir until smooth. Add to skillet. Cook until thick, stirring constantly. Stir in peaches; heat through. Add ham slice and heat for 2-3 minutes. Cut into serving-size pieces. Serve over rice. **Yield:** 4-6 servings.

CASHEW PORK STIR-FRY

Betty Ruenholl, Syracuse, Nebraska

You don't have to pass up pork when you're in a hurry. This hearty main dish will serve up fast!

3/4 cup orange juice
1/3 cup corn syrup
3 tablespoons soy sauce
1 tablespoon cornstarch
1 tablespoon grated orange peel
1/4 teaspoon ground ginger
2 large carrots, sliced
2 celery ribs, sliced
2 tablespoons cooking oil, *divided*
1 pound pork tenderloin, cut into thin strips
1/2 cup cashews
Hot cooked rice

Combine the first six ingredients; set aside. In a large skillet or wok over medium heat, stir-fry carrots and celery in 1 tablespoon oil for 3 minutes. Remove vegetables and set aside. In the same skillet, stir-fry pork in remaining oil for 3 minutes or until no longer pink. Return vegetables to skillet. Stir orange juice mixture; add to skillet. Stir in cashews. Cook and stir for 2 minutes or until sauce is thickened. Serve over rice. **Yield:** 4 servings.

SAUSAGE CASSEROLE FOR TWO

Kathryn Curtis, Lakeport, California

I don't know if my mother made up this German-style recipe or if it was handed down to her. Either way...it's simply scrumptious!

2 smoked fully cooked Polish sausages (about 6 ounces)
1/4 cup sliced fresh mushrooms
1/4 cup finely chopped onion

1 tablespoon butter *or* margarine
2 tablespoons whipping cream
1-1/2 teaspoons Dijon mustard
1/8 teaspoon garlic powder
1/2 cup shredded cheddar cheese
4 tomato slices

Cut sausages in half lengthwise and place in a greased 1-1/2-qt. baking dish. In a saucepan over medium heat, saute mushrooms and onion in butter until lightly browned. Stir in cream, mustard and garlic powder; bring to a boil. Cook and stir until slightly thickened. Pour over sausages; top with cheese. Bake, uncovered, at 450° for 15-20 minutes or until cheese is melted. Garnish with tomatoes. **Yield:** 2 servings.

MEXICAN PIZZA

Matt Walter, Grand Rapids, Michigan

Growing up, I was encouraged to learn my way around the kitchen. Now I do most of the cooking for me and my wife.

2 flour tortillas (10 inches)
3 ounces sliced pepperoni
2 medium tomatoes, chopped
1/2 cup salsa
1 can (2-1/4 ounces) sliced ripe olives, drained
1 cup (4 ounces) shredded Monterey Jack cheese
1 cup shredded lettuce

Place one tortilla on a microwave-safe plate. Layer with half of the pepperoni, tomatoes, salsa, olives and cheese. Microwave on high for 1-1/2 to 2 minutes or until cheese melts. Top with half of the lettuce. Repeat for second pizza. **Yield:** 2 servings. **Editor's Note:** This recipe was tested in a 700-watt microwave.

MANDARIN PORK MEDALLIONS

Dawn Doyle, Easton, Minnesota

(PICTURED ABOVE)

My daughter demonstrated this recipe at the state fair and received lots of compliments. Since she is involved in both food and swine projects, she took great pleasure in promoting Minnesota pork.

1 pork tenderloin (about 1 pound)
1 tablespoon cooking oil
3/4 cup orange juice
1 tablespoon cornstarch
1/4 cup orange marmalade
2 tablespoons lemon juice
1 teaspoon prepared horseradish
1/4 to 1/2 teaspoon salt
Hot cooked noodles
1 can (11 ounces) mandarin oranges, drained

Cut tenderloin into four pieces; flatten to 1/3 in. thickness. In a large skillet over medium heat, cook tenderloin in oil for 3 minutes per side; remove and set aside. Combine orange juice and cornstarch; add to the skillet along with marmalade, lemon juice, horseradish and salt. Bring to a boil. Reduce heat; cook and stir for 2 minutes. Return pork to skillet; cover and cook for 8-10 minutes or until meat juices run clear. Serve over noodles; garnish with oranges. **Yield:** 4 servings.

HAM, RED BEANS AND RICE

Vanita Davis, Camden, Arkansas

Red beans and rice is a popular dish here in the South. This version also features ham.

   3 cans (15 ounces *each*) red beans, rinsed and drained
   1 can (14-1/2 ounces) Mexican *or* Cajun stewed tomatoes
   2 cups cubed fully cooked ham
   1/2 cup water
   1/2 teaspoon garlic powder
   1/2 teaspoon ground cumin
   1/2 teaspoon dried oregano
   1/2 teaspoon dried thyme
   1/2 teaspoon salt
   1/4 teaspoon pepper
   2 to 5 dashes hot pepper sauce
Hot cooked rice

In a large saucepan, combine first 11 ingredients. Bring to a boil; reduce heat. Cover and simmer for 25 minutes. Serve over rice. **Yield:** 6-8 servings.

PASTA WITH SAUSAGE AND TOMATOES

Michelle Fryer Dommel, Quakertown, Pennsylvania

As speedy as tomato dishes are, this recipe puts even more of an emphasis on convenience.

   1 pound bulk Italian sausage
   2 cans (16 ounces *each*) diced tomatoes, undrained
1-1/2 teaspoons chopped fresh basil *or* 1/2 teaspoon dried basil
   1 package (12 ounces) pasta, cooked and drained

In a skillet over medium heat, cook sausage until browned; drain. Add tomatoes and basil. Reduce heat; simmer, uncovered, for 10 minutes. Serve over pasta. **Yield:** 4 servings.

CABBAGE GOULASH

Emma Lee Norris, Memphis, Tennessee

Even people who don't like cabbage love this dish along with bread or hard rolls.

1-1/4 pounds bulk pork sausage
   3/4 pound ground beef
   1 large onion, chopped
   1 can (28 ounces) diced tomatoes, undrained
   1 can (6 ounces) tomato paste
   2 tablespoons vinegar
   1 tablespoon chili powder
   1 teaspoon garlic powder
   1/4 teaspoon crushed red pepper flakes, optional
  10 cups shredded cabbage

In a large kettle over medium heat, brown sausage, beef and onion; drain. Add the next six ingredients; mix well. Stir in cabbage. Reduce heat and simmer for 15-20 minutes or until the cabbage is tender. **Yield:** 6-8 servings.

CHERRY-ALMOND HAM SAUCE

Julie Sterchi, Fairfield, Illinois

This glaze works fine with any meat...and its cheery color adds a festive touch to the table!

   1 jar (12 ounces) cherry preserves
   1/4 cup vinegar
   2 tablespoons corn syrup
   1/4 teaspoon ground cinnamon
   1/4 teaspoon ground cloves
   1/4 teaspoon ground nutmeg
   1/3 cup slivered almonds
   3 tablespoons water
Hot cooked ham slices

In a saucepan, combine the first six ingredients; bring to a boil over medium heat. Reduce heat; simmer for 2 minutes, stirring frequently. Stir in the almonds and water; heat through. Serve with ham. **Yield:** about 1-1/2 cups.

PORK PARTICULARS. When selecting fresh pork, look for firm meat with a moderate amount of fat and marbling. The color can range from light pink to deep rose.

PORK WITH MUSTARD SAUCE

Irma Pomeroy, Enfield, Connecticut

I couldn't wait to grow up and start cooking for my own family! Now that I do, I really enjoy using pork.

   1 pound pork tenderloin
   2 tablespoons butter *or* margarine
   1/2 cup beef broth
   3/4 teaspoon dried tarragon
   1/2 cup whipping cream
   1 tablespoon Dijon mustard
Salt and pepper to taste
Hot cooked noodles, optional

Cut tenderloin into eight pieces. Slice each piece again, but do not cut all of the way through; open each piece and flatten slightly with meat mallet. In a large skillet over medium-high heat, cook the pork in butter until meat juices run clear, 5-6 minutes per side. Remove to a serving platter and keep warm; discard drippings. In the same skillet, cook broth and tarragon over high heat until reduced by half. Reduce heat; stir in cream and mustard. Season with salt and pepper. Spoon over pork. Serve over noodles if desired. **Yield:** 4 servings.

SOUTHWESTERN GRILLED CHOPS

Margaret Pache, Mesa, Arizona

Jalapeno peppers are quite abundant in this area of the country. I think this recipe will appeal to folks who like their food a little hotter.

   1 cup salsa
   1/2 cup chopped onion
   1/4 cup molasses
   1/4 cup lime juice
   1/4 cup chicken broth
   2 garlic cloves, minced
   1 to 3 tablespoons chopped seeded
      jalapeno peppers
   2 teaspoons sugar
   2 pork chops *or* 4 lamb chops (1 inch thick)
Sour cream

In a saucepan, combine the first eight ingredients. Simmer, uncovered, for 15-20 minutes. Meanwhile, grill chops, uncovered, over medium coals, turning once and basting with sauce during the last few minutes of grilling. Grill pork for 15 minutes or until juices run clear. Grill lamb for 10-14 minutes for rare, 14-16 minutes for medium or 16-20 minutes for well-done. Serve with sour cream. **Yield:** 2 servings.

SAUSAGE AND VEGETABLE SKILLET

Ruby Williams, Bogalusa, Louisiana

(PICTURED ABOVE)

The variety of vegetables makes this an attractive dish, and the cooking time is minimal.

   1/2 pound Italian sausage links, cut into
      1/2-inch slices
   1 tablespoon cooking oil
   1 cup cubed yellow summer squash
   1/2 cup chopped green onions
   2 garlic cloves, minced
 1-1/2 cups chopped tomatoes
   2 teaspoons Worcestershire sauce
   1/8 teaspoon cayenne pepper

In a skillet over medium heat, cook sausage in oil until no longer pink; drain. Add squash, onions and garlic; cook for 2 minutes. Stir in the tomatoes, Worcestershire sauce and cayenne pepper; heat through. **Yield:** 2 servings.

Fish & Seafood

LEMON HERBED SALMON

Perlene Hoekema, Lynden, Washington

(PICTURED AT RIGHT)

We sometimes send our delicious Washington salmon all the way to Michigan for my sister to use in this family-favorite dish! The tasty topping can be used on other types of fish, too.

2-1/2 cups fresh bread crumbs
4 garlic cloves, minced
1/2 cup chopped fresh parsley
6 tablespoons grated Parmesan cheese
1/4 cup chopped fresh thyme *or* 1 tablespoon dried thyme
2 teaspoons grated lemon peel
1/2 teaspoon salt
6 tablespoons butter *or* margarine, melted, *divided*
1 salmon fillet (3 to 4 pounds)

In a bowl, combine bread crumbs, garlic, parsley, Parmesan cheese, thyme, lemon peel and salt; mix well. Add 4 tablespoons butter and toss lightly to coat; set aside. Pat salmon dry. Place, skin side down, in a greased baking dish. Brush with remaining butter; cover with crumb mixture. Bake, uncovered, at 350° for 20-25 minutes or until fish flakes easily with a fork. **Yield:** 8 servings.

PAN-FRIED TROUT

Felicia Cummings, Raymond, Maine

(PICTURED AT RIGHT)

I originally devised this recipe for the grill when we were on vacation. Now it's a favorite at home on the stove.

4 trout fillets (about 8 ounces *each*)
1/2 cup grated Parmesan cheese
1/2 cup bacon-flavored crackers, crushed
1/2 cup cornmeal
1/4 to 1/2 teaspoon garlic salt
Pinch pepper
2 eggs

1/2 cup milk
1/2 cup vegetable oil
Lime wedges, celery leaves *and/or* fresh chives *or* parsley for garnish, optional

Rinse fish in cold water and pat dry. In a shallow bowl, combine Parmesan cheese, cracker crumbs, cornmeal, garlic salt and pepper. In another bowl, beat eggs; add milk. Dip fish in the egg mixture, then gently roll in the crumb mixture. In a skillet, fry fish in oil for 5-7 minutes or until it flakes easily with a fork, turning once. Garnish as desired. **Yield:** 4 servings.

NORTH CAROLINA SHRIMP SAUTE

Teresa Hildreth, Stoneville, North Carolina

Seafood is very popular in my state. I found this recipe in a magazine years ago and I've altered it many times to come up with a winning combination.

1 pound fresh shrimp, peeled and deveined
1/2 pound fresh mushrooms, sliced
1 small green pepper, chopped
3 garlic cloves, minced
1/4 cup butter *or* margarine
8 ounces linguini *or* spaghetti, cooked and drained
1/2 cup grated Romano cheese
1/2 teaspoon salt
1/4 teaspoon pepper
Minced fresh parsley
Lemon slices

In a skillet, saute shrimp, mushrooms, green pepper and garlic in butter for 3-5 minutes or until shrimp turn pink. Put hot pasta on a large serving platter. Top with shrimp mixture. Sprinkle with cheese, salt, pepper and parsley; toss. Garnish with lemon. **Yield:** 4 servings.

> **CATCH OF THE DAY.** *Pictured at right, top to bottom: Lemon Herbed Salmon and Pan-Fried Trout (both recipes on this page).*

SHRIMP WIGGLE

Lucille Nicholls, Hurricane, Utah

(PICTURED ABOVE)

Since canned shrimp was very expensive when I was growing up, this special dish always seemed like a real treat. It's still a treat today because it's delicious.

1 cup chopped onion
1/4 cup butter *or* margarine
3 tablespoons all-purpose flour
2 cups milk
4 ounces process American cheese, cubed
1 can (14-1/2 ounces) diced tomatoes, undrained
2 cans (4-1/4 ounces *each*) shrimp, rinsed and drained
1 cup frozen peas, thawed
Salt to taste
Chow mein noodles
Paprika

In a medium saucepan, saute onion in butter until tender. Add flour; stir until thickened and bubbly. Add milk all at once; cook and stir for 2 minutes. Stir in cheese until melted. Add tomatoes, stirring constantly. Add shrimp, peas and salt; heat through. Serve over chow mein noodles; sprinkle with paprika. **Yield:** 6 servings.

TUNA-CHIP CASSEROLE

Janis Plourde, Smooth Rock Falls, Ontario

The addition of asparagus and a special topping gives traditional tuna casserole a new twist.

1 package (7 ounces) plain potato chips, *divided*
1 can (6 ounces) tuna, drained and flaked
1 can (19 ounces) asparagus tips, drained *or* 10 ounces frozen asparagus tips, cooked for 3 minutes, drained
SAUCE:
2/3 cup evaporated milk
1 tablespoon lemon juice
1/4 teaspoon ground mustard
1/8 teaspoon white pepper
TOPPING:
1/4 cup shredded cheddar cheese
1/2 cup sliced almonds

Crush chips and place half in a greased 11-in. x 7-in. x 2-in. baking dish. Top with tuna and asparagus. Cover with remaining chips. Combine sauce ingredients and pour over all. Sprinkle with cheese and almonds. Bake, uncovered, at 325° for 20-25 minutes. Remove from oven; let stand 5 minutes before serving. **Yield:** 6 servings.

BAKED FISH

Lynn Mathieu, Great Mills, Maryland

I created this quick recipe after enjoying a similar dish at a restaurant. Parmesan cheese gives it extra "zip".

✓ This tasty dish uses less sugar, salt and fat. Recipe includes *Diabetic Exchanges*.

1/2 pound panfish fillets (perch, trout *or* whitefish)
4 teaspoons grated Parmesan cheese
1/2 teaspoon dill weed

Place fish in a 10-in. pie plate that has been coated with nonstick cooking spray. Sprinkle with

Parmesan cheese and dill. Bake, uncovered, at 350° for 8-10 minutes or until fish flakes easily with a fork. **Yield:** 2 servings. **Diabetic Exchanges:** One serving (prepared with perch) equals 3 very lean meat; also, 119 calories, 131 mg sodium, 104 mg cholesterol, 0 carbohydrate, 23 gm protein, 2 gm fat.

SALMON CAKES

Imogene Hutton, Norton, Texas

Mama liked to serve these on Sundays. We ate them as fast as she could fry them!

     2 eggs
  1/4 cup whipping cream
  1/4 cup cornmeal
     2 tablespoons sliced green onions
     2 tablespoons all-purpose flour
  1/4 teaspoon baking powder
Pinch pepper
  1/2 teaspoon salt, optional
     1 can (14-3/4 ounces) salmon, drained, boned and flaked
     1 to 2 tablespoons butter *or* margarine

In a medium bowl, beat the eggs. Add cream, cornmeal, onions, flour, baking powder, pepper and salt if desired. Add salmon; mix well. Melt butter in a skillet or griddle; drop salmon mixture by one-third cupfuls and cook over medium heat for 5 minutes on each side or until lightly browned. Serve hot. **Yield:** 3-4 servings (six patties).

CATFISH WITH LEMON-BUTTER SAUCE

Rita Futral, Ocean Springs, Mississippi

(PICTURED BELOW)

I created this recipe for a catfish cooking contest by modifying a recipe for shrimp and spaghetti, which I also developed.

  3/4 cup butter
  1/2 pound fresh mushrooms, sliced
     1 garlic clove, minced
  1/2 cup chicken broth
     2 tablespoons lemon juice
  1/4 to 1/3 cup minced fresh parsley
     1 teaspoon salt
  1/2 teaspoon pepper
1-1/2 pounds catfish fillets, cut into bite-size pieces
    16 ounces spaghetti, cooked and drained
  1/2 cup grated Parmesan cheese
Lemon slices *or* wedges, optional
Additional parsley, optional

In a large skillet, melt butter over medium heat. Saute mushrooms and garlic for 5 minutes. Add broth, lemon juice, parsley, salt and pepper; cook for 3 minutes, stirring occasionally. Add catfish; simmer, uncovered, for 6-8 minutes or until fish flakes easily with a fork. (Butter sauce will be thin.) Serve over hot spaghetti. Sprinkle with Parmesan cheese. Garnish with lemon and parsley if desired. **Yield:** 6-8 servings.

SALMON CROQUETTES

Mary McGuire, Graham, North Carolina

These crisp croquettes are a delightful, fun way to serve salmon.

  1 can (14-3/4 ounces) pink salmon,
    drained, boned and flaked
  1 cup evaporated milk, *divided*
1-1/2 cups cornflake crumbs, *divided*
  1/4 cup dill pickle relish
  1/4 cup finely chopped celery
  2 tablespoons finely chopped onion
Cooking oil for deep-fat frying
TARTAR SAUCE:
  2/3 cup evaporated milk
  1/4 cup mayonnaise
  2 tablespoons dill pickle relish
  1 tablespoon finely chopped onion

In a medium bowl, combine salmon, 1/2 cup milk, 1/2 cup crumbs, relish, celery and onion; mix well. With wet hands, shape one-fourth cupfuls into cones. Dip into remaining milk, then into remaining crumbs. Heat oil to 365° in an electric skillet or deep-fat fryer. Fry croquettes, a few at a time, for 2 to 2-1/2 minutes or until golden brown. Drain on paper towels; keep warm. Combine the sauce ingredients in a medium saucepan; cook over medium-low heat until heated through and slightly thickened. Serve warm with croquettes. **Yield:** 4-6 servings.

HONEY WALLEYE

Kitty McCue, St. Louis Park, Minnesota

(PICTURED BELOW)

Fishing is a favorite recreation here. This recipe is a quick way to prepare all the fresh walleye that's hooked by the anglers in our family.

  1 egg
  2 teaspoons honey
  2 cups crushed butter-flavored crackers
    (45 to 50)
  1/2 teaspoon salt
  4 to 6 walleye fillets (1-1/2 to 2 pounds)
  1/3 to 1/2 cup cooking oil
Lemon wedges, optional

In a shallow bowl, beat egg; add honey. In another shallow bowl, combine cracker crumbs and salt. Dip fillets in egg mixture, then in crumbs until coated. In a skillet, fry fillets in oil for 3-5 minutes per side or until fish flakes easily with a fork. Serve with lemon wedges if desired. **Yield:** 4-6 servings.

GOLDEN FISH CAKES

Madeline Waldron, Walhalla, South Carolina

(PICTURED AT RIGHT)

Our family loves fish, so I've tried many recipes. I came up with this combination and it's been a hit at our house.

**1 pound fish (whitefish, cod *or* haddock), cooked and flaked
1-1/2 cups soft bread crumbs
1 medium onion, chopped
3 eggs
2 to 4 tablespoons water
2 tablespoons mayonnaise
1-1/2 teaspoons ground mustard
1 teaspoon dried parsley flakes
3/4 teaspoon salt
1-1/2 cups Italian-seasoned dry bread crumbs
2 tablespoons cooking oil
Tartar sauce and lemon wedges, optional**

In a bowl, combine the first nine ingredients; mix well. Shape into 12 patties, adding additional water if needed; coat with the bread crumbs. In a large skillet over medium-high heat, fry the patties in oil for 4-5 minutes on each side or until lightly browned. Serve with tartar sauce and lemon if desired. **Yield:** 4-6 servings.

2 servings. **Diabetic Exchanges:** One serving (prepared with margarine and without salt) equals 4 lean meat, 1 fat; also, 254 calories, 156 mg sodium, 98 mg cholesterol, 2 gm carbohydrate, 31 gm protein, 14 gm fat.

LIME BROILED CATFISH

Nick Nicholson, Clarksdale, Mississippi

To serve a reduced-calorie dish that is ready in about 15 minutes, I came up with this fast simple recipe. Lime juice adds a different fresh flavor to the mild taste of the fish.

✓ This tasty dish uses less sugar, salt and fat. Recipe includes *Diabetic Exchanges*.

**1 tablespoon butter *or* margarine
2 tablespoons lime juice
1/2 teaspoon salt, optional
1/4 teaspoon pepper
1/4 teaspoon garlic powder
2 catfish fillets (6 ounces *each*)
Lime slices *or* wedges, optional
Fresh parsley, optional**

In a saucepan over medium heat, melt butter. Stir in lime juice, salt if desired, pepper and garlic powder; mix well. Remove from the heat and set aside. Place fillets in an ungreased shallow baking dish. Generously brush each fillet with the lime-butter sauce. Broil for 5-8 minutes or until the fish flakes easily with a fork. Remove to a warm serving dish; spoon pan juices over each fillet. Garnish with lime and parsley if desired. **Yield:**

OVEN-FRIED FISH

Ann Berg, Chesapeake, Virginia

The secret to this recipe is buttering the fish first before dusting it with flour. That seals in the moisture of the fish, making it succulent and absolutely delicious.

**4 orange roughy, red snapper, catfish *or* trout fillets (1-1/2 to 2 pounds)
6 tablespoons butter *or* margarine, melted, *divided*
1 tablespoon all-purpose flour
Paprika
3 tablespoons lemon juice
1 tablespoon minced fresh parsley
2 teaspoons Worcestershire sauce**

Place fish on a broiler rack that has been coated with nonstick cooking spray. Brush tops of fish with 3 tablespoons of the butter; dust with flour and sprinkle with paprika. Broil 5-6 in. from the heat for 5 minutes or until fish just begins to brown. Combine lemon juice, parsley, Worcestershire sauce and remaining butter; pour over the fish. Broil 5 minutes longer or until fish flakes easily with a fork. **Yield:** 4 servings.

Vegetables & Side Dishes

HERB-BUTTERED CORN

Donna Smith, Victor, New York

(PICTURED AT RIGHT)

My husband and I love fresh corn on the cob and spreading this delicious herb butter on it makes it even better.

> 1/2 cup butter *or* margarine, softened
> 1 tablespoon snipped chives
> 1 tablespoon snipped fresh dill
> 1 tablespoon snipped fresh parsley
> 1/2 teaspoon dried thyme
> 1/4 teaspoon salt
> Dash garlic powder
> Dash cayenne pepper
> 10 ears fresh corn, husked and cooked

In a bowl, combine the first eight ingredients and mix well. Spread over each ear of hot corn. **Yield:** 10 servings.

CHEESE POTATOES

Deborah Amrine, Grand Haven, Michigan

(PICTURED AT RIGHT)

Don't let the basic ingredients fool you—this recipe has anything but ordinary taste. The hearty potatoes have a wonderful cheesy flavor and melt in your mouth. They're simple to prepare and impressive to serve.

> 6 large potatoes, peeled and thinly sliced
> 3 tablespoons butter *or* margarine
> 1 teaspoon salt
> 1/4 teaspoon pepper
> 1 cup milk
> 2 cups (8 ounces) shredded cheddar cheese

In a large skillet over medium heat, saute potatoes in butter until almost tender and lightly browned. Sprinkle with salt and pepper. Add milk; simmer, uncovered, until milk is absorbed. Top with cheese; heat until melted. Stir before serving. **Yield:** 6 servings.

VEGETABLES PROVENCALE

Bobbie Jo Yokley, Franklin, Kentucky

(PICTURED AT RIGHT)

My sister created this recipe and shared it with me. Somehow she always comes up with a new dish that's both colorful and delicious!

> 1 small onion, chopped
> 2 tablespoons cooking oil
> 2 medium zucchini, cubed
> 1/3 cup diced green pepper
> 1 garlic clove, minced
> 1/4 teaspoon salt
> 1/8 teaspoon pepper
> 2 large tomatoes, peeled and quartered
> 1/4 cup grated Parmesan cheese
> 1 tablespoon minced fresh parsley

In a skillet over medium heat, saute onion in oil until tender. Stir in zucchini, green pepper, garlic, salt and pepper. Reduce heat to low; cover and cook for 5-6 minutes or until the vegetables are almost tender. Stir in tomatoes; heat through. Sprinkle with Parmesan cheese and parsley. **Yield:** 4-6 servings.

SESAME ZUCCHINI

Mary Bliss, Canton, Ohio

Although short on ingredients and preparation time, this side dish is long on flavor.

> 4 cups thinly sliced zucchini
> 2 tablespoons sesame seeds
> 2 tablespoons cooking oil
> Salt and garlic powder to taste

In a skillet, saute zucchini and sesame seeds in oil for 2-3 minutes. Season with salt and garlic powder. **Yield:** 6 servings.

> **SAVORY SIDE SHOWS.** *Pictured at right, top to bottom: Herb-Buttered Corn, Cheese Potatoes and Vegetables Provencale (all recipes on this page).*

CORN WITH BASIL

Ronda Lambert, Vandervoort, Arkansas

Our family enjoys eating lots of corn fresh from our garden...and this is one of our favorite ways to serve it.

3-1/2 cups fresh corn
   1 medium onion, chopped
1/2 cup thinly sliced celery
   1 garlic clove, minced
   2 tablespoons butter *or* margarine
   1 jar (2 ounces) diced pimientos, drained, optional
   1 teaspoon dried basil
1/2 teaspoon salt

In a skillet over medium heat, saute corn, onion, celery and garlic in butter for 10 minutes. Stir in pimientos if desired, basil and salt; cover and simmer, stirring occasionally, for 15-20 minutes or until corn is tender. **Yield:** 4-6 servings.

SWEET POTATO CASSEROLE

Eleanor Sherry, Highland Park, Illinois

(PICTURED BELOW)

I've used this recipe a lot since I got it from a friend years ago. I always make it for Thanksgiving and for dinners when I'm serving ham.

4 cups mashed cooked sweet potatoes
   (2-1/4 to 2-1/2 pounds)
1/2 cup sugar
1/2 cup milk
1/3 cup butter *or* margarine, melted
   2 eggs
   1 teaspoon vanilla extract
TOPPING:
1/2 cup chopped nuts
1/2 cup shredded coconut
1/2 cup packed brown sugar
   3 tablespoons butter *or* margarine, melted

In large mixing bowl, combine potatoes, sugar, milk, butter, eggs and vanilla. Spread into a greased 1-1/2-qt. casserole. Combine topping ingredients; sprinkle over potatoes. Bake, uncovered, at 375° for 25 minutes or until heated through. **Yield:** 6-8 servings.

BROCCOLI IN HERBED BUTTER

Norma Apel, Dubuque, Iowa

A delicate herbed butter easily and deliciously dresses up plain broccoli.

✓ This tasty dish uses less sugar, salt and fat. Recipe includes *Diabetic Exchanges*.

   1 pound fresh broccoli, cut into spears
   2 tablespoons butter *or* margarine
1-1/2 teaspoons lemon juice

1-1/2 teaspoons finely chopped onion
1/4 teaspoon salt, optional
1/8 teaspoon *each* dried thyme, marjoram
and savory

Cook broccoli in a small amount of water until crisp-tender. Drain; remove to a serving dish. Melt butter; add lemon juice, onion, salt and herbs. Pour over broccoli. **Yield:** 6 servings. **Diabetic Exchanges:** One serving (prepared with margarine and without salt) equals 1 fat, 1/2 vegetable; also, 51 calories, 42 mg sodium, 0 cholesterol, 3 gm carbohydrate, 2 gm protein, 4 gm fat.

CANDY-COATED CARROTS

Lavonne Hartel, Williston, North Dakota

I really believe putting some zing into vegetables is one of the best ways to get children to eat them. Everyone enjoys this recipe's sweet, tangy glaze.

1 pound baby carrots
1/4 cup butter *or* margarine
1/4 cup packed brown sugar
1 teaspoon lemon juice
1/8 to 1/4 teaspoon hot pepper sauce
1/8 teaspoon salt

In a saucepan, cook carrots in a small amount of water until crisp-tender; drain. Remove carrots; set aside and keep warm. In the same saucepan, cook butter and brown sugar until bubbly. Stir in lemon juice, hot pepper sauce and salt. Return carrots to pan and heat through. **Yield:** 4-6 servings.

ZUCCHINI-GARLIC PASTA

Shelley Smail, Chico, California

(PICTURED ABOVE)

My Italian neighbor gave me a list of the ingredients for this recipe, but he didn't have the measurements written down. I experimented and came up with this side dish, which is nice with many meals.

1 package (16 ounces) wagon wheel-*or*
other small pasta
1/2 pound sliced bacon, diced
1 medium onion, chopped
4 to 6 garlic cloves, minced
2 to 3 medium zucchini, halved and sliced
1/2 teaspoon salt
3 tablespoons lemon juice
1/4 cup grated Romano *or* Parmesan cheese

Cook the pasta according to package directions. Meanwhile, in a large skillet over medium heat, cook bacon until crisp. Drain, reserving 2 tablespoons drippings in skillet. Saute onion and garlic in drippings until tender. Add the zucchini and salt; cook until tender. Rinse and drain pasta; add to the zucchini mixture. Add lemon juice and bacon; toss. Transfer to a serving bowl or platter; sprinkle with cheese. **Yield:** 6-8 servings.

MAKE-AHEAD BACON BITS. When time allows, cook and crumble a package of bacon and then freeze. Use these pieces as a quick and easy topping for baked potatoes, salads and casseroles.

CHEESY GREEN BEANS

Betty Shaw, Weirton, West Virginia

(PICTURED ABOVE)

A family favorite for years, this recipe is one I make often because it can easily be doubled and prepared ahead. It's a must on the menu when my nephews come for dinner!

> **3 tablespoons butter *or* margarine, *divided***
> **1 tablespoon all-purpose flour**
> **1 teaspoon dried minced onion**
> **1 teaspoon sugar**
> **1/4 teaspoon salt**
> **1/4 teaspoon pepper**
> **1 cup (8 ounces) sour cream**
> **4 to 6 cups French-style green beans, cooked and drained**
> **1/2 cup crushed cornflakes**
> **1 cup (4 ounces) shredded sharp cheddar *or* Swiss cheese**

Melt 2 tablespoons of butter in a large saucepan. Stir in flour, onion, sugar, salt and pepper to form a smooth paste. Bring to a boil; cook and stir for 1 minute or until thickened. Reduce heat; add the sour cream and stir until smooth. Cook and stir over low heat for 2 minutes (do not boil). Fold in the beans. Spread into a greased shallow 1-1/2-qt. baking dish. Melt remaining butter and toss with cornflake crumbs; sprinkle cheese and crumb mixture over bean mixture. Bake, uncovered, at 400° for 20 minutes or until heated through. **Yield:** 6-8 servings.

FRIED GREEN TOMATOES

Judy Benson, Granite Falls, Minnesota

When I was growing up, these were a summertime favorite with my family. Back then, we just dipped the tomato slices in flour and fried them in butter.

> **1/2 cup all-purpose flour**
> **1/4 cup cornmeal**
> **1/4 cup grated Parmesan cheese**
> **1/2 teaspoon dried oregano**
> **1/2 teaspoon salt**
> **1/8 teaspoon pepper**
> **3 to 4 green tomatoes, cut into 1/2-inch slices**

Cooking oil

Combine the flour, cornmeal, Parmesan cheese, oregano, salt and pepper. Coat tomato slices with flour mixture. In a skillet over medium heat, cook tomatoes in oil for 2-3 minutes on each side or until tender and lightly browned. Drain on paper towels. **Yield:** 4-6 servings

CABBAGE-POTATO SAUTE

Jeann Jones, Ogema, Wisconsin

You'll come to rely on this recipe when you need a side dish in a hurry. It adds plenty of substance to a simple meal.

> **4 cups shredded cabbage**
> **1/2 cup water**
> **1/4 cup grated uncooked peeled potato**

1 tablespoon butter *or* **margarine**
Pinch salt and pepper
1 tablespoon vinegar

In a saucepan, cook cabbage in water until tender, stirring occasionally; drain. Add potato, butter, salt and pepper. Stir in vinegar. Cook and stir over low heat for 5 minutes. **Yield:** 4 servings.

ZESTY BUTTERED PEAS

Claire Talone, Morrisville, Pennsylvania

(PICTURED ON FRONT COVER)

The lively, pungent flavor of savory turns plain peas into a special treat that my guests love.

✓ This tasty dish uses less sugar, salt and fat. Recipe includes *Diabetic Exchanges*.

2 tablespoons butter *or* **margarine**
1 package (10 ounces) frozen peas, thawed
1 cup sliced celery
1/2 cup chopped onion
1 tablespoon minced fresh savory *or* **1 teaspoon dried savory**
1/2 teaspoon salt, optional
2 tablespoons diced pimientos

Melt butter in a heavy saucepan; add peas, celery, onion, savory and salt if desired. Cover and cook over medium heat for 6-8 minutes or until vegetables are tender. Stir in pimientos. **Yield:** 6 servings. **Diabetic Exchanges:** One serving (prepared with margarine and without salt) equals 1 fat, 1/2 starch; also, 74 calories, 93 mg sodium, 0 cholesterol, 8 gm carbohydrate, 2 gm protein, 4 gm fat.

DOWN-HOME SUCCOTASH

Marian Platt, Sequim, Washington

(PICTURED BELOW)

If you grow your own corn, you can have it really fresh for this recipe if you make sure everything is ready before you pick the corn! That's the way I like it.

5 bacon strips, diced
2 cups fresh corn
1/2 pound fresh lima beans
1 medium green pepper, chopped
1 medium onion, chopped
2 medium tomatoes, cut into wedges

In a skillet, cook bacon until crisp. Drain, reserving 1 tablespoon drippings in the skillet. To the skillet, add corn, lima beans, green pepper and onion. Simmer for 10-15 minutes or until vegetables are almost tender, adding water if necessary. Stir in tomatoes and bacon; heat through. **Yield:** 12-14 servings.

CORN OKRA CREOLE

Ruth Aubey, San Antonio, Texas

(PICTURED BELOW)

This dish is representative of my area of the country, particularly the Texas-Louisiana border. Corn, okra and Creole seasonings are all popular here.

  1 cup chopped green pepper
  1/2 cup chopped onion
  3 tablespoons cooking oil
  2 cups fresh *or* frozen corn
  1-1/2 cups fresh sliced okra *or* 1 package (16 ounces) frozen okra
  3 medium tomatoes, peeled and chopped (about 1-1/2 cups)
  1 tablespoon tomato paste
  1/4 teaspoon dried thyme
Salt to taste
  1/4 teaspoon pepper
  1/2 teaspoon hot pepper sauce, optional

In a skillet, saute green pepper and onion in oil for 5 minutes. Add corn and okra; cook over medium heat for 10 minutes, stirring occasionally. Add tomatoes, tomato paste, thyme, salt, pepper and hot pepper sauce if desired; mix well. Cover and simmer for 3-5 minutes, stirring occasionally. **Yield:** 4-6 servings.

HERBED RICE

John Davis, Mobile, Alabama

Through the years, I've compiled quite a few recipes specifically for folks who cook for themselves. This nicely seasoned rice is a favorite.

✓ This tasty dish uses less sugar, salt and fat. Recipe includes *Diabetic Exchanges.*

  1/4 cup uncooked long grain rice
  1 green onion with top, cut into 1-inch pieces
  1 tablespoon butter *or* margarine
  1/8 teaspoon *each* dried tarragon, thyme, basil, parsley flakes and pepper
  1/2 cup chicken broth
Salt to taste, optional

In a small saucepan, cook rice and onion in butter until onion is tender. Add the seasonings; cook for 1 minute. Add broth and salt if desired; bring to a boil. Cover and simmer for 15 minutes or until liquid is absorbed and rice is tender. **Yield:** 1 serving. **Diabetic Exchanges:** One serving (prepared with

margarine and low-sodium broth and without salt) equals 2-1/2 starch, 2 fat; also, 284 calories, 129 mg sodium, 0 cholesterol, 39 gm carbohydrate, 5 gm protein, 12 gm fat.

ORANGE-KISSED BEETS

Bonnie Baumgardner, Sylva, North Carolina

(PICTURED AT RIGHT)

This is an original recipe I developed a few years ago. It's one of my husband's favorites.

   1/3 cup orange juice
   2 tablespoons brown sugar
   1 tablespoon butter *or* margarine
   1/2 teaspoon cornstarch
   1/8 teaspoon ground ginger
   1/8 teaspoon salt
   1/8 teaspoon pepper
   1 can (8-1/4 ounces) sliced beets, drained
   2 tablespoons golden raisins
Orange peel strips, optional

In a saucepan, combine orange juice, brown sugar, butter, cornstarch, ginger, salt and pepper. Cook and stir over medium heat until thickened. Add the beets and raisins; heat through. Garnish with orange peel if desired. **Yield:** 2 servings.

ASPARAGUS POLONAISE

Miriam Hershberger, Holmesville, Ohio

I found this recipe in our local newspaper, and it has been a family favorite ever since.

   3 slices white *or* whole wheat bread, crumbed
   1/4 cup butter *or* margarine
   1 hard-cooked egg, peeled and chopped
   1/2 cup chopped fresh parsley
   1/4 teaspoon salt
   2 pounds fresh asparagus, trimmed

In a skillet, saute bread crumbs in butter until golden. Stir in egg, parsley and salt. Meanwhile, cook asparagus in a small amount of water until crisp-tender; drain. Remove to a serving platter; top with crumb mixture. **Yield:** 8 servings.

QUICK BAKED BEANS

Connie Tiesenausen, Demmitt, Alberta

When I don't have time to make old-fashioned baked beans, I turn to this speedy variation. Folks are always delighted with the results.

   1 pound sliced bacon, diced

   1 large onion, chopped
   3 cans (28 ounces *each*) pork and beans, undrained
   1 cup barbecue sauce
   1/2 cup packed brown sugar
   1/3 cup prepared mustard

In a large skillet, cook bacon and onion until the bacon is crisp and the onion is tender; drain. Add remaining ingredients; simmer for 10 minutes. **Yield:** 10-12 servings.

SPICED POTATOES

Mary Fitch, Lakewood, Colorado

Red pepper flakes give a little "zip" to this buttery potato dish. It's especially good with fish.

   6 to 8 medium unpeeled red potatoes, thinly sliced
   1/2 cup butter *or* margarine, melted
   1 tablespoon dried oregano
   1 garlic clove, minced
   1/2 teaspoon crushed red pepper flakes

Place potatoes in an ungreased 11-in. x 7-in. x 2-in. baking dish. In a bowl, combine the butter, oregano, garlic and red pepper flakes; pour over potatoes. Bake, uncovered, at 450° for 25 minutes or until potatoes are tender, stirring every 10 minutes. **Yield:** 4-6 servings.

CAULIFLOWER AU GRATIN

Jacki Ricci, Ely, Nevada

(PICTURED BELOW)

This dish will make a vegetable lover out of anyone. Whenever I serve it, everyone just raves about it and asks for the recipe. Sometimes I'll substitute broccoli for all or half of the cauliflower, and it tastes just as good!

    1/2 cup chopped fully cooked ham
      1 to 2 garlic cloves, minced
      6 tablespoons butter *or* margarine
      1 head cauliflower, broken into florets
      2 tablespoons all-purpose flour
1-1/2 cups whipping cream
    1/4 teaspoon salt
Pepper to taste
Pinch cayenne pepper
1-1/2 cups (6 ounces) shredded Swiss cheese
      2 to 3 tablespoons minced fresh parsley

In a large skillet over medium heat, saute ham and garlic in butter for 2 minutes. Add cauliflower and cook just until crisp-tender. Combine flour and cream until smooth; stir into skillet and blend well. Add salt, pepper and cayenne. Bring to a boil; cook and stir for 2 minutes or until thickened and bubbly. Pour into a greased 2-qt. baking dish. Sprinkle with cheese. Broil 4 in. from the heat for 2-4 minutes or until lightly browned. Sprinkle with parsley. **Yield:** 6-8 servings.

SKILLET SQUASH AND POTATOES

Bonnie Milner, DeRidder, Louisiana

My niece suggested I try cooking squash and potatoes together. I found that potatoes really do enhance the flavor of squash.

      1 small potato, peeled and thinly sliced
    1/4 cup chopped onion
      1 tablespoon cooking oil
      1 small yellow summer squash, sliced
    1/4 teaspoon salt
    1/8 teaspoon pepper
Dash paprika

In a skillet over medium-low heat, cover and cook the potato and onion in oil for 12 minutes. Add squash; cook, uncovered, for 8-10 minutes or until vegetables are tender, stirring occasionally. Season with salt, pepper and paprika. **Yield:** 2 servings.

MINTY PEAS AND ONIONS

Santa D'Addario, Brooklyn, New York

(PICTURED ABOVE)

Mother could always rely on peas and onions when she was in a hurry and needed a quick side dish. Besides being easy to prepare, this dish was loved by everyone in our family.

✓ This tasty dish uses less sugar, salt and fat. Recipe includes *Diabetic Exchanges*.

> **2 large onions, cut into 1/2-inch wedges**
> **1/2 cup chopped sweet red pepper**
> **2 tablespoons cooking oil**
> **2 packages (16 ounces *each*) frozen peas**
> **2 tablespoons minced fresh mint *or* 2 teaspoons dried mint**

In a large skillet, saute onions and red pepper in oil until tender. Add peas; cook, uncovered, stirring occasionally, for 10 minutes or until heated through. Stir in mint and cook for 1 minute. **Yield:** 8 servings. **Diabetic Exchanges:** One serving equals 1 starch, 1 fat; also, 114 calories, 118 mg sodium, 0 cholesterol, 15 gm carbohydrate, 6 gm protein, 4 gm fat.

GERMAN-STYLE SPINACH

Joan Hutter, Warnick, Rhode Island

Grandma's spinach dish is flavored with her Austrian heritage. It's tasty and always looks so pretty on the plate. We children never had to be told to eat our spinach at Grandma's house!

> **2 packages (10 ounces *each*) frozen chopped spinach**
> **1 large onion, chopped**
> **2 garlic cloves, minced**
> **2 tablespoons butter *or* margarine**
> **6 bacon strips, cooked and crumbled**
> **1/2 teaspoon ground nutmeg**
> **1/2 teaspoon salt**
> **Pepper to taste**

Cook spinach according to package directions. Drain; set aside. In a large skillet, saute onion and garlic in butter until tender. Stir in the spinach, bacon, nutmeg, salt and pepper; heat through. **Yield:** 6-8 servings.

FRESH VEGETABLE KABOBS

Suzanne McKinley, Lyons, Georgia

These are quick and easy to prepare, and a fun way to eat vegetables—our kids love them! In summer, we like to put the kabobs on the grill.

> **2 medium ears fresh corn, cut into 2-inch pieces**
> **2 medium zucchini, cut into 1-inch pieces**
> **8 pearl onions *or* 1 package (8 ounces) pearl onions, cooked**
> **1/2 cup butter *or* margarine, melted**
> **2 tablespoons minced chives**
> **2 tablespoons minced fresh parsley**
> **1/2 teaspoon garlic salt**

Thread the corn, zucchini and onions alternately onto four large skewers. Combine butter, chives, parsley and garlic salt. Broil kabobs for 8-10 minutes, turning and brushing often with butter mixture. **Yield:** 4 servings.

CARROT-APPLE SIDE DISH

Martina Knowles, Grand Forks, North Dakota

(PICTURED ABOVE)

Pairing carrots and apples with sugar and spice gives this dish its mouth-watering appeal.

1-1/2 cups diced carrots (about 6 medium)
1/2 cup water
1 tablespoon butter *or* margarine
1/4 cup packed brown sugar
1 tablespoon lemon juice
1/8 teaspoon ground cinnamon
1 cup diced peeled apple
1 tablespoon cornstarch
2 tablespoons cold water

In a saucepan, cook carrots in water until crisp-tender; drain. Add butter, brown sugar, lemon juice and cinnamon; mix well. Stir in apple. Cover and simmer for 10 minutes, stirring occasionally. Combine cornstarch and cold water; stir into carrot mixture. Bring to a boil; cook and stir for 1 minute or until thickened. Simmer, uncovered, for 2 minutes or until glazed, stirring constantly. **Yield:** 4 servings.

CREAMED POTATOES

Mary Lewis, Memphis, Tennessee

We always had mashed potatoes with our traditional Sunday roast beef. The secret to making them light and fluffy is in the whipping!

3-1/2 to 4 pounds potatoes, peeled and quartered
1/4 cup butter *or* margarine
1 ounce cream cheese, softened
1/3 to 2/3 cup evaporated milk *or* whipping cream
Salt and pepper to taste

In a large saucepan, cook potatoes in boiling salted water until tender; drain. Add butter, cream cheese and 1/3 cup milk. Mash the potatoes, adding additional milk if needed. Season with salt and pepper. **Yield:** 8-10 servings.

BROCCOLI WITH RED PEPPER

Karen Davies, Wanipigow, Manitoba

The crisp snap of water chestnuts adds to the great taste of this colorful side dish.

✓ This tasty dish uses less sugar, salt and fat. Recipe includes *Diabetic Exchanges*.

4 cups broccoli florets
2 teaspoons minced fresh gingerroot or 1/2 teaspoon ground ginger
2 garlic cloves, minced
2 tablespoons cooking oil
1 medium sweet red pepper, julienned
1 can (8 ounces) sliced water chestnuts, drained

In a skillet, stir-fry broccoli, ginger and garlic in oil until broccoli is crisp-tender, about 2 minutes. Add red pepper and water chestnuts; stir-fry until heated through, about 1 minute. **Yield:** 4 servings. **Diabetic Exchanges:** One serving equals 2 vegetable, 1-1/2 fat; also, 117 calories, 28 mg sodium, 0 cholesterol, 17 gm carbohydrate, 3 gm protein, 7 gm fat.

CREAMY NOODLES AND CABBAGE

Gail Nero, Canton, Georgia

When the weather turns cooler, you can find me preparing this old-fashioned fare for my family. It's a comforting and delicious side dish.

- 1 small head cabbage, chopped (about 1 pound)
- 1 medium onion, chopped
- 1/4 teaspoon salt
- 1/4 teaspoon pepper
- 6 tablespoons butter *or* margarine
- 1 tablespoon all-purpose flour
- 2 cups half-and-half cream
- 1 package (12 ounces) noodles *or* fettuccine, cooked and drained
- 1 cup (4 ounces) shredded Parmesan cheese
- 1/2 cup crumbled cooked bacon

In a Dutch oven, saute cabbage, onion, salt and pepper in butter until vegetables are crisp-tender, about 10 minutes. Combine flour and cream until smooth. Add to vegetables; bring to a boil and boil for 1 minute. Stir in noodles and Parmesan cheese; heat through. Sprinkle with bacon. **Yield:** 10-12 servings.

TORTELLINI BAKE

Donald Roberts, Amherst, New Hampshire

(PICTURED BELOW)

Summer in New Hampshire brings plenty of fresh zucchini and squash…one year I had so much that I was searching for different ways to prepare it, and that's when I came up with this recipe.

- 1 small zucchini, diced
- 1 small yellow summer squash, diced
- 1 small onion, diced
- 1 medium sweet red pepper, diced
- 1 teaspoon dried basil
- 1/2 teaspoon salt
- 1/2 teaspoon pepper
- 1 tablespoon olive *or* vegetable oil
- 1 package (10 ounces) refrigerated cheese tortellini, cooked and drained
- 1 cup (4 ounces) shredded mozzarella cheese
- 1 cup half-and-half cream

In a skillet, saute zucchini, squash, onion, red pepper, basil, salt and pepper in oil until vegetables are crisp-tender. Transfer to a 1-1/2-qt. baking dish; stir in pasta, cheese and cream. Bake, uncovered, at 375° for 20 minutes or until heated through. **Yield:** 6-8 servings.

WESTERN BEANS

Catherine Skelton, Seligman, Missouri

Whenever we're invited to a potluck, I'm asked to bring this dish. I don't mind because it's so simple to make.

1-1/2 pounds ground beef
1/2 cup chopped onion
2 garlic cloves, minced
2 cans (16 ounces *each*) pork and beans, undrained
1/3 cup chopped dill pickle
1/3 cup chili sauce
1 teaspoon Worcestershire sauce
1 teaspoon salt
1/2 teaspoon pepper
1/8 teaspoon hot pepper sauce

In a Dutch oven over medium heat, brown beef, onion and garlic; drain. Add remaining ingredients and heat through. **Yield:** 10-12 servings.

HUSH PUPPIES

Mary McGuire, Graham, North Carolina

(PICTURED BELOW)

Mom is well known for her wonderful hush puppies. Her recipe is easy to prepare and gives tasty results. The onion adds to the great flavor.

1 cup yellow cornmeal
1/4 cup all-purpose flour
1-1/2 teaspoons baking powder
1/2 teaspoon salt
3/4 cup milk
1 egg, beaten
1 small onion, finely chopped
Oil for deep-fat frying

In a medium bowl, combine cornmeal, flour, baking powder and salt; mix well. Add the milk, egg and onion; stir just until moistened. In a deep-fat fryer or electric skillet, heat oil to 365°. Drop batter by teaspoonfuls into oil. Fry for 2 to 2-1/2 minutes or until golden brown. Drain on paper towels. **Yield:** 4-6 servings.

CREAMED ASPARAGUS AND TOMATO

Phyllis Clinehens, Maplewood, Ohio

Since asparagus freezes well, you can treat your family to this dish no matter what time of year.

2 pounds fresh asparagus, trimmed
1/3 cup mayonnaise *or* salad dressing
1-1/4 teaspoons lemon juice
1/4 teaspoon salt
Pinch pepper
1 medium tomato, peeled, seeded and diced

In a skillet, cook asparagus in boiling water until crisp-tender, about 6-8 minutes. Meanwhile, in a saucepan over low heat, combine mayonnaise, lemon juice, salt and pepper; heat through. Stir in tomato. Drain asparagus; place on a serving platter. Top with tomato mixture. **Yield:** 6-8 servings.

BROCCOLI-POTATO PANCAKES

Patty Kile, Greentown, Pennsylvania

I came up with this recipe by combining two recipes for broccoli and potato "latkes". These are easy to prepare and make a delicious side dish.

    1 cup fresh *or* frozen finely chopped
      broccoli
    1 cup boiling water
    3 eggs
    2 tablespoons all-purpose flour
    2 green onions, sliced
  1/2 teaspoon salt
  1/8 teaspoon pepper
    1 large uncooked potato, peeled and
      finely shredded
Cooking oil

In a bowl, combine broccoli and boiling water. Let stand for 5 minutes; drain thoroughly. In another bowl, beat eggs. Add flour, onions, salt and pepper; mix well. Add broccoli and potato. In a large skillet, heat 1/4 in. of oil over medium-high heat. Drop batter by 1/2 cupfuls into hot oil. Cook

until lightly browned on both sides. Drain on paper towels. **Yield:** 2 servings.

SKILLET ZUCCHINI AND SAUSAGE

LaBelle Doster, Vancouver, Washington

(PICTURED ABOVE)

I often turn to this dish when folks drop by because it takes little time to prepare. And judging by the requests I receive for the recipe, everyone seems to love it!

  1/2 pound fully cooked smoked Polish
      sausage, cut into 1/2-inch slices
    2 tablespoons cooking oil
    1 cup chopped onion
    1 cup sliced celery
  1/2 cup chopped green pepper
    1 garlic clove, minced
  1/2 teaspoon dried oregano
  1/2 teaspoon pepper
    4 to 5 medium zucchini, sliced
    4 to 5 medium tomatoes, coarsely chopped
Italian seasoning to taste

In a large skillet, lightly brown sausage in oil. Add onion, celery, green pepper, garlic, oregano and pepper. Cook and stir until vegetables are almost tender. Add zucchini and tomatoes; cook and stir until zucchini is just tender. Sprinkle with Italian seasoning. **Yield:** 8-10 servings.

PARSLEY POTATOES

Adeline Piscitelli, Sayreville, New Jersey

The fresh flavor of parsley is perfect with hot buttered potatoes. I used this recipe when I did all the cooking at the restaurant that we once ran, and customers loved it.

**2 pounds potatoes, peeled and cut into
2-inch pieces
1/2 cup butter *or* margarine, melted
1/4 cup minced fresh parsley
Salt and pepper to taste**

Place potatoes in a saucepan and cover with water. Bring to a boil and cook until tender; drain. Combine butter and parsley; pour over the potatoes and toss to coat. Season with salt and pepper. **Yield:** 6-8 servings.

ORANGE RICE PILAF

Joyce Sitz, Wichita, Kansas

(PICTURED BELOW)

This is a delicious and different way to prepare rice. I usually make this recipe when I have guests.

**1 cup diced celery
3 tablespoons chopped onion
1 tablespoon grated orange peel
1/4 cup butter *or* margarine
1/2 teaspoon salt
1-1/3 cups water
3 tablespoons orange juice
1-1/2 cups uncooked instant rice**

In a 3-qt. saucepan, saute celery, onion and orange peel in butter until tender. Add salt. Combine water and orange juice; add to celery mixture. Bring to a boil. Stir in the rice. Remove from the heat; cover and let stand for 10 minutes or until liquid is absorbed. Fluff with a fork. **Yield:** 4-6 servings.

APRICOT-GLAZED SWEET POTATOES

Joan Huggins, Waynesboro, Mississippi

I usually serve this side dish with poultry or pork. Its wonderful aroma always brings my family to the table extra hungry.

**3 pounds sweet potatoes, cooked, peeled
and sliced
1 cup packed brown sugar
5 teaspoons cornstarch
1/4 teaspoon salt
1/8 teaspoon ground cinnamon
1 cup apricot nectar
1/2 cup hot water
2 teaspoons grated orange peel
2 teaspoons butter *or* margarine
1/2 cup chopped pecans**

Place sweet potatoes in a greased 13-in. x 9-in. x 2-in. baking dish; set aside. In a saucepan, combine brown sugar, cornstarch, salt and cinnamon; stir in apricot nectar, water and orange peel. Bring to a boil; cook and stir for 2 minutes. Stir in butter and pecans. Pour over sweet potatoes. Bake, uncovered, at 350° for 20 minutes or until heated through. **Yield:** 8-10 servings.

FANCY BRUSSELS SPROUTS

Dorothy Anderson, Ottawa, Kansas

Parsley, sugar and crisp water chestnuts make the brussels sprouts fresh tasting and festive looking, especially for the holidays.

✓ This tasty dish uses less sugar, salt and fat. Recipe includes *Diabetic Exchanges*.

    1 cup water
1/4 cup minced fresh parsley
    1 teaspoon sugar
1/2 teaspoon salt, optional
    2 pints fresh brussels sprouts, halved *or*
    2 packages (10 ounces *each*) frozen
      brussels sprouts, thawed
    1 can (8 ounces) water chestnuts, drained
      and diced
    1 tablespoon butter *or* margarine

In a saucepan, combine water, parsley, sugar and salt if desired; bring to a boil over medium heat. Add brussels sprouts. Cover and simmer for 6-8 minutes or until tender; drain. Add water chestnuts and butter; heat through. **Yield:** 6 servings. **Diabetic Exchanges:** One serving (prepared with margarine and without salt) equals 2 vegetable, 1/2 fat; also, 67 calories, 34 mg sodium, 0 cholesterol, 11 gm carbohydrate, 3 gm protein, 2 gm fat.

HARVARD BEETS

Stella Quade, Carthage, Missouri

We grow beets in our own garden, and they're so good in this recipe. They have such a nice flavor and are very pretty when served.

    2 cans (15 ounces *each*) sliced beets
1/2 cup sugar
    1 tablespoon all-purpose flour
1/2 teaspoon salt
1/2 cup vinegar
    2 tablespoons butter *or* margarine

In a saucepan, cook beets until heated through. Drain, reserving 1/4 cup juice; set aside. In a 3-qt. saucepan, combine sugar, flour and salt. Stir in

vinegar and reserved beet juice until smooth. Bring to a boil; cook and stir for 2 minutes or until thickened. Add beets and butter; cook over low heat for 4-5 minutes or until heated through. **Yield:** 6-8 servings.

ASPARAGUS WITH BLUE CHEESE SAUCE

Leona Luecking, West Burlington, Iowa

(PICTURED ABOVE)

My sister introduced me to this recipe years ago because she knows I love blue cheese. I make this dish every spring when we have fresh home-grown asparagus.

1/2 pound fresh asparagus, trimmed
    2 ounces cream cheese, softened
    3 tablespoons evaporated milk *or*
      half-and-half cream
1/8 teaspoon salt
    1 to 2 tablespoons crumbled blue cheese

In a skillet, cook asparagus in a small amount of water until crisp-tender, about 6-8 minutes. Meanwhile, in a saucepan, cook and stir cream cheese, milk and salt over low heat until smooth. Stir in blue cheese and heat through. Drain asparagus; place on a serving platter. Top with blue cheese sauce. **Yield:** 2 servings.

> **LOSE THE LEAVES.** When purchasing root vegetables like carrots and beets with leaves attached, remove them as soon as you get home. These leaves draw moisture from the vegetable.

BREADED TOMATOES

Marion Stanley, Gilroy, California

(PICTURED ABOVE)

If we were lucky enough to have meat on Sunday, Mother would fix this side dish using Dad's garden-fresh tomatoes. The sauce adds a different and delicate flavor.

      8 to 10 medium firm tomatoes
      1 cup crushed saltines
      1 tablespoon grated Parmesan cheese
      1/2 cup butter *or* margarine, melted
CHEESE SAUCE:
      2 tablespoons butter *or* margarine
      2 tablespoons all-purpose flour
      1/4 teaspoon salt
Dash white pepper
1-1/2 cups milk
      3 tablespoons grated Parmesan cheese

Peel and core tomatoes. In a small bowl, combine saltine crumbs and Parmesan cheese. Dip each tomato in butter, then roll in the crumb mixture, gently pressing crumbs onto tomato. Arrange tomatoes in a single layer in a greased shallow baking dish. Sprinkle any remaining crumbs or butter over the tomatoes. Bake, uncovered, at 475° for 15 minutes or until tomatoes begin to brown and are heated through (watch closely). Meanwhile, for cheese sauce, melt butter in a medium saucepan. Stir in flour, salt and pepper. Add milk; cook and stir over medium heat for 2 minutes. Stir in Parmesan cheese. Serve over tomatoes. **Yield:** 8-10 servings.

MICROWAVE SPAGHETTI SQUASH

Lina Vainauskas, Shaw Air Force Base, South Carolina

One of the pleasant surprises about squash is that it's so low in calories. That means I can "splurge" a little with the other ingredients in the recipe. Spaghetti squash is fun to work with...and so "tender tasty"!

      1 spaghetti squash (about 1-1/2 pounds)
      1 medium sweet red pepper, thinly sliced
      1 small onion, thinly sliced
      2 garlic cloves, minced
      1 tablespoon olive *or* vegetable oil
      1 medium tomato, chopped
      1 medium zucchini, thinly sliced
      1 cup sliced fresh mushrooms
      1 tablespoon tarragon *or* cider vinegar
      1 teaspoon dried tarragon
1/2 teaspoon salt
1/4 teaspoon pepper

Pierce squash with a fork. Place on paper towel in microwave; cook on high for 6 minutes per pound or until squash is soft. Let stand for 5-10 minutes. Cut in half; remove seeds. Scoop out pulp and set aside. In a 2-qt. microwave-safe baking dish, toss red pepper, onion, garlic and oil. Cover and microwave on high for 2 minutes or until tender. Add remaining ingredients; cover and microwave on high for 3 minutes or until crisp-tender. Toss with squash. **Yield:** 6-8 servings. **Editor's Note:** This recipe was tested in a 700-watt microwave.

GARLIC PASTA

Sandi Pichon, Slidell, Louisiana

This is one of many recipes I acquired while living in France. It's a simple, tasty side dish.

>   1 whole garlic bulb, separated into cloves
>   and peeled
>   1/2 cup olive *or* vegetable oil
>   1/2 cup minced fresh parsley
>   1/4 cup chopped fresh oregano *or* 4
>   teaspoons dried oregano
>   1 teaspoon salt
>   1/4 teaspoon pepper
>   1 pound pasta, cooked and drained

In a large skillet over low heat, saute garlic in oil for 20 minutes or until golden brown. Remove from the heat; add parsley, oregano, salt and pepper. Toss with hot pasta. **Yield:** 4 servings.

GARDEN MEDLEY

Suzanne Pelegrin, Ocala, Florida

This dish complements any meal. Feel free to mix-and-match your favorite vegetables.

✓ This tasty dish uses less sugar, salt and fat. Recipe includes *Diabetic Exchanges*.

>   1 medium yellow summer squash
>   1 medium zucchini
>   1 medium onion, halved
>   1 medium green pepper
>   3 garlic cloves, minced
> 1-1/2 teaspoons minced fresh oregano *or*
>   1/2 teaspoon dried oregano
> 1-1/2 teaspoons minced fresh basil *or*
>   1/2 teaspoon dried basil
>   1/2 cup chicken broth
>   2 cups cherry tomatoes, halved

Cut vegetables into 2-in. x 1/2-in. strips. In a skillet or wok over medium heat, cook and stir the vegetables, garlic, oregano and basil in broth until vegetables are crisp-tender, about 7 minutes. Add tomatoes; heat through. **Yield:** 8 servings. **Diabetic Exchanges:** One serving (prepared with low-sodium broth) equals 1-1/2 vegetable; also, 36 calories, 11 mg sodium, 0 cholesterol, 8 gm carbohydrate, 2 gm protein, trace fat.

FIVE-VEGETABLE SKILLET

Julia Trachsel, Victoria, British Columbia

(PICTURED BELOW)

This is a vegetable dish that I enjoyed as a child and still remember with pleasure. It's a hearty complement to most entrees.

>   6 cups water
>   2 teaspoons salt, *divided*
>   1 pound fresh green beans, cut into 1-inch
>   pieces
>   6 medium carrots, cut into 1-inch pieces
>   3 medium potatoes, peeled and quartered
>   2 cups fresh *or* frozen peas
>   1 cup fresh *or* frozen corn
>   2 cups whipping cream
>   6 tablespoons butter *or* margarine
>   2 tablespoons minced chives
>   1/2 teaspoon pepper
>   1/4 teaspoon paprika

In a large saucepan or Dutch oven, bring water and 1 teaspoon salt to a boil. Add beans, carrots, and potatoes; cook for 15 minutes. Add peas and corn; cook 3-5 minutes longer or until tender. Drain, reserving 2 cups liquid. Set vegetables aside. In the same pan, combine reserved liquid, cream, butter, chives, pepper, paprika and remaining salt. Add vegetables and heat through. **Yield:** 8-10 servings.

SWEET-AND-SOUR RED CABBAGE

Barbara White, Cross Plains, Wisconsin

I helped Mother shred the cabbage and cut up the apples for this recipe. This is one part of the meal that is even tastier if it can be made ahead.

    1 cup water
1/4 cup packed brown sugar
    3 tablespoons vinegar
    2 tablespoons bacon drippings *or*
        cooking oil
1/4 teaspoon salt
Dash pepper
    4 cups shredded red cabbage
    2 medium tart apples, peeled and sliced

In a large skillet, combine water, brown sugar, vinegar, drippings, salt and pepper. Cook for 2-3 minutes or until hot, stirring occasionally. Add cabbage; cover and cook over medium-low heat for 10 minutes, stirring occasionally. Add apples; cook, uncovered, for 10 minutes or until tender, stirring occasionally. **Yield:** 6-8 servings.

GRILLED MUSHROOMS

Melanie Knoll, Marshalltown, Iowa

(PICTURED BELOW)

Mushrooms cooked over hot coals always taste good, but this easy recipe makes the mushrooms

taste fantastic. I love to spend time outdoors and cook entire meals on the grill.

1/2 pound medium fresh mushrooms
1/4 cup butter *or* margarine, melted
1/2 teaspoon dill weed
1/2 teaspoon garlic salt

Thread mushrooms onto skewers. Combine butter, dill and garlic salt; brush over mushrooms. Grill over hot coals for 10-15 mintues, basting and turning every 5 minutes. **Yield:** 4 servings.

PARSNIP SAUTE

Janice Van Wassehnova, South Rockwood, Michigan

Even folks who turn up their noses at parsnips come running to the kitchen when they smell the aroma of this special saute.

    3 large parsnips, peeled and diced
1/2 cup diced carrot
1/2 cup sliced celery
1/2 cup diced onion
    2 tablespoons butter *or* margarine
3/4 teaspoon salt
1/8 teaspoon pepper

Place parsnips in a saucepan and cover with water. Bring to a boil and cook until crisp-tender. Meanwhile, in a skillet, saute carrot, celery and onion in butter until crisp-tender, about 6 minutes. Drain parsnips; add to carrot mixture. Add salt and pepper. Cook and stir for 4 minutes or until vegetables are tender. **Yield:** 6 servings.

HERBED GREEN BEANS

Bernice Morris, Marshfield, Missouri

The herb butter makes this green bean side dish so pleasant. I like to serve it with a ham dinner.

✓ This tasty dish uses less sugar, salt and fat. Recipe includes *Diabetic Exchanges*.

1-1/2 pounds fresh green beans
1/2 cup finely chopped onion
    2 tablespoons butter *or* margarine
    3 tablespoons lemon juice
    1 tablespoon minced fresh parsley
1-1/2 teaspoons chopped fresh thyme *or* 1/2
        teaspoon dried thyme
    1 teaspoon salt, optional
1/4 teaspoon paprika

In a saucepan, cover beans with water; cook until crisp-tender. Meanwhile, in a skillet, saute onion in butter until tender. Add lemon juice, parsley, thyme, salt if desired and paprika. Drain beans;

add herb butter and stir to coat. **Yield:** 6 servings. **Diabetic Exchanges:** One serving (prepared with margarine and without salt) equals 1 vegetable, 1 fat; also, 76 calories, 42 mg sodium, 0 cholesterol, 10 gm carbohydrate, 2 gm protein, 4 gm fat.

GARLIC MASHED POTATOES

Myra Innes, Auburn, Kansas

People who try these potatoes say they rival varieties served at restaurants.

    6 medium potatoes, peeled and quartered
    4 to 5 garlic cloves, peeled
    5 cups water
    2 tablespoons olive *or* vegetable oil
    1/2 to 1 teaspoon salt
Pinch pepper

In a saucepan, bring potatoes, garlic and water to a boil. Reduce heat; cover and cook for 20 minutes or until potatoes are tender. Drain, reserving 2/3 cup cooking liquid. Mash the potatoes. Add oil, salt, pepper and reserved liquid; stir until smooth. **Yield:** 4-6 servings.

COPPER CARROTS

Billie Scoggins, Long Beach, Mississippi

When I prepare this delicious carrot recipe, I'm reminded of a fabulous church supper our family attended back in 1942, where this was one of the side dishes served.

    3 medium carrots, julienned
    2 teaspoons sugar
    1/2 teaspoon cornstarch

    1/4 teaspoon salt
    1/8 teaspoon ground ginger
    2 tablespoons orange juice
    1 tablespoon butter *or* margarine
Minced fresh parsley, optional

In a small saucepan, cook carrots in water until crisp-tender; drain. Remove carrots; set aside and keep warm. In the same saucepan, combine sugar, cornstarch, salt and ginger. Gradually stir in orange juice; bring to a boil. Cook and stir for 2 minutes. Add butter. Return carrots to pan and heat through. Sprinkle with parsley if desired. **Yield:** 2 servings.

CORN FRITTERS

Auton Miller, Piney Flats, Tennessee

(PICTURED ABOVE)

During the Depression, we made do with what we had. Mother always looked for ways to add variety to our meals, and these corn fritters were her special treat.

    1/3 cup all-purpose flour
    1/8 teaspoon salt
    1/4 teaspoon baking powder
    1/4 teaspoon paprika
    1 egg, *separated*
    3/4 cup frozen corn, thawed
Oil for deep-fat frying

In a bowl, combine flour, salt, baking powder and paprika. In another bowl, beat egg yolk; stir in corn. Add to flour mixture and mix well. Beat egg white until soft peaks form; fold into flour mixture. In a deep-fat fryer or electric skillet, heat oil to 375°. Drop batter by heaping tablespoonfuls into oil; fry for 3-4 minutes or until golden brown. Drain on paper towels. **Yield:** 2-4 servings.

ONION POTATO PANCAKES

Joan Hutter, Warnick, Rhode Island

(PICTURED ABOVE)

When Grandma prepared potato pancakes, she used an old-fashioned grater, great for potatoes but not for knuckles! With homemade apple-sauce, this side dish complements a meal so well.

> 2 eggs
> 1 medium onion, quartered
> 2 tablespoons all-purpose flour
> 3/4 teaspoon salt
> 1/4 teaspoon pepper
> 1/4 teaspoon baking powder
> 4 medium potatoes (about 1-1/2 pounds), peeled and cubed
> 2 tablespoons minced fresh parsley
> 3 to 4 tablespoons cooking oil

In a blender or food processor, place the eggs, onion, flour, salt, pepper, baking powder and 1/2 cup of potatoes. Cover and process on high until smooth. Add parsley and remaining potatoes; cover and pulse 2-4 times until potatoes are chopped. Pour 1 to 2 tablespoons oil onto a hot griddle or skillet. Pour batter by 1/3 cupfuls onto griddle; flatten slightly to a 4-in. to 5-in. diameter. Cook until golden on both sides, adding oil as needed. **Yield:** 6-8 servings (12 pancakes).

SWEET POTATO BALLS

Lois Hoof, Houston, Texas

My mother would serve these sweet potato balls at Thanksgiving. As I recall, she always had to double the recipe!

> 2 cups cold mashed sweet potatoes
> 1 egg
> 4 tablespoons butter *or* margarine, melted, *divided*
> 1 tablespoon whipping cream
> 1/2 teaspoon salt
> 1/4 teaspoon ground nutmeg
> 6 to 8 marshmallows
> 1-1/2 cups crushed cornflakes

Mix sweet potatoes, egg, 2 tablespoons butter, cream, salt and nutmeg. Divide into six to eight portions; shape each into a ball around a marshmallow. Dip in remaining butter, then roll in cornflakes. Place in a greased 9-in. pie plate. Bake at 400° for 15 minutes. **Yield:** 6-8 servings.

CREAMY CABBAGE

Alice Lewis, Los Osos, California

This recipe, which was handed down to me from my grandmother, has been happily received at potluck suppers.

4 cups shredded cabbage
1/2 cup diced bacon
1 tablespoon all-purpose flour
1/2 teaspoon salt
1/4 teaspoon paprika
1/8 teaspoon pepper
1 cup milk
1 cup soft bread crumbs

In a 3-qt. saucepan, cook cabbage for 7 minutes in boiling water; drain. In a skillet, cook bacon until crisp. Drain, reserving 1 tablespoon drippings. Add flour, salt, paprika and pepper to drippings. Gradually add milk; cook and stir for 2 minutes or until thickened. Place cabbage in a 1-qt. casserole. Top with sauce. Sprinkle crumbs and bacon on top. Bake, uncovered, at 400° for 15 minutes. **Yield:** 4 servings.

GREEN BEAN MEDLEY

Janice Cox, Smithfield, Kentucky

My family looks forward to summer because that's when I prepare this much-requested recipe with fresh green beans from our garden.

✓ This tasty dish uses less sugar, salt and fat. Recipe includes *Diabetic Exchanges*.

1-1/2 pounds fresh green beans, halved
2 medium carrots, cut into 2-inch strips
1 medium onion, cut into rings
1 celery rib, sliced
1 cup water
2 to 3 tablespoons minced fresh savory
  ***or* 2 to 3 teaspoons dried savory**
1 teaspoon salt, optional
1/8 teaspoon pepper

In a large saucepan, combine all ingredients; bring to a boil. Reduce heat; cover and simmer for 5-10 minutes or until vegetables are tender, stirring occasionally. Remove to a serving bowl with a slotted spoon. **Yield:** 6 servings. **Diabetic Exchanges:** One serving (prepared without salt) equals 1-1/2 vegetable; also, 41 calories, 20 mg sodium, 0 cholesterol, 9 gm carbohydrate, 2 gm protein, trace fat.

SQUASH AND BROCCOLI STIR-FRY

Erlene Cornelius, Spring City, Tennessee

(PICTURED AT RIGHT)

The first summer that my husband and I were retired, we had an abundance of squash. I was raised on a farm and taught nothing should go to waste, so I hunted in my recipe file and found this one. I've made it often ever since.

✓ This tasty dish uses less sugar, salt and fat. Recipe includes *Diabetic Exchanges*.

1 tablespoon lemon juice
2 teaspoons honey
1 pound butternut squash, peeled, seeded and cut into 1/4-inch slices
1 garlic clove, minced
1/4 teaspoon ground ginger
2 tablespoons cooking oil
1 cup broccoli florets
1/2 cup sliced celery
1/2 cup thinly sliced onion
2 tablespoons sunflower seeds

Combine lemon juice and honey; set aside. In a large skillet, saute squash, garlic and ginger in oil for 3 minutes. Add the broccoli, celery and onion; cook 3-4 minutes longer or until vegetables are crisp-tender. Add the honey mixture and toss; sprinkle with sunflower seeds. **Yield:** 6 servings. **Diabetic Exchanges:** One serving equals 2 vegetable, 1-1/2 fat; also, 113 calories, 20 mg sodium, 0 cholesterol, 13 gm carbohydrate, 2 gm protein, 7 gm fat.

Short & Sweet Treats

OATMEAL RAISIN COOKIES

Wendy Coalwell, Abbeville, Georgia

(PICTURED AT RIGHT)

I was given this recipe by a dear friend. The secret is to measure exactly (no guessing on the amounts) and to bake for the time indicated.

- 1/2 cup shortening
- 1/2 cup packed brown sugar
- 1/2 cup sugar
- 1 egg
- 1/2 teaspoon vanilla extract
- 1-1/4 cups all-purpose flour
- 1 cup rolled oats
- 1 teaspoon baking soda
- 1/2 teaspoon salt
- 1/2 cup raisins
- 1/2 cup coarsely chopped pecans, optional

In a large mixing bowl, cream shortening and sugars. Add egg and vanilla; mix well. Combine flour, oats, baking soda and salt; add to creamed mixture. Stir in raisins and pecans if desired. Shape into 1-in. balls. Place on ungreased baking sheets; flatten with a spoon. Bake at 350° for 10-11 minutes or until golden brown. Do not overbake. Remove to wire racks to cool. **Yield:** about 3 dozen.

HOT APPLE SUNDAES

Betty Matthews, South Haven, Michigan

(PICTURED AT RIGHT)

These sundaes have wonderful fall flavor and are a perfect way to round out a menu—economically.

- 1/2 cup sugar
- 1/2 cup orange juice
- 1/4 cup lemon juice
- 1/2 teaspoon ground cinnamon
- 5 cups sliced peeled apples
- 5 cups vanilla ice cream
- Additional cinnamon, optional

In a saucepan over medium heat, bring sugar, juices and cinnamon to a boil. Reduce heat; sim-

mer, uncovered, for 5 minutes. Add apples and return to a boil. Reduce heat; cover and simmer for 10 minutes or until the apples are tender. Serve warm over ice cream. Sprinkle with cinnamon if desired. **Yield:** 5 servings (2-1/2 cups topping).

STRAWBERRY SHORTCAKE

Sue Gronholz, Columbus, Wisconsin

(PICTURED AT RIGHT)

This recipe is special to me because it's my grandma's. It's the first thing I bake when my strawberries ripen in spring.

✓ This tasty dish uses less sugar, salt and fat. Recipe includes *Diabetic Exchanges*.

- 2 cups all-purpose flour
- 2 tablespoons sugar
- 4 teaspoons baking powder
- 1/2 teaspoon salt
- 1/2 teaspoon cream of tartar
- 1/2 cup cold butter *or* margarine
- 1 egg
- 2/3 cup milk
- 2 pints fresh strawberries, sliced
- Whipped cream, optional

In a bowl, combine flour, sugar, baking powder, salt and cream of tartar. Cut in butter until mixture resembles coarse crumbs. Beat egg and milk; stir into flour mixture just until moistened. Spread into a greased 8-in. square baking pan. Bake at 375° for 20-25 minutes. Cut into squares; top with strawberries and whipped cream if desired. **Yield:** 9 servings. **Diabetic Exchanges:** One serving (prepared with margarine and skim milk and served without whipped cream) equals 2 fat, 1-3/4 starch; also, 217 calories, 436 mg sodium, 24 mg cholesterol, 27 gm carbohydrate, 5 gm protein, 11 gm fat.

> **FANTASTIC FINALES.** *Pictured at right, clockwise from top: Oatmeal Raisin Cookies, Hot Apple Sundaes, Strawberry Shortcake (recipes on this page) and One-Bowl Brownies (recipe on page 188).*

One-Bowl Brownies

Becky Albright, Norwalk, Ohio

(PICTURED ON PAGE 187)

There's no brownie recipe or mix I've ever tried that tastes better than this! Besides, you can mix it in one bowl in just a few minutes. My husband's grandmother passed the recipe on; now our son makes these brownies for after-school snacks.

    2 cups sugar
1-1/3 cups all-purpose flour
  3/4 cup baking cocoa
    1 teaspoon baking powder
  1/2 teaspoon salt
  1/2 cup chopped nuts
  2/3 cup vegetable oil
    4 eggs, beaten
    2 teaspoons vanilla extract

In a large bowl, combine sugar, flour, cocoa, baking powder, salt and nuts. Add oil, eggs and vanilla; stir just until moistened. Do not overmix. Spread in a greased 13-in. x 9-in. x 2-in. baking pan. Bake at 350° for 20-25 minutes or until a toothpick inserted near the center comes out clean. **Yield:** 2 to 2-1/2 dozen.

Coconut Macaroons

Penny Ann Habeck, Shawano, Wisconsin

(PICTURED BELOW)

These cookies earned me a first-place ribbon at the county fair. Whenever I make them to give away, my husband always asks me where his batch is!

1-1/3 cups flaked coconut
  1/3 cup sugar
    2 tablespoons all-purpose flour
  1/8 teaspoon salt
    2 egg whites
  1/2 teaspoon vanilla extract

In a small bowl, combine coconut, sugar, flour and salt. Stir in egg whites and vanilla; mix well. Drop by rounded teaspoonfuls onto greased baking sheets. Bake at 325° for 18-20 minutes or until golden brown. Cool on wire racks. **Yield:** about 1-1/2 dozen.

Candy Bar Pie

Rosalind Hamilton, Iowa, Louisiana

This is the recipe I reach for when I just can't wait to satisfy a craving for something oh-so-chocolaty!

    6 chocolate bars with almonds (1.45 ounces *each*)
    1 carton (8 ounces) frozen whipped topping, thawed
    1 tablespoon vanilla extract
    1 graham cracker crust (9 inches)
Grated semisweet chocolate, optional

In a double boiler or microwave oven, melt chocolate bars. Fold the whipped topping into chocolate. Stir in vanilla. Spoon into pie crust; garnish with

grated chocolate if desired. Chill until ready to serve. **Yield:** 6-8 servings.

CHOCOLATE CRUNCHIES

Vanessa Pieper, Bradford, Vermont

Mother used to make these candies when I was young, using Grandmother's recipe. Now my daughters make them...with delicious results!

> 2 cups (12 ounces) semisweet chocolate chips
> 2 cups (12 ounces) butterscotch chips
> 1/2 teaspoon vanilla extract
> 3 cups chow mein noodles

In the top of a double boiler over simmering water, melt chips and vanilla; stir until smooth. Fold in noodles. Drop by teaspoonfuls onto waxed paper. Cool. **Yield:** 2-1/2 dozen.

BUTTERSCOTCH PUDDING

Audrey Wall, Industry, Pennsylvania

Everyone always raves how much better this pudding tastes than the kind you make from a box.

> 1 cup packed dark brown sugar
> 1/4 cup all-purpose flour
> 2 cups milk
> 2 eggs
> 1/8 teaspoon salt
> 1 teaspoon vanilla extract

In a saucepan, combine sugar, flour, milk, eggs and salt. Cook over medium heat, stirring constantly,

for 2 minutes or until thickened. Remove from the heat; stir in vanilla. **Yield:** 4 servings.

BLUEBERRY SLUMP

Eleanore Ebeling, Brewster, Minnesota

(PICTURED ABOVE)

My mother-in-law used to make slump with wild blueberries and serve it warm with a pitcher of farm cream on the table.

> 3 cups fresh *or* frozen blueberries
> 1-1/4 cups water
> 1/2 cup sugar
> 1 tablespoon lemon juice
> 1 teaspoon finely grated lemon peel
> 1 cup all-purpose flour
> 2 tablespoons sugar
> 2 teaspoons baking powder
> 1/2 teaspoon salt
> 1 tablespoon cold butter *or* margarine
> 1/2 cup milk
> Cream *or* whipped cream, optional

In a large saucepan, combine blueberries, water, sugar, lemon juice and peel; bring to a boil. Reduce heat and simmer, uncovered, for 5 minutes. Meanwhile, combine flour, sugar, baking powder and salt; cut in butter until mixture resembles coarse crumbs. Add milk, mixing just until moistened. Drop six spoonfuls onto the simmering berries. Cover and cook over low heat for 10 minutes. Do not lift lid. Spoon dumplings into individual serving bowls and spoon some sauce over each. Serve warm with cream or whipped cream if desired. **Yield:** 6 servings.

1 can (14 ounces) sweetened condensed
  milk
1 cup cold water
1 cup whipping cream, whipped
Additional whipped cream, optional

In a large mixing bowl, combine pudding mix, milk and water. Beat until well mixed. Chill for 5 minutes. Fold in whipped cream. Spoon into individual serving dishes. Garnish with whipped cream if desired. **Yield:** 4-6 servings.

HAZELNUT CHOCOLATE CHIP COOKIES

Mrs. Selmer Looney, Eugene, Oregon

(PICTURED ON FRONT COVER)

Oregon has an abundance of nuts, and these nutty cookies are popular with the ladies at my craft club. I grew up during the Depression, and my mother taught us to use what was available and said, "It doesn't have to be expensive to be good." She was right!

1 cup butter *or* margarine, softened
1 cup packed brown sugar
1/2 cup sugar
2 eggs
1 teaspoon vanilla extract
2-1/3 cups all-purpose flour
1 teaspoon baking soda
1/2 teaspoon salt
1 cup (6 ounces) semisweet chocolate chips
3/4 cup chopped hazelnuts

In a large mixing bowl, cream butter and sugars. Add eggs, one at a time, beating well after each addition. Add vanilla. Combine flour, baking soda and salt; stir into creamed mixture. Fold in chips and nuts. Drop by heaping tablespoonfuls 3 in. apart onto ungreased baking sheets. Bake at 375° for 10-12 minutes or until light brown. Remove to a wire rack to cool. **Yield:** 3 dozen.

MARSHMALLOW DELIGHTS

Diane Hixon, Niceville, Florida

When you bake these snacks, the marshmallow inside disappears and creates a gooey, yummy cinnamon roll. They're so easy!

1 tube (8 ounces) refrigerated crescent
  rolls
1/4 cup sugar
1 tablespoon ground cinnamon
8 large marshmallows
1/4 cup butter *or* margarine, melted

QUICK AMBROSIA

Eleanor Lock, Escondido, California

(PICTURED ABOVE)

This dessert has become a favorite for many of our family's meals. Fruit is a refreshing finale.

1/4 cup flaked coconut, toasted
2 tablespoons confectioners' sugar
1 medium orange, peeled and sectioned
1 medium firm banana, sliced
1/4 cup orange juice
Maraschino cherries, optional

Combine coconut and sugar. Divide orange and banana between two bowls; pour juice over fruit. Sprinkle with coconut mixture. Garnish with cherries if desired. **Yield:** 2 servings.

CHOCOLATE MOUSSE

Elsie Shell, Topeka, Indiana

This recipe is especially convenient when unexpected guests arrive. It's so easy to whip up and looks pretty with a mint leaf garnish.

1 package (3.9 ounces) instant chocolate
  pudding mix

Separate rolls into eight triangles. Combine sugar and cinnamon. Dip each marshmallow into butter, roll in cinnamon-sugar and place on a triangle. Pinch dough around marshmallow, sealing all edges. Dip tops of dough into the remaining butter and cinnamon-sugar. Place with sugar side up in greased muffin cups. Bake at 375° for 13-15 minutes. **Yield:** 8 servings.

RASPBERRY TRIFLE

Marcy Cella, L'Anse, Michigan

(PICTURED BELOW)

Beautiful and luscious, this trifle is an impressive way to use your fresh raspberries. Plus, with purchased pound cake or ladyfingers, it's nice and easy to prepare—your guests will never know!

1 package (16 ounces) pound cake, cut into 18 slices *or* 2 packages (3 ounces *each*) ladyfingers
2 packages (3.4 ounces *each*) instant vanilla pudding mix
1 jar (18 ounces) raspberry jam
1-1/2 pints fresh raspberries
Whipped cream and additional raspberries

Arrange one-third of the cake slices on the bottom of a trifle dish or large decorative bowl. Prepare pudding according to package directions. Place another third of the cake slices around the inside of bowl, using half of the pudding to hold them in place. Gently combine jam and raspberries; spoon half over the pudding. Layer with remaining cake, pudding and raspberry mixture. Chill. Garnish with whipped cream and additional raspberries. **Yield:** 8-10 servings.

CHOCOLATE PEANUT BUTTER PIE

Carole Taylor, Mason City, Iowa

One of the best things about this pie is that I don't have to turn on the oven. It's a hit each summer.

1 package (3.9 ounces) instant chocolate pudding mix
1-3/4 cups cold milk
1 chocolate crumb crust (8 to 9 inches)
2 cups whipped topping
2 packages (1.6 ounces *each*) peanut butter cups, crumbled

In a mixing bowl, beat pudding and milk until blended, about 2 minutes. Pour into crust. Refrigerate for 20 minutes or until thickened. Cover with whipped topping; sprinkle with peanut butter cups. **Yield:** 6-8 servings.

PEACHY DESSERT SAUCE

Helene Belanger, Denver, Colorado

(PICTURED BELOW)

We love this pretty peach sauce over ice cream and also served on angel food cake. It's delicious.

1 teaspoon cornstarch
1/4 cup water
2 tablespoons apricot jam *or* preserves
1-1/2 teaspoons sugar
1/2 teaspoon lemon juice
3/4 cup sliced fresh *or* canned peaches
Vanilla ice cream
Fresh mint, optional

In a small saucepan, mix cornstarch and water until smooth. Add jam, sugar and lemon juice; bring to a boil. Cook and stir for 1-2 minutes; reduce heat. Add peaches; heat through. Serve over ice cream. Garnish with mint if desired. **Yield:** 3/4 cup.

RASPBERRY DUMPLINGS

Jeanette Redman, Newark, Ohio

These scrumptious dumplings are very easy to fix. I like to prepare them just before a meal and then set them aside to be served warm for dessert. They're good cold, too!

1 quart fresh *or* frozen raspberries
1 cup sugar
1 cup water

3 tablespoons cornstarch
3 cups biscuit/baking mix
1/4 cup sugar
1 cup milk
Additional sugar and ground nutmeg, optional

In a 6-qt. kettle, combine raspberries, sugar, water and cornstarch; stir to blend. Bring to a boil, stirring often. Reduce heat. Meanwhile, combine biscuit mix and sugar; stir in milk just until moistened. Drop by spoonfuls onto boiling berries. Cook over low heat, uncovered, for 10 minutes; cover. Cook 10-15 minutes longer or until dumplings test done. Sprinkle with sugar and nutmeg if desired. **Yield:** 10 servings.

CRISPY COCONUT BALLS

Elaine Wilkins, Jasper, Alabama

For satisfying a sweet tooth, these light bite-size snacks are our favorite on-the-road treats.

1/4 cup butter *or* margarine
40 large marshmallows *or* 4 cups miniature marshmallows
5 cups crisp rice cereal
1 cup flaked coconut

Melt butter in a saucepan over low heat. Add the marshmallows and cook, stirring constantly, until melted. Remove from the heat; stir in cereal until well coated. With buttered hands, shape mixture into 1-in. balls. Roll in coconut, pressing gently to coat. **Yield:** about 3 dozen.

WHITE CHRISTMAS CANDY

Carol Hammond, Helena, Alabama

(PICTURED ABOVE)

During the holiday season several years ago, my husband brought this wonderful candy home from work. The co-worker who'd shared it graciously included the recipe...and I've been making it ever since.

2 pounds white confectionery coating*, cut into small chunks
1/2 pound crushed candy canes *or* crushed peppermint candies

Melt confectionery coating over medium-low heat, stirring until smooth. Stir in candy. Spread on waxed paper-lined baking sheets; refrigerate for 8-10 minutes. Break into small pieces; store in airtight containers. **Yield:** 2-1/2 pounds. ***Editor's Note:** White confectionery coating is found in the baking section of most grocery stores. It is sometimes labeled "almond bark" or "candy coating" and is often sold in bulk packages of 1 to 1-1/2 pounds.

SCRUMPTIOUS S'MORES

Anne Sherman, Orangeburg, South Carolina

This dessert takes everyone back to their childhood. You can make them in advance, then wrap in plastic wrap and store at room temperature.

8 ounces semisweet chocolate
1 can (14 ounces) sweetened condensed milk
1 teaspoon vanilla extract
1 package (16 ounces) graham crackers
2 cups miniature marshmallows

In a heavy saucepan, melt chocolate over low heat. Stir in milk and vanilla; cook and stir until smooth. For each dessert, spread 1 tablespoon chocolate mixture on two whole graham crackers. Place 5-6 marshmallows on one cracker; top with second cracker. Gently press together. Repeat. **Yield:** 16 servings.

RASPBERRY-LIME PIE

Jane Zempel, Midland, Michigan

This refreshing pie was an immediate hit when I first served it. It's a slightly tart dessert we enjoy in warm weather.

1 can (14 ounces) sweetened condensed milk
1/2 cup lime juice
1 carton (8 ounces) frozen whipped topping, thawed
Few drops red food coloring, optional
1 cup fresh raspberries
1 graham cracker crust (9 inches)
Additional raspberries and fresh mint, optional

In a bowl, combine milk and lime juice (mixture will begin to thicken). Fold in whipped topping, food coloring if desired and raspberries. Pour into pie crust; chill. Garnish with raspberries and mint if desired. **Yield:** 8 servings.

RAISIN CUSTARD PIE

Ruth Ann Stelfox, Raymond, Alberta

(PICTURED ABOVE)

A comforting, old-fashioned dessert, this custard pie is one of my mom's best. The fluffy meringue makes it look so special, and the raisins are a nice surprise.

1/2 cup sugar
3 tablespoons cornstarch
3 egg yolks, beaten
2 cups milk
1/2 cup raisins
2 teaspoons lemon juice
1 pastry shell (9 inches), baked
MERINGUE:
3 egg whites
1/4 cup sugar

In a saucepan, combine sugar and cornstarch. Whisk in the egg yolks and milk. Cook over medium heat, stirring constantly, until mixture comes to boil; boil for 1 minute. Add raisins and lemon juice. Pour into pie shell. For meringue, beat egg whites until foamy. Gradually add sugar, beating until stiff and glossy. Spread over hot filling, sealing to edges. Bake at 350° for 10-15 minutes or until light brown. Store leftovers in the refrigerator. **Yield:** 8 servings.

RHUBARB COCONUT COOKIES

Betty Claycomb, Alverton, Pennsylvania

At our garden club fund-raiser, each group within the club serves a different kind of food. These cookies are made by the "rhubarb group"...and they are always the first to sell out!

1/2 cup shortening
1-1/3 cups packed brown sugar
1 egg
2 cups all-purpose flour

1 teaspoon ground cinnamon
1/2 teaspoon baking soda
1/2 teaspoon ground cloves
1/2 teaspoon ground nutmeg
1/2 teaspoon salt
1/4 cup milk
1 cup finely diced rhubarb
1 cup chopped pecans *or* walnuts
1 cup raisins
1/2 cup flaked coconut

In a mixing bowl, cream shortening and brown sugar. Add egg; beat well. Combine dry ingredients. Add to the creamed mixture alternately with milk and mix well. Stir in rhubarb, nuts, raisins and coconut. Drop by tablespoonfuls onto greased baking sheets. Bake at 375° for 12-15 minutes or until golden. Cool on wire racks. **Yield:** 3 dozen.

APPLE-HONEY TAPIOCA PUDDING

Amy Kraemer, Glencoe, Minnesota

I'm glad that apple season is long, since my family requests this pudding quite often!

4 large tart apples, peeled and cut into 1-inch slices
3/4 cup honey
3 tablespoons butter *or* margarine
1 tablespoon lemon juice
1/2 teaspoon salt
1/2 teaspoon ground cinnamon
1/3 cup quick-cooking tapioca

2-1/2 cups water
Ice cream

In a saucepan, combine the first six ingredients. Cover and simmer just until apples are tender. Using a slotted spoon, remove apples to a bowl. Add tapioca and water to saucepan. Cook and stir until thickened and clear; pour over apples. Serve with ice cream. **Yield:** 6 servings.

FUDGE SUNDAES

Tammy Mackie, Seward, Nebraska

(PICTURED BELOW)

My father-in-law introduced this recipe to the family. The fudgy sauce has a nice flavor and is a special favorite of our four children.

2 cups (12 ounces) semisweet chocolate chips
2 squares (1 ounce *each*) unsweetened chocolate
1 cup whipping cream
1/4 cup cold coffee
Dash salt
1 teaspoon vanilla extract
Ice cream
Maraschino cherries, optional

In a medium saucepan, combine the first five ingredients. Heat on low, stirring constantly, until chocolate is melted. Remove from the heat; stir in vanilla. Serve over ice cream. Top with a cherry if desired. **Yield:** 2-1/2 cups topping.

SWISS CHERRY DESSERT

Laura Mae Peterson, Salem, Oregon

(PICTURED BELOW)

My beloved Swiss mother-in-law gave me this recipe years ago. It's quick and easy to prepare and, as she was so frugal, easy on the pocketbook!

  4 tablespoons butter *or* margarine,
    divided
  2 to 3 slices day-old bread, cut into
    1-inch cubes
  1 can (15 ounces) pitted dark sweet *or*
    Bing cherries
2-1/2 teaspoons cornstarch
1-1/2 teaspoons sugar
  1/2 teaspoon vanilla extract
  1/4 teaspoon almond extract
Whipped cream and fresh mint, optional

In a medium skillet, melt 2 tablespoons butter. Add bread cubes; cook and stir until browned. Remove from the heat; set aside. Drain cherries, reserving syrup. Set cherries aside. In a medium saucepan, combine cherry syrup, cornstarch, sugar, extracts and remaining butter; bring to a boil. Cook and stir for 2 minutes. Remove from the heat; cool slightly. Stir in cherries. Divide bread cubes between two serving dishes and top with the cherry mixture. Garnish with whipped cream and mint if desired. **Yield:** 2 servings.

APPLE FRITTERS

Katie Beechy, Seymour, Missouri

Our children ask for these fritters each fall when there are plenty of apples available.

2-1/2 cups all-purpose flour
  1/2 cup instant nonfat dry milk powder
  1/3 cup sugar
    2 teaspoons baking powder
    1 teaspoon salt
    2 eggs
    1 cup water
    2 cups chopped peeled tart apples
Oil for deep-fat frying
Confectioners' sugar

In a mixing bowl, combine the first five ingredients. Beat eggs and water; stir into dry ingredients just until moistened. Fold in apples. In a deep-fat fryer or electric skillet, heat oil to 375°. Drop batter by teaspoonfuls into oil and fry until golden brown; drain. Dust with confectioners' sugar. Serve warm. **Yield:** about 3-1/2 dozen.

Fudgy Christmas Wreath

Nancy Maguire, Stony Plain, Alberta

Although the directions state to form the chocolate mixture into a wreath, you can be creative and use any shape you like to make this a year-round treat.

1 can (14 ounces) sweetened condensed milk
2 cups (12 ounces) semisweet chocolate chips
1 cup chopped walnuts
1/2 teaspoon vanilla extract
Red and green maraschino cherries

In a saucepan over low heat, cook and stir milk and chocolate chips until chocolate melts and mixture is slightly thickened, about 6 minutes. Remove from the heat; stir in nuts and vanilla. Cool for 15 minutes or until mixture begins to set. Line a baking sheet with waxed paper. Spoon chocolate mixture by 2 tablespoonfuls into small mounds to form a wreath. Decorate with cherries. Chill until firm. **Yield:** about 24 servings.

Peppermint Cookies

Donna Lock, Fort Collins, Colorado

When the holidays creep up on me, this recipe fills my cookie jar with goodies in a hurry.

2/3 cup butter-flavored shortening
1/4 cup sugar
1/4 cup packed brown sugar
1 egg
1-1/2 cups all-purpose flour
1/2 teaspoon baking powder
1/2 teaspoon salt
1/2 cup crushed peppermint candy

In a mixing bowl, cream shortening and sugars; beat in egg. Combine flour, baking powder and salt; stir into the creamed mixture. Fold in peppermint candy. Drop by teaspoonfuls onto greased baking sheets. Bake at 350° for 10-12 minutes or until edges begin to brown. Cool on wire racks. **Yield:** 3-1/2 dozen.

Chocolate Pizza

Norma Oosting, Holland, Michigan

(PICTURED ABOVE)

No one can resist hearty slices of pizza...especially when they feature chocolate! This dessert is delicious as well as eye-catching.

8 ounces white confectionery coating*, *divided*
1-1/3 cups (8 ounces) semisweet chocolate chips
1/2 cup *each* salted peanuts, miniature marshmallows, crisp rice cereal, coconut, red and green candied cherries

In a heavy saucepan, melt 6 oz. confectionery coating and the chips. Stir in peanuts, marshmallows and cereal. Spread evenly onto a greased 10-in. pizza pan. Sprinkle with coconut; top with cherries. Melt remaining confectionery coating; drizzle over pizza. Chill. **Yield:** 16-20 servings. ***Editor's Note:** White confectionery coating is found in the baking section of most grocery stores. It is sometimes labeled "almond bark" or "candy coating" and is often sold in bulk packages of 1 to 1-1/2 pounds.

SUGAR SUBSTITUTE. If you don't have brown sugar on hand, you can substitute 1 tablespoon of molasses and 1/4 cup of sugar for every 1/4 cup of brown sugar called for in the recipe.

MINI CHOCOLATE CUPCAKES

Annette Stevens, Olds, Alberta

I like to make these treats for a change of pace. People love the hint of chocolate in every bite.

> 1 cup butter *or* margarine, softened
> 1-1/2 cups sugar
> 1-1/2 teaspoons vanilla extract
> 4 eggs
> 2-1/2 cups all-purpose flour
> 2-1/2 teaspoons baking powder
> 1/2 teaspoon salt
> 1 cup milk
> 1 cup (6 ounces) miniature semisweet chocolate chips

In a mixing bowl, cream butter and sugar. Add vanilla. Add eggs, one at a time, beating well after each addition. Combine flour, baking powder and salt; add alternately with milk to creamed mixture. Stir in chocolate chips. Fill paper-lined muffin cups two-thirds full. Bake at 400° for 14-16 minutes or until cupcakes test done. Cool. **Yield:** 4 dozen mini or 2 dozen regular cupcakes.

PEACH BLUEBERRY COBBLER

Ramona Banfield, Harrison, Arkansas

I once made a triple recipe of this cobbler for a picnic and it was still warm when I served it. Everyone loved it!

> 2 cups fresh *or* frozen sliced peaches
> 1/3 to 1/2 cup sugar
> 4 teaspoons quick-cooking tapioca
> 2 teaspoons lemon juice
> 1 cup fresh *or* frozen blueberries
> Ground nutmeg
> **DUMPLINGS:**
> 1 cup all-purpose flour
> 2 tablespoons sugar
> 1 teaspoon grated lemon peel
> 1-1/2 teaspoons baking powder
> 1/8 teaspoon salt
> 1/4 cup cold butter *or* margarine
> 1/2 cup half-and-half cream *or* evaporated milk
> Vanilla ice cream, optional

In a 1-1/2-qt. baking dish, combine peaches, sugar, tapioca and lemon juice. Sprinkle blueberries and nutmeg on top; set aside. For dumplings, combine the first five ingredients in a mixing bowl; cut in butter until mixture resembles fine crumbs. Add cream; stir just until moistened. Drop by teaspoonfuls onto fruit mixture. Sprinkle with nutmeg. Bake at 400° for 20-25

CREAMY VANILLA PUDDING

Jeanne Bullard, Charlotte, North Carolina

(PICTURED ABOVE)

This creamy pudding turns out perfect every time! It's quick and easy to make, and the result is an old-fashioned pudding that's great for an after-school snack or to use as a base for many delicious desserts.

> 1/2 cup sugar
> 3 tablespoons cornstarch
> Pinch salt
> 2-1/2 cups milk
> 2 egg yolks, beaten
> 1 tablespoon butter *or* margarine
> 1 teaspoon vanilla extract

In a saucepan, combine sugar, cornstarch and salt. Stir in milk until smooth. Bring to a boil over medium heat. Reduce heat; cook and stir for 2 minutes. Add 1/2 cup milk mixture to yolks; return all to pan. Cook and stir for 1 minute or until thickened. Remove from the heat; stir in butter and vanilla. **Yield:** 4 servings.

minutes or until golden brown. Serve with ice cream if desired. **Yield:** 8 servings.

QUICK TOFFEE BARS

Jeanette Wubbena, Standish, Michigan

These buttery, beautiful, quick bars are my all-time favorite...and a fast way to fill the cookie jar when company's coming!

12 graham crackers, broken into quarters
1 cup butter *or* margarine
1/2 cup sugar
1 cup chopped nuts
1 cup (6 ounces) semisweet chocolate chips, melted

Line a 15-in x 10-in. x 1-in. jelly roll pan with waxed paper and grease the paper. Arrange graham crackers in pan and set aside. In a saucepan, melt butter and sugar over medium heat; simmer for 3 minutes. Spread evenly over graham crackers. Sprinkle nuts on top. Bake at 325° for 10 minutes. Cool. Spread chocolate over bars and allow to cool. Invert pan; remove waxed paper. **Yield:** 4 dozen.

STICK TO THESE GUIDELINES. Unopened *regular* peanut butter will keep in a cool dry place for at least 1 year. Once opened, it will keep for 3 months. *Natural* peanut butter should be refrigerated and used within 6 months.

FLOURLESS PEANUT BUTTER COOKIES

Maggie Schimmel, Wauwatosa, Wisconsin

(PICTURED BELOW)

These cookies never stick around long. People can't believe they're made without flour.

1 cup sugar
1 cup creamy peanut butter
1 egg

In a large bowl, mix all ingredients. Roll into 24 balls; place on ungreased baking sheets and flatten with a fork. Bake at 350° for 16-18 minutes. Cool on wire racks. **Yield:** 2 dozen.

MAPLE BISCUIT DESSERT

Leslie Malter, Waterbury, Vermont

(PICTURED BELOW)

These biscuits have been made by the women in my family for a long time. We use the maple syrup we boil each sugaring season from the trees on our land.

> **2 cups all-purpose flour**
> **1 tablespoon baking powder**
> **1/2 teaspoon salt**
> **1/4 cup shortening**
> **3/4 cup milk**
> **1-1/2 cups maple syrup**

In a bowl, combine flour, baking powder and salt; cut in shortening until mixture resembles coarse crumbs. Add milk; stir just until moistened. On a floured surface, roll dough to 1/2-in. thickness; cut with a 2-in. biscuit cutter. Pour syrup into an 11-in. x 7-in. x 2-in. baking dish. Place biscuits on top of syrup. Bake at 450° for 12-15 minutes or until biscuits are golden brown. **Yield:** 10-12 servings.

CHEWY CHOCOLATE COOKIES

Sheri Ziesemer, Olympia, Washington

This cookie recipe—a favorite of our four children—has been in my collection for years. Sometimes I'll substitute mint-flavored chips for the semisweet chocolate ones.

> **1-1/4 cups butter *or* margarine, softened**
> **2 cups sugar**
> **2 eggs**
> **2 teaspoons vanilla extract**
> **2 cups all-purpose flour**
> **3/4 cup baking cocoa**
> **1 teaspoon baking soda**
> **1/2 teaspoon salt**
> **2 cups (12 ounces) semisweet chocolate chips**

In a mixing bowl, cream butter and sugar. Add eggs, one at a time, beating well after each addition. Add vanilla. Combine dry ingredients; gradually add to creamed mixture. Stir in chocolate chips. Drop by teaspoonfuls onto lightly greased baking sheets. Bake at 350° for 8-10 minutes (do not overbake). Cool for 1 minute before removing to wire racks. **Yield:** about 4-1/2 dozen.

WHITE CHOCOLATE FUDGE

Jan Lutz, Stevens Point, Wisconsin

This recipe is similar to one of my favorite dark fudge recipes. I'll frequently make my white fudge to give as gifts for Christmas and Valentine's Day. It's an interesting contrast to all of the darker candies—and the cream cheese gives it such a nice rich and creamy texture!

> **1 package (8 ounces) cream cheese, softened**
> **4 cups confectioners' sugar**
> **1-1/2 teaspoons vanilla extract**
> **12 ounces white confectionery coating*, cut into small chunks**
> **3/4 cup chopped pecans**

In a mixing bowl, beat cream cheese, sugar and vanilla until smooth. In a microwave or double boiler, melt confectionery coating. Fold into cream cheese mixture; add pecans. Spread into a greased 8-in. square pan. Chill until serving; cut into squares. **Yield:** about 4 dozen. **Editor's Note:**

White confectionery coating is found in the baking section of most grocery stores. It is sometimes labeled "almond bark" or "candy coating" and is often sold in bulk packages of 1 to 1-1/2 pounds.

YOGURT LEMON PIE

Elsie Culver, Big Arm, Montana

This tasty recipe came about by experimenting in my kitchen. When I'm not baking for relatives or friends, I'm busy tending my cherry orchard or skiing, bowling or dancing!

> 1 package (8 ounces) cream cheese, softened
> 1/3 cup milk
> 2 cups (16 ounces) plain yogurt
> 1 package (3.4 ounces) instant lemon pudding mix
> 1 pie shell (9 inches), baked
> Whipped topping and lemon peel strips, optional

In a mixing bowl, beat cream cheese and milk until smooth; stir in yogurt. Add pudding mix and blend until mixture begins to thicken. Pour into crust. Garnish with whipped topping and lemon peel if desired. **Yield:** 8 servings.

LAST-MINUTE SHORTCAKE

Sharon Nichols, Brookings, South Dakota

This sweet treat is so quick because you make it in the microwave. Top it with fruit—fresh strawberries are my favorite!

> 1 cup all-purpose flour
> 3 tablespoons sugar
> 1 teaspoon baking powder
> 1/4 teaspoon salt
> 1/4 cup cold butter *or* margarine
> 1 egg
> 1/3 cup milk
> Fresh *or* frozen sliced strawberries
> Whipped cream

In a bowl, combine dry ingredients; cut in butter until mixture resembles coarse crumbs. Beat egg and milk; stir into flour mixture. Spoon into five microwave-safe 4-oz. custard cups. Microwave on medium for 3 minutes. Microwave on high for 2-3 minutes or until cake tests done with a toothpick. Serve with strawberries and whipped cream. **Yield:** 5 servings. **Editor's Note:** This recipe was tested in a 700-watt microwave.

PRALINE SUNDAES

Valerie Cook, Hubbard, Iowa

(PICTURED ABOVE)

Necessity can be the mother of recipes, too! I came up with this one as a way of using up the extra evaporated milk I had from making fudge.

> 1-1/4 cups packed brown sugar
> 1/4 cup butter *or* margarine
> 16 large marshmallows
> 2 tablespoons light corn syrup
> Dash salt
> 1 cup evaporated milk
> 1/2 cup chopped pecans, toasted
> 1 teaspoon vanilla extract
> Ice cream

In a saucepan, combine brown sugar, butter, marshmallows, corn syrup and salt. Cook and stir over low heat until marshmallows are melted and mixture comes to a boil. Boil for 1 minute. Remove from the heat; cool for 5 minutes. Stir in evaporated milk, pecans and vanilla; mix well. Serve over ice cream. Store leftovers in the refrigerator. **Yield:** 2-1/2 cups topping.

NEW ORLEANS PECAN PIE

Mitzi Adkinson, Albany, Georgia

(PICTURED ABOVE)

Although this pie is named for New Orleans, our town is the world's "pecan capital", so it fits us, too!

- 2 eggs, *separated*
- 1 cup (8 ounces) sour cream
- 1 cup sugar
- 1/4 cup all-purpose flour
- 1/2 teaspoon vanilla extract
- 1/4 teaspoon salt
- 1 pastry shell (9 inches), baked
- 1 cup packed brown sugar
- 1 cup chopped pecans

In saucepan, combine egg yolks, sour cream, sugar, flour, vanilla and salt. Cook and stir over medium heat until thickened, about 5 minutes (do not boil). Pour into pie shell; set aside. In a mixing bowl, beat egg whites until soft peaks form. Gradually add brown sugar; beat until stiff. Spread over hot filling, sealing to edges. Sprinkle with pecans. Bake at 375° for 12-15 minutes or until golden brown. **Yield:** 8 servings.

SAUCEPAN BROWNIES

Dorelene Doddridge, Kirk, Colorado

Brownies are a favorite treat to prepare—just combine a few ingredients, pour into a pan and pop in the oven. Nothing could be easier!

- 1 cup (6 ounces) semisweet chocolate chips
- 1/4 cup butter *or* margarine
- 2 cups biscuit/baking mix
- 1 can (14 ounces) sweetened condensed milk
- 1 egg
- 1 cup chopped walnuts

In a saucepan, melt chocolate chips and butter over low heat. Add biscuit mix, milk and egg; stir until smooth. Add nuts. Pour into a greased 13-in. x 9-in. x 2-in. baking pan. Bake at 350° for 25 minutes. **Yield:** 2-1/2 dozen.

PEACHY ANGEL FOOD DESSERT

Lois Walters, Beaconsfield, Iowa

By varying the pie filling, you can use this recipe for several occasions throughout the year. Plus, it's sure to appeal to everyone's palate.

- 1 prepared angel food cake (10 inches)
- 2 envelopes (1.3 ounces *each*) whipped topping mix
- 2 packages (3 ounces *each*) cream cheese, softened
- 1 cup confectioners' sugar
- 1 can (21 ounces) peach *or* cherry pie filling

Tear cake into bite-size pieces; set aside. Prepare whipped topping according to package directions; set aside. In a large mixing bowl, beat cream cheese and confectioners' sugar; fold in whipped topping. Add cake pieces; stir gently to coat evenly. Spoon into a 13-in. x 9-in. x 2-in. baking pan. Top with pie filling. Chill until ready to serve. **Yield:** 12 servings.

GLAZED APPLE COOKIES

Marietta Saladin, Woodstock, Illinois

I've had this recipe since my first child was little …now it's a favorite of my grandchildren. I like to use Jonathan apples in the recipe, but you can use the apple of your choice.

  1/2 cup shortening
1-1/2 cups packed brown sugar
  1 teaspoon baking soda
  1 teaspoon salt
  1 teaspoon ground cinnamon
  1 teaspoon ground cloves
  1/2 teaspoon ground nutmeg
  1 egg
  1 cup finely chopped peeled apples
  1 cup chopped walnuts
  1 cup raisins
  1/4 cup apple juice *or* milk
  2 cups all-purpose flour
VANILLA GLAZE:
1-1/2 cups confectioners' sugar
  1 tablespoon butter *or* margarine

  1/4 teaspoon vanilla extract
  1/8 teaspoon salt
2-1/2 tablespoons half-and-half cream

In a large mixing bowl, cream shortening, sugar, baking soda, salt, spices and egg. Stir in apples, nuts, raisins, juice and half of the flour; mix well. Blend in remaining flour. Drop by heaping tablespoonfuls onto greased baking sheets. Bake at 400° for 10-12 minutes. Remove to wire racks. Combine glaze ingredients and spread over cookies while warm. **Yield:** about 3 dozen.

BING CHERRY ICE CREAM SAUCE

Jane Thibeault, Oxford, Massachusetts

(PICTURED BELOW)

Pour this over your favorite ice cream for a sweet-tart treat!

  1 can (15 ounces) pitted dark sweet *or*
    Bing cherries
  2 tablespoons cornstarch
  1/4 teaspoon almond extract
Ice cream, sponge cake *or* pound cake

Drain cherries, reserving juice. Set cherries aside. Place juice and cornstarch in a saucepan. Cook, stirring constantly, until thickened. Stir in extract and cherries. Serve over ice cream, sponge cake or pound cake. **Yield:** 2 cups topping.

INDEX